The Complete Idiot's Reference Card

Taking C.A.R.E. Checklist

Every single parent has more than a handful to handle. So here's an easy-to-manage list of reminders that you can use to take CARE: finding the best ways to Communicate, Adapt, Respect, and Expect. Post this list on the fridge, tape it by the phone, make copies for every family member.

1. Be a parent first.

   COMMUNICATE: Let your kids know that you're there for them, no matter what.

   ADAPT: Kids may be the losers when you "win" a nasty and protracted court fight, so weigh carefully what details are actually worth battling over.

   RESPECT: Kids need to be kids—respect their right to have their own growing-up time, protected from "grownup" behavior.

   EXPECT: Your "personal life" may need to be on hold temporarily while you tend to your family.

2. Remember that the facts are on your side.

   COMMUNICATE: Make contact with as many single parents and groups as possible.

   ADAPT: Adapt your life. Take advantage of the flexible policies offered by many schools and employers.

   RESPECT: Give yourself credit for making independent decisions and managing difficult situations.

   EXPECT: Expect to succeed. Tell yourself, "Others do t..."

3. Put your feelings to go...

   COMMUNICATE: It's O... nest about your e..., letting your kids see your feelings gives them per... to feel, too.

   ADAPT: Turn fear into ac... turn pride into creat...

   RESPECT: Know that you... s are NOT you; thei... ngs are their own.

   EXPECT: Know that... ms are norma... r yo... nd your kids.

4. Find the help that...

   COMMUNICATE: ... you ne... mily, friends, support networks.

   ADAPT: Find way... ad with oth... arents in your situation.

   RESPECT: Respect... ds and remember that we gain strength by leaning on others; balance by reachi...

   EXPECT: Everybod... sometimes! You can "repay" a favor by giving help back to other parents in yo...

5. Go for goals that ma... r kids and you.

   COMMUNICATE: ... oals together. Let your kids see that you have life goals for yourself. Help you... eirs.

   ADAPT: Remember... e is what happens while you're making other plans," so be prepared to chan... als or plans as your life situation changes.

   RESPECT: Help yo... t goals that are right for *them*... necessarily goals that *you* want for them.

   EXPECT: If you kn... ere you're going, you'll probably get there—but perhaps not within the timeframes you p... ct. Be realistic.

alpha books

Taking C.A.R.E. Checklist

6. Plan your space and time to best fit your special needs.

    COMMUNICATE: Explain the goals of organization to your family.

    ADAPT: The needs and abilities of each family member vary. Be flexible!

    RESPECT: Acknowledge the values and priorities of your kids in your efforts to organize their lives.

    EXPECT: Accept the fact that your lifestyle may never be featured on a magazine cover, but it works for you.

7. Find work that's right for all of you.

    COMMUNICATE: Discuss your needs with your employers.

    ADAPT: Change your goals to meet present demands.

    RESPECT: Remember your children's needs when you make your own plans.

    EXPECT: Know the policies your employer offers, and expect your employer to make good on promised benefits.

8. Make your money work for you.

    COMMUNICATE: Talk with professionals or others who can help you make sense of your financial situation.

    ADAPT: Find ways to bring more money in, spend less, and balance your "wants" and your "needs."

    RESPECT: Your kids' "wants" may be important; find ways to meet some of them.

    EXPECT: Be prepared to keep working at getting finances in order for the long term. Have a positive attitude—it helps!

9. Create a family—and freedom.

    COMMUNICATE: Let people know you value their friendship; let kids know it's okay for them to care about their "other" family.

    ADAPT: The people you meet among your neighbors, support groups, and new acquaintances can create bonds as strong as "family ties"—be quick to establish relationships.

    RESPECT: Your kids need as much family contact as they can get—let them have it, regardless of your feelings about your ex or your ex's family.

    EXPECT: Any family you create can foster comfort, growth, and joy—great "family values."

10. Build from the basics. The bottom line is love; the most profitable approach is with a positive attitude.

    COMMUNICATE: Tell your kids, "I love you" and "I'm proud of you," and "Thank you"—A LOT!

THE COMPLETE IDIOT'S GUIDE® TO

Single Parenting

by Sara Dulaney

alpha books

A Division of Macmillan General Reference
A Simon & Schuster Macmillan Company
1633 Broadway, New York, NY 10019-6785

©1998 by Sara Dulaney

All rights reserved. No part of this book shall be reproduced, stored in a retrieval system, or transmitted by any means, electronic, mechanical, photocopying, recording, or otherwise, without written permission from the publisher. No patent liability is assumed with respect to the use of the information contained herein. Although every precaution has been taken in the preparation of this book, the publisher and author assume no responsibility for errors or omissions. Neither is any liability assumed for damages resulting from the use of information contained herein. For information, address Alpha Books, 1633 Broadway, 7th Floor, New York, NY 10019-6785.

THE COMPLETE IDIOT'S GUIDE TO and design are trademarks of Prentice-Hall, Inc.

Macmillan Publishing books may be purchased for business or sales promotional use. For information please write: Special Markets Department, Macmillan Publishing USA, 1633 Broadway, New York, NY 10019.

International Standard Book Number: 0-02-862409-2
Library of Congress Catalog Card Number: 98-85423

00 99 98   8 7 6 5 4 3 2 1

Interpretation of the printing code: the rightmost number of the first series of numbers is the year of the book's printing; the rightmost number of the second series of numbers is the number of the book's printing. For example, a printing code of 98-1 shows that the first printing occurred in 1998.

Printed in the United States of America

Note: This publication contains the opinions and ideas of its author. It is intended to provide helpful and informative material on the subject matter covered. It is sold with the understanding that the author and publisher are not engaged in rendering professional services in the book. If the reader requires personal assistance or advice, a competent professional should be consulted.

The author and publisher specifically disclaim any responsibility for any liability, loss or risk, personal or otherwise, which is incurred as a consequence, directly or indirectly, of the use and application of any of the contents of this book.

Alpha Development Team

Publisher
Kathy Nebenhaus

Editorial Director
Gary M. Krebs

Managing Editor
Bob Shuman

Marketing Brand Manager
Felice Primeau

Senior Editor
Nancy Mikhail

Development Editors
Phil Kitchel
Jennifer Perillo
Amy Zavatto

Editorial Assistant
Maureen Horn

Production Team

Production Editor
Mark Enochs

Copy Editor
Michael Cunningham

Cover Designer
Mike Freeland

Photo Editor
Richard H. Fox

Illustrator
Jody P. Schaeffer

Designer
Glenn Larsen

Indexers
Chris Barrick
Nadia Ibrahim

Layout/Proofreading
Angela Calvert
Kim Cofer
Mary Hunt

Contents at a Glance

Part 1: You are NOT Alone   1

    1 Facing Facts   3
Millions of single parents like you share common concerns and joys.

    2 What, You Worry?   13
Scared and worried feelings are facts of life in the single-parent family. The trick is to put them to good use.

    3 It's About You   21
Getting to know you—getting to know all about you; better be getting to like who you are.

Part 2: Keeping an Eye on the Kids   31

    4 Growing Patterns   33
Your children are unique—yet at the same time, they follow patterns of development similar to all other kids. Here's what you should watch for.

    5 Dealing with Discipline   41
At every stage, your kids—like everyone's—have developmental challenges to meet—and create challenges for you.

    6 Your Children, Yourself?   55
Being a "parent first" is key—and it doesn't mean putting the kids in charge! How to mind the boundaries.

    7 Whose Rights? What's Right? Support and Custody   65
The letter of the law is often filled with typos. But by paying attention, you can make support and custody choices that work for you and your kids.

    8 Caring About Caretakers   83
Who's minding the kids? You are when you follow steps to ensure good childcare.

Part 3: Finding Space and Time   89

    9 Designs for Living   91
How to make you and your kids comfortable, no matter where you live.

    10 First Things First: Getting Organized   101
How to get organized in a way that suits your needs.

    11 Handling Housework   107
Managing what needs to be managed—and eliminating what doesn't.

    12 Making Time   117
Arranging and rearranging your schedules to meet everyone's changing needs.

Part 4: Money Matters — 125

13 Facing Your Financial Facts — 127
Figuring out what money you have, and what you need.

14 Balancing Your Budget — 139
Finding the best ways to manage the money you have.

15 What Works — 151
Setting and achieving career goals that meet your needs for today—and tomorrow.

Part 5: The Buddy System: Friends — 161

16 Connections: That's What Friends Are For — 163
Friendship means fun—and a lot more—for both single parents and their children.

17 Creating a Single-Parent Community — 173
You are not alone—part two. How to make the most of the people you do have in your life.

18 Intimate Arrangements: Sex and Dating — 181
How to share the joys and avoid the pitfalls of getting personal—for both you and your kids.

Part 6: You Are Family — 191

19 Sharing Your Children—With Their Other Parent — 193
"Being a parent first" really counts here: How to work it out so your kids have all the love and support they need.

20 Sharing Your Children—With All of Their Family — 203
Family matters—to your kids and their relatives. How to make the most of it.

21 Family First — 209
"Happy families are all alike." How can you make your special family happy? This is it!

22 Re: Marriage — 215
Most divorces end in remarriage. A majority of remarriages end in divorce. How to improve your odds.

A Resources — 223
Where the single parent can find the in-depth information in print, online, and in-person.

B Meaning? Glossary — 235
All the terms relating to single parenting.

C Checklist Checkup — 238
A series of worksheets to show you how far you've come.

D Single Parent Problem Solver — 261
Frequently asked questions and where to get the answers.

Index — 265

Contents

Part 1: You Are NOT Alone — 1

1 Facing Facts — 3

Single Parenting by the Numbers 4
    Single Parents on the Rise 5
    Single by Choice 5
    Single Parent Profiles 6
    Singles in Your Neighborhood 7
Suddenly Single? 7
Common Concerns 9
Singular Joys 10
The Least You Need to Know 11

2 What, You Worry? — 13

The Feelings of the Single-Parent Family 14
    Feeling Fear 14
    Pride in the Name of Love 14
Reality Check 14
Simple Solutions 16
    Face Your Fears 16
    Accentuate the Positive 17
What Are Your Kids Feeling? 18
    Facing a New Reality 20
The Least You Need to Know 20

3 It's About You — 21

Going Through Changes 22
Personal Profiling 23
    Why Take Stock? 23
    Taking Your Personal Inventory 23
Where Are You Going? 28
The Least You Need to Know 30

Part 2: Keeping an Eye on the Kids — 31

4 Growing Patterns — 33

Child Psychology 101 34
Climbing the Developmental Ladder 35
Possible Problems 35
    Expressing Themselves 35
    Acting Out 36
    Role Reversal 37
    Sexual Identity Crisis 38
    Stress Proofing 38
The Secrets of Successful Single Parents 38
Focus on Your Family 39
    Listen to Your Kids 39
The Least You Need to Know 40

5 Dealing with Discipline — 41

Tracking Trouble 42
The Ages and Stages of Discipline 42
Is Your Kid "Normal?" 43
Why Kids Misbehave 45
Discipline as They Grow 45
    Discipline for Young Ones 45
    Discipline for Pre-Teens 46
    Discipline for Teens 47
Disciplinary Tools for Any Age 49
    Positive Consequences 49
    Corporal Punishment? 49
    "I" Messages 50
    Picking Battles 50
    Advice from the Frontlines 51
You and Your Ex: Discipline Duo 52
HELP! And How to Find It 52
    Choosing a Therapist 53
    Other Sources for Extra Support 54
The Least You Need to Know 54

6 Your Children, Yourself? 55

The Importance of Self-Esteem 55
   Building Self-Esteem in Your Kids 56
   Building Your Own Self-Esteem 58
Getting a Life 59
   Creating Success 59
   Separate Togetherness 60
The Good, the Bad, and the Co-Dependent 60
   Feelings or Facts? 61
   Parent or Pal? 61
Setting Priorities 62
   Putting Kids First 62
   Being a Parent First 62
The Least You Need to Know 64

7 Whose Rights? What's Right? Support and Custody 65

Ignorance of the Law 66
   Protecting Your Kids 67
   The Best Interests… 67
Custody: Who Decides? 68
   The Rules 68
   How Custody Decisions Are Made 69
   What Works: Joint Custody 69
Fund Fights: Support 72
   Getting Support 72
   Getting Help 74
Going Mobile: Can You Move? 75
   Moving On 76
   Staying Put 76
Do You Have to Go to Court? 76
   Conflict Resolution 76
   Doing It Yourself 77
Battling It Out in Court 77
Your Kids Are Key 78
The Final Word: Your Will 80
The Least You Need to Know 81

8 Caring About Caretakers — 83

Is Childcare Good for Children? — 84
Your Childcare Options — 84
Affording Childcare — 85
Getting Quality Childcare — 86
Checking Up on Childcare — 87
Childcare Through The Ages — 88
The Least You Need to Know — 88

Part 3: Finding Space and Time — 89

9 Designs for Living — 91

Relax: Make Yourselves Comfortable — 92
Stretching Space and Money — 93
Private Space, Private Time — 94
Time for Togetherness — 96
Safety First — 97
Wish Lists — 98
The Least You Need to Know — 99

10 First Things First: Getting Organized — 101

Getting Organized — 102
Goal-Setting Checklist — 102
Organization: A Family Affair — 103
What Needs To Be Organized? — 104
  Simplify Your Life — 105
The Least You Need to Know — 106

11 Handling Housework — 107

In Praise of Housework — 108
What Kids Can't Do — 109
Getting the Kids Involved — 110
  Getting Organized — 111
  Making the Most of It — 111
Housekeeping How-To — 112
  Hiring Help — 113
Sharing Chores — 113
Chores Checklists — 114
The Least You Need to Know — 115

12 Making Time — 117

Divide Time to Double It 118
    Where Does Your Time Go? 118
Timely Tips 118
sKIDules 120
Who Gets to See the Kids? 121
    Rearranging Custody 122
    Rearranging Visitation 122
Beating Burnout 122
The Least You Need to Know 123

Part 4: Money Matters — 125

13 Facing Your Financial Facts — 127

Steps to Financial Freedom 128
    Calculating Your Expenses 128
    Adding Up Your Assets 131
Collecting Child Support and Alimony 132
    Desperately Seeking Support 132
    Improving Your Support 133
Other Sources of Support 134
Charge It! Using Credit Carefully 134
Your Money and Your Life 136
Your Assets and Liabilities Checklist 137
The Least You Need to Know 138

14 Balancing Your Budget — 139

Getting What You Want—and What You Need 140
Budgeting Basics 141
Sticking to Your Budget 142
More Money 143
    Boosting Your Income 143
    Decreasing Your Outgo 144
Keeping Records 147
The Big Picture: Setting Goals 148
Building Your Savings 149
The Least You Need to Know 150

15 What Works — 151

- Finding a Job That Fits 152
  - Dare to Dream 152
  - Earning Income 153
  - Exploring the Possibilities 153
  - Taking Action 154
- Finding a Company That's Family Friendly 154
  - Flex Time 156
  - Family Leave Laws 157
- Optimizing Your Earning Power 157
  - Back to School 157
  - Working at Home 159
- The Family That Works Together… 160
- The Least You Need to Know 160

Part 5: The Buddy System: Friends — 161

16 Connections: That's What Friends Are For — 163

- What Friends Are For 163
- Who Are Your Friends? 164
- Making New Friends 165
- Getting Your Kids Involved 166
- Holding On to Old Friends 166
- Your Kids' Connections 167
- When Kids Are Home Alone 168
- Family Fun: Shared Activities 169
- The Least You Need to Know 172

17 Creating a Single-Parent Community — 173

- Networking 174
- Support Groups 174
  - Religious Groups 175
  - Clubs—Yours and Your Kids 175
  - Starting Your Own Group 176
- True Pals 176
- School Days 177
- The People in Your Neighborhood 177
- Community-Resource Checklist 178
- The Least You Need to Know 179

18 Intimate Arrangements: Sex and Dating — 181

- Are You Ready to Date Again? 181
- What Will Your Kids Think? 182
- Dating: Don't Ask, Don't Tell? 183
- The Dating Double Standard 184
- Sex and the Single Parent 185
- Should You Bring Your Kids on a Date? 185
- Your Kids and Your Dates: Can They All Get Along? 186
  - First Date Jitters 187
  - Dating Other Parents 187
- Intimacy Issues 188
- The Final Word 188
- The Least You Need to Know 189

Part 6: You Are Family — 191

19 Sharing Your Children—With Their Other Parent — 193

- Successful Child Sharing: A Win-Win Situation 194
- Cooperative Parenting 195
- Sharing Fairly 196
  - Consistency Counts 197
  - Staying in the Loop 198
  - Parenting from a Distance 199
- When Visitation Doesn't Work 200
- Should Children Choose? 201
- The Least You Need to Know 202

20 Sharing Your Children—With All of Their Family — 203

- Extending the Net 204
- What's Holding You Back? 205
- Making the Most of What You've Got 206
  - When Families Fight for Rights 206
- Keeping It All in the Family 207
- The Least You Need to Know 207

21 Family First — 209

- Making a Permanent Home 210
- Building a Future 211

What Matters Most 211
   Happy Kids 211
   Joyful Journey 212
   Making Memories 212
The "Ideal" Family: Yours! 212
The Least You Need to Know 213

22 Re: Marriage 215

Should You Get Married? 216
Living Together 217
You're Still a Parent First 218
Blending Families: Can't You All Just Get Along? 219
   Playing Favorites 219
   Dealing with Jealousy 220
Sibling Rivalry 220
   New Parent, Old Parent 220
   Testing, Testing 221
When Your Ex Remarries 222
The Least You Need to Know 222

A Resources 223

You Are Not Alone: Single-Parent Info and Support 223
   Hotlines 223
   Websites 224
   Single-Parent Groups 225
   Books 225
Whose Rights? What's Right? Support And Custody 226
   Websites 226
   Groups 226
   Books 227
Being a Parent First: Guides to Raising Healthy,
   Confident Kids 228
   Groups 228
   Books 230
Professional Help and How to Find It 231
   Websites 231
   Groups 231
   Facing Your Financial Facts 231
   Websites 231
   Books 232

xiii

  What Works 232
   Groups 232
   Books 233
  First Things First: Getting Organized 233
   Books 233
  Re: Marriage 233
   Websites 233
   Groups 234
   Books 234

B Meaning? Glossary   **235**

C Checklist Checkup   **238**

D Single Parent Problem Solver   **261**

Index   **265**

Foreword

If you are reading this, congratulations! You're curious and interested in learning, and you have already taken the first (and one of the most important) steps in assuring that you will be the best single parent that you can be.

Too often people (wrongly) believe that parenting is something instinctive, something natural, something that we just know without being taught. Well, I can assure you that that is a myth. I'm a certified psychotherapist; yet when I became a single parent seventeen years ago, I didn't have a clue about what I should do.

I was overwhelmed at times and quite surprised at the intensity of the challenges of day-to-day parenting. I realized fairly quickly that I needed lots of help to meet those demands.

All first-time parents are in the same boat. We have to learn from the on-the-job training. But single parents, who often have already faced some rough times, have some especially complex challenges. Your self-esteem may need a bit of healing, and at the same time you may also be concerned about how to help your kids through the adjustment to a new phase of their lives.

Sure, most of us do, somehow, manage to get through each day learning by trial and error, but why try to reinvent the wheel when you could actually enjoy parenting?

Sara Dulaney understands children in a rare and wonderful way, but she also understands single parents, and with this gift she helps us to see complicated situations clearly and realistically from both the childrens' and the parent's points of view. She understands and appreciates our worries and fears, and speaks to them with practical and wise advice.

Discipline is a particularly important issue for single parents. Most of us don't want to criticize or scold our children, but we often don't really know what else to do. Sara shares positive approaches which work, which can help make your household a happier one, and which ultimately can lead to a closer and more healthy relationship with your child.

By reading this book you can learn a lot and perhaps be spared hours of the "guilts" and that awful feeling of "If only I'd realized that sooner." It contains a wealth of valuable tips for coping with the practical and emotional challenges of single parenting. Sara covers custody issues, sexuality, discipline, money, stress, getting organized, having fun with your child and so much more, and she does so in a readable, humorous, and clear style.

My son is now a very grown-up and independent teenager about to go off to college, and looking back over the years I'm shocked at how quickly they've flown by. Although some days do seem endless (like when you're having a rough time yourself or trying to deal with a sick or cranky child), parenting actually is a relatively short phase of our lives, and so each of those days are quite precious. Reading and learning how to do your best early on can help assure that you make the most of them.

Enjoy!

Jane Mattes, C.S.W.

Author, *Single Mothers by Choice*, and founder, Single Mothers by Choice

Introduction

"Happy families are all alike; every unhappy family is unhappy in its own way." That famous line, which introduces Tolstoy's *Anna Karenina*, could updated for single parents as:

"Single-parent families have much in common, but each single-parent family has to handle its own hassles."

The fact that modern society abounds in single-parent families may make it easier, in a general way, to cope as a single parent. Afterall, 13 million-plus single parents do make a statement. But as an individual, coping on a daily basis still can be, shall we say, a challenge.

This book knows you can meet that challenge and was written to help you do so.

A key feature of this *Complete Idiot's Guide* is its *attitude*. An attitude that's positive, not pitying; that focuses on what you can do without wasting good energy on what you can't. An attitude that says sure this is tough, but lots of folks manage, so you can, too. All you need is a little help from your friends.

The only "idiotic" thing a single parent can do is *not* use all the help that's around. Experts report that single-parent families that have the most problems are the ones who sought help least often. In other words, asking for help gets help. And needing help is normal. That's what this book is here for.

And as for "happy families?" Happiness is a choice, a matter of attitude. And contrary to Tolstoy, each single-parent family can be happy in its own way.

So let's get started!

How to Use This Book

The goal of this book is to help you as a single parent optimize your life and your children's healthy growth (pretty good goals for all parents, not just single parents).

Though it covers a lot of ground and draws on a lot of resources, this book doesn't pretend to give the final word on anything—in the end, only you can determine what's best for you and your family. So in the spirit of the 21st century, this book is truly interactive. Within these pages you'll find lots of questionnaires, checklists, and self-quizzes to figure out how the material relates to you. You'll also find detailed directions for access to more in-depth resources: Websites and chatrooms, books and magazines, and support groups and experts.

Introduction

The book moves from the very general to the very personal. Each section provides appropriate facts and information, but also expertise from professionals and advice and experience from the "real" experts—other single parents who've been there.

Part 1, "You Are NOT Alone," give you facts on the overall single parenting situation and states the facts of life that are common to all single parent families.

Part 2, "Keeping an Eye on the Kids," focuses on your children—their natural development and how to guide it, as well as advice on how to handle support, custody, and childcare issues.

Part 3, "Finding Space and Time," discusses a wide range of very practical matters, from arranging space that always seems too small to managing schedules that always seem too busy.

Part 4, "Money Matters," is about all matters related to money: whether you need help budgeting what you've got or changing your career to bring in more; having enough for today and planning for tomorrow's security.

Part 5, "The Buddy System: Friends," focuses on fun! You'll learn the importance of friendships for both you and your kids, and how to develop a caring community of parents like yourself.

Part 6, "You Are Family," shows you how to make the most of the family you've got, how to make sure your children benefit from the best you and your ex have to offer, and how to handle remarriage.

You'll find specific help and support for all these issues—and a lot more—throughout the book.

This is a lot! But then you deal with a lot, each and every day. Because I know how busy and hassled you are, all of this material is presented in a fashion that's fast to grab hold of. You can read the whole book from beginning to end—great. If you have a specific topic of concern, go for it. But each chapter is laid out so that you can easily get everything from a quick nugget of information on a topic that concerns you to an in-depth discussion of it.

Extras

To help guide you through the successes and pitfalls of raising a family as a single parent, this book offers additional tips, warnings, and words of advice from single parents who've been there. You'll find extra information in the following boxes:

The Complete Idiot's Guide to Single Parenting

Singular Successes
Firsthand experiences and anecdotes from or about other single parents and their families.

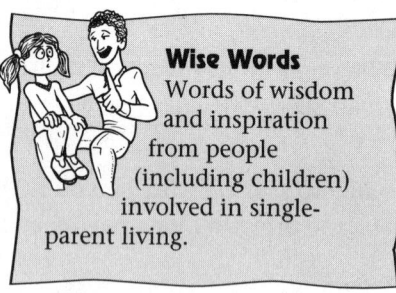

Wise Words
Words of wisdom and inspiration from people (including children) involved in single-parent living.

Meaning?
Definitions of technical terms related to parenting, psychological development, financial planning, and more.

Parent Pitfalls
Warnings signs of destructive patterns or behavior in both single parents and their kids.

Expert-Ease
Practical tips on making the most of single parenting.

In addition to the main text and sidebars, you'll find plenty of checklists and self-tests that make this book an interactive experience. You'll have the chance to put the information and ideas you've gotten from each chapter to work in your own life. Hopefully, by the end you'll be able to pull all your new knowledge—about single parenting in general and about your own individual situation—together.

Acknowledgments

The author acknowledges with special thanks the contributions of many professionals, including: therapists Mary-Alice Olson of Pennsylvania; Jane Mattes, C.S.W. of New York; and M. Taylor Bach of Kentucky.

Margot Cohn and Marion Flomenhaft of the Center for Career Education and Life Planning at New York University.

Kathy Ward Cameron of Action for Children in Columbus, OH, and Terry Gilliam of the Delaware Prevention Institute.

Phyllis Burlage, CPA of Burlage Associates in Millersville, MD and President of the Maryland Association of Acts; financial consultant George Klander, RFC. Vice President of Money Management Advisory Inc.

As well as all the "non professionals"—moms and dads and kids who have shared their stories and firsthand observations about life in single parent families: Daniel, Lavern, Julie, Tracy, Rachel, Joe, Nicole, Jason, Jean, and the others, as well as many members of Parents without Partners, Single Parents On Line and the Single Parents Association. And with thanks to Ian and, of course, Sean.

Special Thanks to the Technical Editor

The Complete Idiot's Guide to Single Parenting was reviewed by an expert who not only reviewed the advice presented in this book, but also provided valuable insight to help ensure that this book tells you everything you need to know about successful single parenting. Our special thanks are extended to Mary-Alice Olson.

Mary-Alice Olson, ACSW, received her masters degree in social work from the University of Pittsburgh in Pittsburgh, Pennsylvania. For the past five years, she has worked in private practice. She specializes in treating eating disorders, cognitive therapy, and depression. For four years, she worked on an inpatient psychiatric floor of St. Francis Medical Center.

Part 1
You Are NOT Alone

Let's be honest: Single parenting is hard. Just because so many people are doing it doesn't make single parenting any easier to deal with emotionally. No matter how smart and together you are, and no matter how surely you know that you made the right decision, you may still succumb to feelings of panic and insecurity.

You may try to ignore your feelings because they are just too scary. Unfortunately, the worst way to deal with feelings is to not *deal with them. Awareness is the first step. This section shows you how to come to terms with your own feelings.*

Chapter 1

Facing Facts

In This Chapter

- ➤ Single parenting: a growing trend
- ➤ How single parents get that way
- ➤ The top five worries of single parents
- ➤ The keys to single-parenting success

It's seven a.m. You're trying to iron the creases out of your best suit while convincing your screaming kid to eat breakfast. Just then the car pool mom calls to say she can't do it this morning—can you? You should be thinking about an important meeting at work, but now you're not even sure you can get to the office.

It's 11 a.m. A call from daycare has just interrupted your big client pitch. Your four-year old has a high fever and you have to go.

It's 6 p.m. Your second-grader is hysterical because nobody showed up for parents' day—but if you'd taken any more time off, you risked being fired.

It's the third time this week you've had to send your son to his room for too much rough-housing—and you're tired of having to be the bad guy and the fun guy all the time.

Part 1 ➤ *You Are NOT Alone*

It's two days till payday. You're sweating out another month of nailbiting tension, worried you won't have enough in the bank to cover the bills. And your support check hasn't arrived—again.

It's another Saturday evening at home. You're the only grownup you know of stuck in front of the TV, and you're wishing your romantic life were half as good as the reruns you're watching with the kids.

At times like these, it's easy for a single parent to feel like a complete idiot. You may wonder, Was I out of my mind?? What made me think I could do this by myself?!

Fact is, all of us who've been there sometimes feel that way, too. That's not surprising. Holding responsibility for another human life is, to put it in its most positive light, a daunting challenge—even for two parents working together. For singles, it gets harder.

Luckily, there's help available—not only from this book and from plenty of professional and expert resources (which you'll learn about as we go), but also from the millions of others who share your situation and can share their experience.

While you're alone in the pre-dawn hours, awake with anxiety about how to make ends meet, or with rage about your situation, it may be some comfort to know that, throughout the country, more than 13 million other single parents are likely to be worrying about the same stuff.

It MAY be a comfort; at the very least, it's a reminder that you are not alone.

Single Parenting by the Numbers

Meaning?
Who qualifies as a *single parent*? Any adult raising one or more children for a period of time without the aid of a partner. That includes: Single moms, single dads, grandparents raising grandkids, single parents by divorce, by widowhood, by adoption, or just by circumstance.

The nation's 13.3 million single parents represent nearly a third of the country's parents. Viewed another way: 32 percent of all families with children under the age of eighteen live in single-parent households, according to 1996 U.S. Census Bureau figures.

From the kids' point of view: over a third of all U.S. children live in single-parent homes—that's 22 million of the country's more than 70 million kids under age 18. At least half of all U.S. children will, at some time, be spending time with a single adult.

That means that at some time, half of all American parents will be in sole charge of a kid or kids—and thus qualify as single parents.

Single Parents on the Rise

Our numbers have been steadily rising through the century. Both single moms and single dads are becoming increasingly more common:

➤ The number of single-parented kids has more than tripled since 1960, and almost doubled in the last 25 years.

➤ The number of single mothers has more than doubled in the past quarter century.

➤ While there still aren't as many single dads as single moms out there, the number of single fathers has increased threefold since 1970 from nearly 800,000 to 2.4 million. That makes single-father households the fastest-growing type of family group in all of American demography. (Is that an honor, or what?)

Why the huge increase? Demographic researchers say that it's not because of some massive increase in teenage pregnancies; rather, it's because of more fundamental and extensive social changes. The divorce rate has soared, and fewer couples who conceive are finding it necessary to marry.

Single by Choice

It wasn't that long ago that single parents—especially those who admitted their status—were an oddity. As recently as the 1970s, it was thought that a single mother couldn't—certainly shouldn't—raise a baby alone. Yet today, millions are choosing to do just that.

The growing numbers of single parents reflect deeper changes in American society. For instance, the number of unmarried couples has soared from just under 200,000 in 1970 to nearly 1.2 million in 1995.

Or, consider that as recently as the 1980s, homosexuality was rarely a topic for open discussion—yet today gays and lesbians are raising children conceived by artificial insemination, and adoptive children are placed with gay and lesbian singles.

How about this: until the '90s, a woman's maximum childbearing age had definite limits. Today, women are able to conceive babies without a partner at ages formerly considered "too late."

> **Parent Pitfalls**
> Although surveys suggest that the idea of out-of-wedlock childbirth is acceptable to most Americans, a strong plurality of the U.S. still thinks that a single parent cannot raise a child as well as two parents can. What do you believe?

For whatever reasons, more women—and men—are choosing to parent without partners (that is, give birth or adopt with no intention of establishing a formally committed relationship with another adult). These people are counted in the Census Bureau's

Part 1 ➤ *You Are NOT Alone*

"never-married" category of both single moms and single dads. This category is up 230 percent in the last 25 years.

The result of having or acquiring a baby by any means? Spending more than 20 years on parenthood (at the least)—and spending at least part of those years "alone," and looking for ways to cope.

> **Singular Successes**
>
> Some statistical profiles of contemporary "single"-parent living arrangements:
>
> Single parents living on their own: 8.1 million.
>
> Single parents living with other family members: 2.2 million.
>
> Single parents living with unrelated others: 3.1 million.

But keep in mind that unmarried doesn't always mean alone: With cohabitation rates booming, just because a child lives with only one parent may not mean that there is no other adult living in the household. As you may already have found out, that live-in arrangement can be good or bad news. (See Chapters 18 and 22 for more on that.)

Single Parent Profiles

Who are these single parents? Everybody! While the Census Bureau snapshot of the "typical" single parent is a white woman in her early thirties living in a greater-metropolitan region with 1.85 children, detailed demographic research shows that across the U.S., people of every age, socioeconomic class, and ethnic and racial group are single parenting.

> **Wise Words**
> You may worry and feel guilty about how your kids are doing—but here's what some young teens of divorced single parents say: "With a good, close relationship with one parent, you can enjoy life just as well—or better." "No matter what happens you don't have to feel ashamed or afraid."

And no matter what your locale or status, your kids are not alone either. In the U.S., 22 million single-parented kids live in every community, large and small, rich and poor.

Because there are so many of us, there's plenty of acceptance and help around for your kids AND you—and lots of broad-based research focusing on their development, your needs, and the best techniques for optimal single-parent living. You'll find the results of those studies throughout this book.

Where once single parents were a tiny minority, today our growing numbers bring security.

Singles in Your Neighborhood

National census numbers don't cut it for you? If you (and/or your kids) still feel like you're the only single-parent household in the world, take your own "census."

Are you really alone? Find out:

➤ How many children in your kids' classes at school are from single-parent homes?

➤ How many single-parent families are in your neighborhood?

➤ How many are in your church or temple?

➤ How many of your coworkers are single parents, too?

You may find a sense of safety in numbers and take comfort in the fact that there are lots of folks like you. You may also find the experiences of other single parents useful to your situation. But even if not, just knowing the facts about your own living situation, and reviewing them with your kids, can help all of you feel more "normal."

> **Expert-Ease**
> Reach out: Find the other single parents you feel comfortable with and create your own social and support network. This can make you feel better and may have practical benefits—group support can affect your child's school's attitudes and policies, for instance, if too many school events seem geared toward two-parent households. And group members may be available for giving and getting back-up childcare.

Suddenly Single?

As you take your own census, you'll likely find a variety of reasons why people become single parents:

➤ By choice

➤ By chance (unintentional pregnancy)

➤ By divorce

➤ By desertion

➤ By the death of a spouse

How you became a single parent may make a difference in how you view and play your role as single parent. For example, single parents by choice may be more confident and prepared to cope. (On the other hand, they may also be more reluctant to admit they need help!)

While those who become single parents by chance may spend a lot of energy on simply coping with the shock, they may also be more open to accepting positive support.

Widow/ers have the advantage of undiluted sympathy and support from society—but they may be completely unprepared for single parenthood, a drawback that could be made worse if they have trouble dealing with their grief.

Deserted spouses may have an additional dose of rage to work through, and their kids may have higher than average levels of insecurity.

Single mothers may be more accepted by society, but they have a more difficult economic row to hoe; single dads may have to struggle to get the social attention and services they need but may have less trouble making it financially.

Seeing how each "type" may bring with it a special set of circumstances and concerns, you'll find it valuable to take a careful look at your own situation. What type are you? Check out the following checklist.

How Do You Feel About Single Parenting?

Are you a single parent by:

_____ Choice   _____ Chance   _____ Death   _____ Desertion

Was your separation from your partner—or decision to not attach to him/her—made:

_____ In an amicable context?   _____ In a hostile context?

What kind of difference does that make in your attitude toward your situation—and perhaps toward your children as well?

Biggest positive impact: _____

_____

Biggest negative impact: _____

_____

It's especially important to be clear—and honest—about these circumstances because recent research indicates that single-parent children tend to experience differing degrees of difficulty depending on the circumstances of the breakup. For example, if negative feelings between the parents continue after a breakup (say, after a hostile divorce), kids suffer from carrying the double burden of loss and rage. On the other hand, if a breakup actually eases household tension and the parents can still support each other after their separation, kids develop as though the family were intact.

And even earlier studies—done when single-parenting was not so common—revealed that in single-parent situations where the separated parents got along well enough to put the child first, the children were as healthy as those in happy, "intact" families—and happier than those in unhappy, "intact" families.

So a big first step toward improving your children's lot is to be clear about how you feel about your situation (and beginning to find ways to dissipate any negativity can certainly help you, too!)

Common Concerns

Single parents, no matter where they live or in what circumstances, share a lot of the same worries:

> **Meaning?**
> *Intact* is a word used in social service professions to refer to married, never-divorced families with children. As such, it's a useful shorthand term, but the suggestion that divorced or non-married parents with kids are "broken" is a holdover from a previous era.

➤ The well-being of their kids

➤ Their finances

➤ Their family's security

➤ Their family's health and safety

➤ Their legal problems

➤ Their jobs

How closely do these match *your* worries? Try this: Write down all the things that you're worried about. Writing out your worries is your first step toward wiping them out.

Single Parent Worry Worksheet

Write down the issues that you are most concerned about in each area of your life:

Your kids _____

Your finances _____

Your family's security _____

Your family's health and safety _____

Your legal problems _____

Your job _____

Your physical and mental health _____

Your relationships _____

Your romantic life _____

9

You've already come a long way toward easing those worries with this book. Future chapters will give you strategies to deal with each of the issues on this list.

You're right to be concerned about you and your child's well-being. Various studies reveal some more hard facts: Children raised by single parents DO reportedly have more difficulties in life now and later than those from intact homes. (Of course, kids raised in UNhappy traditional homes have problems, too.)

Good news for single parents: The most recent studies indicate that the difficulties faced by single-parent kids stem less from their living arrangements than from poverty, external stress, and a poor environment. Since single-parent families are much more likely to be economically disadvantaged, the better you can manage to improve your living situation, the less "troubled" your kids are likely to be.

Plus, studies show that the kind of difficulties faced by these kids—difficulties with school, sleep, or relationships, for instance—are similar to those encountered by kids in intact families whose parents are largely absent due to the demands of work schedules.

The message? The better you as a single parent can cope with life, the better off your kids will be. That means you should focus on what you can do to stabilize your daily life (for example, improving your child custody arrangements, your social supports, and your financial status). Fortunately, a great deal of practical help is available to work through those issues, and this book is a great place to start.

> **Wise Words**
> Tracy's Mom struggles. Her job is solid but not high paying; she's got a long commute; and now there's school to deal with. She gives Tracy as much as she can—maybe more—and sometimes she resents it. Then she found a note from Tracy: "Dear Mom: Thank you for the paper-doll book. And thank you for being such a great Mom. I know it would be easier if we had a Daddy, but you are a great Mom. I love you."

Singular Joys

Not that it's all struggle! There's a lot more than numbers and issues and late-night brooding to this single parenting business. There's joy and growth and possibility, too: The satisfaction of meeting and overcoming a challenge; of helping a life unfold—and getting the help you need to make it the best life possible; and of learning all you can from your kids, and from the experience of parenting them.

Sure there are days when simple survival is a victory—when nothing seems to work out. And the tips in this book will help you through them. But you'll read here how others in your situation have gone beyond simple survival.

Take a cue from Evelyn, a divorced mother of ten: "In the beginning life was very difficult for all of us, but as we gradually pulled together to make ourselves a strong family, we learned to put negative feelings behind us. I assumed the positive attitude that my kids could move confidently through life. It worked for us: Accenting the positive (plus a good sense of humor) kept our family going when things were toughest and kept us growing as life became smoother."

The Least You Need to Know

- ➤ Single parenting is not easy, but it's not impossible.
- ➤ Growing numbers of single parents mean that there are growing sources of support and information for you to draw on.
- ➤ Your outlook as a single parent will be affected by how you became a single parent. The sooner you can work through any lingering negativity, the better for you and your kids.
- ➤ Experts suggest that kids of single parents are more negatively affected by socioeconomic factors (poverty, external stress, and a poor environment) than they are by their single parent status. If you can improve those factors, you can improve your child's chances for healthy, successful development.
- ➤ Remember that there are joys to single parenting, too. If you think of family life as a chore or a tragedy, you'll miss all the adventure of helping your children to grow.

Chapter 2
What, You Worry?

In This Chapter

- ➤ The fears of every single parent
- ➤ Realistic versus destructive fears
- ➤ Facing your fears
- ➤ What are your children feeling?

Did you ever keep tropical fish? Ever change the water in the fish tank? The fish become very agitated. The more delicate ones may not even recover from the experience. And it's easy to understand why: Their entire universe has been disrupted. You know that it's for their own good and that they'll be better and happier afterward—but they have no idea what's happening and what the outcome will be.

So if fish can have those kinds of feelings when their world is in an uproar, why not humans? If you—and even more so, your kids—have gone through a major upheaval, you'd be crazy not to have feelings about it. Feelings are normal. Even the nature of those feelings is fairly predictable; single-parent status nearly always creates some sense of vulnerability.

This chapter helps you explore some of those feelings—and what you can do about them.

The Feelings of the Single-Parent Family

Psychological experts observe several emotional characteristics common to the single-parent family. They use complex diagnostic definitions like "abandonment injury," "pathologenic," and "anxiety reaction."

The feelings that single parents and their families most commonly recognize are actually very simple: fear and its flipside—pride.

In normal doses, fear is understandable and pride is necessary. Problems arise only when the fears are incapacitating or the pride cuts us off from others.

Feeling Fear

Kids can admit they're afraid their parent can't handle things. They seem worried when their parent goes out, even for short errands. They're overanxious about school. At their core, experts observe, these expressed fears are all communicating the underlying, unexpressed one: At any age, the child wonders, "What if something happens to the one parent I have? What will happen to me?"

Parents express fears about money, about their kids, about the safety of their neighborhoods. All these may be justified, but they also serve as expressions of the unspoken fear: "What if I can't handle this?"

Pride in the Name of Love

This is where (for better or worse) pride kicks in. "Of course I/Mom/Dad can handle this!" That's great as an expression of a positive attitude, but to the extent that it prevents you from getting help and advice when you could use it, it's not so great. Pride goads us—parents and children—to do well, to look good, to make outstanding lemonade from bitter lemons, perhaps. And that's fine. Pride also expresses itself as anger: How could my ex/my parent do this to me?! And sometimes pride causes the diffusion of too much energy, by not allowing you to ask for help when you need it.

Reality Check

It may be time for a diagnostic self-test. As a start—Do you hear yourself or your children saying "I'm fine!" a little too often? You don't have to be fine until you really are. In the meantime, your troubles may be real.

When fear of financial insecurity, for instance, causes you to be thrifty and get careful financial advice, that's great. But when it leads to continual anxiety and a constant denial of necessary items to your kids, it's not productive. Then pride can step in and prevent you from asking for a loan. That, in turn, can create more fear about your situation.

Some fears—especially those self-generated ones without any firm basis in reality—can be a big waste of emotional energy, and can lead to actions that are less than wise. Here are some common fears:

- "What will people think?"
- "Are my kids ruined forever?"
- "How will I pay for my infant's college?"
- "Will my ex get married and try to get the kids?"
- "What if no one wants a relationship with someone with children?"
- "Since my first wife died, so will anyone else I marry."

> **Wise Words**
> Single-parent kids express certain worries privately—and need to learn whether they have basis in fact: "I was afraid Dad would leave, too."…"I was afraid the kids at school would make fun of me."…"I was afraid we'd become homeless."…"I was afraid I'd never be happy again."

Do any of these sound familiar? Which of your anxieties are tied to "reality now"—and which are "what ifs?"

Real fears include:

- Not being able to keep your job and care properly for your kids.
- Not having enough money.
- What to do in the case of an illness or accident that requires hospitalization or long-term care.
- A variety of unpredictable crises.

Real fears require appropriate actions. For example, start looking or negotiating now for work that provides flexibility with security (see Chapter 15 for ideas). Get financial advice from an expert (many are low-cost or cost-free, as noted in Chapter 13). Be sure you have a back-up network of care, as noted in Chapter 8. Whatever the worry or fear, appropriate action should eliminate it.

You and your children can derive justifiable pride from unexpected accomplishments, such as learning how to perform new tasks—from bedmaking to home maintenance. Get successfully involved in some brand new activity despite your everyday struggles and concerns. Help someone else get through problems you've already experienced. These kinds of actions are worth more than a pat on the back and should be reinforced.

Part 1 ➤ *You Are NOT Alone*

Simple Solutions

If you're feeling paralyzed by fear or false pride, therapists suggest you try to find the source. Irrational fears are not usually about what they appear to be. They may simply be an expression of an underlying and understandable anxiety over your single-parent situation.

> **Wise Words**
> "Never be afraid to admit if something is troubling you or on your mind. Talk to your kids. They don't have to understand the details of your problem but they will understand what it's like to have problems."
> —A single dad with joint custody of a teenage son

Often just acknowledging them and seeing them for what they really are can help. For instance, you'll get one of those "Of course!" or "Aha!" glows when you've looked at a specific fear over, say, money and tracked it down to its real source.

Talking with or listening to other people in your situation—even "lurking" in a single-parent newsgroup on the Internet—can often provide all the reassurance you need that others are in your boat, too.

Counsellors agree that it's important to be open with your kids, but on a level they will understand. They should be told what they need to know in order for them to deal with their issues. They should not be used as a support system or avenue to vent.

Face Your Fears

"We have nothing to fear but fear itself." Franklin D. Roosevelt was right on the money. Often we—adults as well as children—are so afraid of what we'll see if we confront our fears that we're afraid to switch on the light and make the boogie man disappear.

> **Expert-Ease**
> You kids can benefit from a fear-list, too. Or use the list idea to help them talk about their fears and rate the reality-level of each.

To shine the light of day on your fears, write them down. Right now—make a list of everything you're afraid of or have been since becoming a single parent. Now, cross out each fear that didn't come true. Next to those (a few?) that are left, rank how likely they are to come true, from five stars (imminently possible) to no stars (not a chance it'll ever happen). Finally, for all the 3-star or better fears, make some notes about actions that you can take to avoid having them come true. Your list might look like this:

Chapter 2 ➤ What, You Worry?

Fear List	
I am afraid about:	Actions I can take:
**Losing the kids	
**Losing my home	
**Facing a nasty custody fight	Try a mediator
Being let down by my family	
Not being able to do my job	
***My kids getting in trouble	Get good counseling
*Never having another relationship	Join groups that interest me
**Not being able to cope	
*Being forced to give up my career	Explore flexible work options
*Not having enough money	Focus on finding a better-paying career
Not having any friends	
Being hated by my kids	

Note that most of your fears probably focus on not getting something you want or need, or losing something you have.

Sometimes it helps to just take a deep breath, look around, and ask, "Is my family all right, right now? Are we safe, warm, and fed? If so, then for right now, there's nothing to be afraid of." "Now" is what you can deal with—not the "if onlys" of the past or the "what ifs" of the future.

Feeling better now?

Accentuate the Positive

Just as you make lists of your fears and worries, make a list of all you've accomplished during the time you've been a single parent. What's your most proud achievement? What steps have you taken to move yourself toward positive accomplishments? Give yourself some gold stars and let yourself feel that, indeed, you can handle things.

> **Wise Words**
> "My son was much more able talk about his dog's feelings and worries than his own. My daughter could discuss feelings when they were "other people's." So that's what I did: We could talk about scary feelings that way and they could find reassurance without having to admit to their own fears."
> —A widowed Mom

17

Part 1 ➤ *You Are NOT Alone*

What Are Your Kids Feeling?

Children tend to express their feelings—perhaps especially the negative ones—in an indirect fashion. A child who's having nightmares about intruders in the home is fairly obviously saying, "I'm feeling scared and insecure." Children who develop repeated ailments to avoid school are probably afraid to leave the house. But it can get even more complex, and you do need to be aware of troubles that may not get "smiled" away. Here are some difficulties child psychologists often see, and their common symptoms:

> **Meaning?**
> *Displaced anger* is anger that is expressed toward people or objects other than the actual source of the anger. Kids who get into many fights on the playground, for instance, may be driven by anger toward a parent who they feel has let them down.

> **Meaning?**
> *Situational* or *reactive depression* is what we commonly refer to as the blues: a down phase tied to a specific event—like a loss from death or divorce. This passes, although professional help is useful to avoid its leading to *chronic* or *major depression,* which can be a serious, long-term emotional disorder which requires professional help.

➤ **Worry.** As mentioned earlier, common worries of children include: worrying that something might happen to the absent parent; worrying they might lose the rest of their family; worrying that something might happen to the parent they live with; worrying that they caused the break-up; or worrying that they caused the death of their parent.

If your child seeks reassurance, respond with continuing affirmation and consistency. When you're away, give details of where you are, and check in regularly.

➤ **Fear** shows itself through a constant need for reassurance and an unwillingness to leave the parent's side.

Children who can't be persuaded to talk about their fears can be helped by practicing being away from the parent or perhaps by acting out fears with toys or expressing them with blocks or paint.

➤ **Anger,** especially *displaced anger*, which is anger directed at safe targets rather than the actual cause. (For example, throwing a tantrum with you, when they are really angry with their other parent for missing a visit.) Watch for a short temper, tantrums, and a general "chip on the shoulder" attitude.

Try to find harmless ways for your child to vent his or her anger while staying calm yourself.

➤ **Depression.** The symptoms of depression in children can include (but are not limited to) irritability, rage, stomachaches, headaches, and dizziness; bedwetting, nightmares, and aggressive behavior. Note that *situational* or *reactive depression* often flares in response to a specific event; *chronic* or *long-term depression* is a serious illness that requires professional help.

- **Obsessive Compulsive Disorders** (OCD) show themselves through symptoms such as repetitive behavior (like repeatedly washing hands or brushing teeth until the gums bleed) and other irrational hygiene-related activities often tied to feelings of guilt.

    Repetitive checking behaviors are also a symptom. The checking often develops out of a need for reassurance and security. These OCD behaviors are not "bad habits," but need professional treatment. Behavioral therapy has great success with OCD.

How to respond to all this emotion? First: Listen. Listen to what your kids are saying—and what they're not saying. Silence is a big clue, therapists say: A child who quits talking and doesn't want to discuss his feelings may be in more trouble than one who is acting out (using inappropriate behavior to express emotions he cannot verbalize).

Or, a child or teen may withdraw more dramatically—not only not talking, but barely responding, and spending as much time out of the house or alone in her room as possible. Yes, we all need "space," especially in trying times—but when the withdrawal is unusual, you need to take note—and get professional help. If you can't reach your child's fear, seek a trained professional.

Also, seeking one-to-one or group psychotherapy can be helpful if you are feeling overwhelmed and beginning to experience anxiety or depression. Therapy can offer an opportunity to address any issues that may be playing themselves out in your parenting. It may also be important to have the child evaluated for therapy if the behavior described above arises.

You'll learn more about the special problems single-parent children face in more detail in Part 2.

> **Wise Words**
> "I had a child in therapy for a year for depression. That depression lasted six to eight years after their father died. And another child had panic attacks, and another a bout with obsessive compulsive behavior. They're much better now. Time heals… with lots of love and professional help when needed."
> —A widowed mother of four

> **Meaning?**
> *Obsessive-Compulsive Disorder (OCD)* is a combination of obsessions (recurrent and persistent thoughts, impulses, or images that cause marked anxiety or distress) and compulsions (repetitive behaviors or mental acts that the person feels driven to perform in response to an obsession) aimed at preventing or reducing distress. OCD is often accompanied by depression, guilty states, and anxiety.

Part 1 ➤ You Are NOT Alone

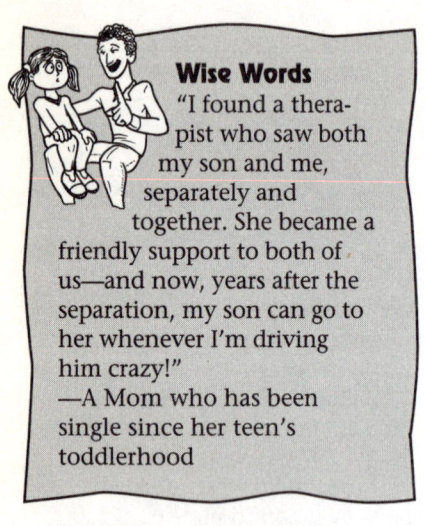

Facing a New Reality

Anyone who told you how lucky you were to have experienced your life-trauma ("That which doesn't kill you, makes you strong") would probably be in line for what seems like a well-deserved punch in the nose. But the fact is, the emotions that we experience do add a richness to life that an untroubled existence misses out on. That is, if we literally work THROUGH them. We learn that we can feel intense emotion and survive. Children learn compassion for others through facing difficulties themselves.

But all of this ultimately cheerful reality may not help much when you or your kids are in the pits. To help them (and you) you need to take all the steps outlined so far: Avoid denial, empathize, practice a positive attitude, and find help from professionals and support groups.

But in addition to those steps, one thing that almost always proves effective is accepting that life is tough, that emotions are excruciating, and that the struggle is a bear. After you've accepted all that, find something new to turn your attention to. That's right: Supporting your child in building a website or joining the soccer club is not an escape. To find some talent that you've been burying is not avoidance. It's simply the way to let go of the past and get on with what matters.

> **Wise Words**
> "I found a therapist who saw both my son and me, separately and together. She became a friendly support to both of us—and now, years after the separation, my son can go to her whenever I'm driving him crazy!"
> —A Mom who has been single since her teen's toddlerhood

> **Wise Words**
> "I found that if I could look at what I do have, instead of what I don't have, I felt a lot better about my life."
> —A teenage boy raised by a single parent.

The Least You Need to Know

➤ Feelings aren't fatal unless they're bottled up. Make sure you encourage your children to express their fears and anger directly.

➤ Examine your fears carefully. Are they rational, or are they covering up deeper insecurities?

➤ Support networks can hold you together when you need it and charge you up when you're ready.

➤ Therapy is likely to be a necessary part of moving from one emotional place to another.

➤ "Life is difficult," a Buddhist saying goes. "And once we have accepted that it is difficult, it is no longer difficult."

Chapter 3

It's About You

In This Chapter

- ➤ Do your kids have a good parent?
- ➤ Taking stock of your personality
- ➤ Evaluating your dreams
- ➤ Setting goals for yourself

Being a parent doesn't mean that your kids are the only concern. Some single parents shy away from focusing on themselves because they think that would be selfish. Some feel so strongly about putting their children first that they seem angry about being asked about their own goals.

If you still have a hard time paying attention to yourself, think of this: Ever notice how when you're on a plane, the flight attendants giving those "in case of emergency" instructions always say that if you are traveling with a small child, put your oxygen mask on first, and then help the child? In other words, if you can't save your own life, you've got no chance of helping your family!

So this chapter gets you to work to ensure the optimum life for yourself by focusing on your dreams. By the time you're done, you'll be amazed at what an interesting role model you can be for your kids (and not to mention a wonderful life companion for yourself)!

Part 1 ➤ *You Are NOT Alone*

Going Through Changes

Becoming a single parent—however it happened—is sure to throw your life into turbulence. Divorce and death represent traumatic losses. Childbirth or adoption are major changes that require more than a quick adjustment. Others who've been there offer suggestions for getting through the changes:

> **Wise Words**
> "If my Mom could get a life I wouldn't feel like she had to be part of mine all the time: hang out with me and my friends, go out together, shop, travel. She needs to meet people her own age!"
> —Teenage son of widow

> **Wise Words**
> Harry Truman once said, "A pessimist is one who makes difficulties of his opportunities and an optimist is one who makes opportunities of his difficulties." And he turned out OK.

> **Parent Pitfalls**
> Self-sacrifice is indeed part of parenting—but parents who sacrifice all for their kids may end up with little but resentment.

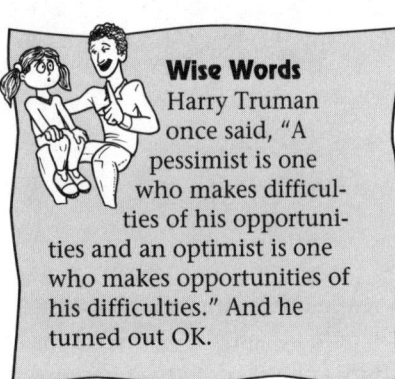

➤ Accept that your life is different—for better or worse, that's a fact that can't be changed. Letting go of the past and moving into the present and toward the future can be tough—but there are actions you can take.

➤ Find ways to rest and renew. Practice relaxation; get as much sleep as you can. If getting to sleep is tough, use less caffeine and take more walks.

➤ Eat well. Good nutrition is as important for you as for your kids. Try avoiding junk food for a few days and see how much your mood improves! Stay away from alcohol and other depressants (and if you can't, get help).

➤ Find a support group that will understand your loss and energize you to move ahead. As you connect with others in similar situations, you'll find that helping others helps you. By sharing experience, you not only share strength; you also give your own self-worth a boost. (Dubious? Hook up with a group like those listed in Appendix A and give it a shot. Can't hurt!)

➤ If you really feel stuck, seek therapy. Counseling alone may help, or your therapist may recommend a temporary prescription for tranquilizers or antidepressants, which can be useful. But beware of self-medicating with alcohol or other drugs.

➤ Practice smiling and thinking positive. Don't dismiss this as gag-me advice without at least trying it. (You'd encourage your kids to try anything new at least once, wouldn't you?).

And if you think you have nothing to smile or think positive about, get busy: Check yourself out with the checklists in this chapter.

Chapter 3 ➤ It's About You

Personal Profiling

The unexamined life may not be worth living, as Plato noted, but in the 2,500 years since then, a lot of people have gone through their lives in blithe self-ignorance. They don't have the time to explore their motivations (sound familiar?). Or they already know who they are (or think they do) and see no need. Wherever you stand on this issue, it's likely that your goals and expectations have been turned upside down by your new role as a single parent. So the life you once knew so well may now be an all-new adventure.

Why Take Stock?

Businesses small and large need to keep track of their stock—especially at the turning of the sales season. Well, you're at a season-turning point right now. You have a life that extends beyond your parenting role. Though it probably seems never ending right now, your kids will grow up fast—and then where will you be?

> **Wise Words**
> "My kids were happy when I got out on my own. Still, keep it in balance, remembering that there will be plenty of private time for yourself later."—Advice from a widow with grown children

Your dreams and goals have probably been shifted out of focus by your single-parent status, however you arrived here. You need to keep your eye so much on the now and the them that it's easy to forget that your own image and dreams may need polishing.

So why not take some of the kind of advice you'd pass on to your kids—and take a look at yourself!

Taking Your Personal Inventory

Modern retailers, of course, have computerized systems that check inventory with each cash register purchase. We older models have to do our evaluations manually and mentally.

You'll find it useful to break the big life-topic into its three primary parts—Love, Creation, and Soul. Or perhaps it's less intimidating to call the parts of life—Relationships, Career, and Self. Each part of life brings assets, liabilities, dreams, and goals.

Use the following forms and questionnaires for clarifying your own profile.

Key advice: Write down your answers. There is great power in putting even your most secret thoughts in writing; you may find that you uncover information you were unaware of. Plus, if it's in writing, you can use the info to develop a checklist at the end of the chapter that can literally help make your dreams come true. For now, take a look, and (in more ways than one) fill in the blanks.

23

Part 1 ▸ *You Are NOT Alone*

Personal Style Self-test

Use a scale of 1 to 8 to profile your own personal style. Begin by rating each descriptive line with "1" for "least like me" to "8" for "most like me."

                                                                          least like me   most like me

I…

P	Tend to work quickly, often impatiently	1 2 3 4 5 6 7 8
O	Like to have a plan to work by	1 2 3 4 5 6 7 8
R	Prefer to use old skills rather than learn new ones	1 2 3 4 5 6 7 8
A	Value making other people happy	1 2 3 4 5 6 7 8
L	Enjoy analyzing things (problems and people)	1 2 3 4 5 6 7 8
S	Enjoy working by myself	1 2 3 4 5 6 7 8
E	Adapt to change easily	1 2 3 4 5 6 7 8
N	Dislike routine	1 2 3 4 5 6 7 8

I…

R	Am precise and detail-oriented	1 2 3 4 5 6 7 8
A	Like to feel that people are getting along well	1 2 3 4 5 6 7 8
E	Tend to take on too many projects to finish comfortably	1 2 3 4 5 6 7 8
P	Focus on results more than process	1 2 3 4 5 6 7 8
O	Dislike working on more than one project at once	1 2 3 4 5 6 7 8
N	Rush work even to the point of carelessness	1 2 3 4 5 6 7 8
S	Find it difficult to remember faces and names	1 2 3 4 5 6 7 8
L	Am uncomfortable interacting emotionally with others	1 2 3 4 5 6 7 8

I…

E	Am influenced in decision-making by personal feelings	1 2 3 4 5 6 7 8
L	Appreciate fairness and rational orderliness	1 2 3 4 5 6 7 8
S	Often have trouble communicating with others	1 2 3 4 5 6 7 8
N	Enjoy learning new techniques more than putting them to use	1 2 3 4 5 6 7 8
A	Tend to work in spurts rather than steadily	1 2 3 4 5 6 7 8
R	Proceed step by step to a result	1 2 3 4 5 6 7 8
O	Need minimal info to initiate projects	1 2 3 4 5 6 7 8
P	Enjoy variety	1 2 3 4 5 6 7 8

Chapter 3 ▶ It's About You

I…

A	Am sensitive to other people's needs	1 2 3 4 5 6 7 8
R	Don't enjoy being presented with new problems	1 2 3 4 5 6 7 8
O	Come to quick decisions about things and people	1 2 3 4 5 6 7 8
S	Dislike being interrupted	1 2 3 4 5 6 7 8
L	Am able to take the "personal" component out of a job	1 2 3 4 5 6 7 8
E	Feel comfortable with open-ended projects and situations	1 2 3 4 5 6 7 8
P	Enjoy working with other people around	1 2 3 4 5 6 7 8
N	Follow my intuitions	1 2 3 4 5 6 7 8

I…

L	Don't have much need for others' approval	1 2 3 4 5 6 7 8
O	Need to come to conclusions about people & situations	1 2 3 4 5 6 7 8
E	Am curious and excited about new situations	1 2 3 4 5 6 7 8
S	Need a quiet setting for work	1 2 3 4 5 6 7 8
A	Avoid unpleasant communications	1 2 3 4 5 6 7 8
N	Can deal calmly with complicated processes	1 2 3 4 5 6 7 8
P	Enjoy interacting with people	1 2 3 4 5 6 7 8
R	Don't rely on intuition	1 2 3 4 5 6 7 8

Now, total the rank-number "scores" for each letter-code:

P = ____
E = ____
R = ____
S = ____
O = ____
N = ____
A = ____
L = ____

Circle the four letter-items with the highest number scores.
Write down those four corresponding letters here:

_____

Each letter represents an aspect of your PERSONAL style:

P or **people-oriented** types tend to turn attention outward, to others, and the environment.

E or **enthusiastic types** are generally spontaneous, curious, and available for new experiences. (They occasionally have difficulty completing more mundane tasks.)

R or **right-now types** dwell in the present and rely on directly observed information.

S or **self-focused types** look inward and focus on their own emotions and ideas. (They may have some difficulty dealing with others.)

O or **organized types** plan step by step approaches to life and appreciate arriving at decisions (and are sometimes put off by unexpected change).

N or **new-facing types** have faith in possibilities and the future (and may perhaps pay less attention to the present).

A or **appreciative types** operate from personal judgments (and sometimes ignore hard facts).

L or **logical types** base their decisions and opinions on rational analysis and tend to focus closely on tasks (sometimes to the exclusion of human factors).

When you tally up your scores, stop and give them some thought. What do they say about how you get along in the world and with other people—about how you feel about your own value?

Career experts know that if your career goals don't match your personality type, success may be elusive (and perhaps not even satisfying, even when you do achieve it). You will have a better chance at happiness when you allow your goals to grow out of your personality.

Chapter 3 ▸ It's About You

Dream Analysis Worksheet

To get a clear view of your personal and emotional assets and liabilities, open up your dreams and take a look at some personality possibilities.

DREAMS
Begin with what you liked playing as a kid. What's your earliest memory of a life-dream? Write it down, even if it seems silly.
_____
_____

MORE DREAMS
What did you want to be when you were in elementary school?
_____

In junior high? _____
In high school? _____

What do you do in your free time? Note what kinds of activities you most enjoy watching or reading about:
_____

What kinds of activities send you into daydreaming? _____
_____

And now, today, if you could do anything at all in life, what would it be? (Forget what you think it OUGHT to be—or what would be good for your children. For just this moment, focus on what YOU want.) _____
_____

What do your dreams, then and now, have in common? Describe in a few words:
_____

DOING: Are you doing something actively, with your hands or body?
_____

RELATING: Are you relating with other people? In what context? (Groups, helping, supervising, one on one...) _____

EXCELLING: What marks excellence in your dreams? Creating a product? Completing a project? Winning at something? Hearing applause?
_____
_____

ACTIVITY LEVEL: How active are you in your dream: Are you sedentary? Vigorous? Moderate? _____

THINKING: How much of your dream work relies on your mind more than the rest of you? (As in creating, thinking, planning, etc.)
_____

SETTING: Where does your dream take place? Outdoors? Inside? In a specific location?
_____

Part 1 ➤ *You Are NOT Alone*

Now, analyze your dreams. What do they tell you about what you most enjoy doing? Are there ways you can translate your dreams into reality? Make a commitment to yourself: start to think about what you want to work toward and how you plan to start.

Where Are You Going?

Now that you're more in touch with your dreams, you can get where you want to be—maybe not this week, but in the future, when you feel that your life is more your own. Take some steps now to make it more your own right now.

Charting Your Goals Worksheet

With your "dreams" in mind, write down one major life-goal for each area:

Relationship-related goal: _____

Work-related goal: _____

Self-related goal: _____

Now, write down three specific steps you could take toward achieving those goals:

Relationship-related goal: _____

_____

_____

Work-related goal: _____

_____

_____

Self-related goal: _____

_____

_____

Now, from the information you've put down, make some to-do lists.

What are the three qualities or characteristics about yourself that you like the most?

_____

_____

_____

List three ways you'll put them to good use:
_____
_____
_____

What are the three that you like the least?
_____
_____
_____

List three ways you'll work to change them:
_____
_____
_____

Where would you like to be in:
5 years: _____
10 years: _____
15 years: _____

And three actions you can take right now toward getting there:
_____
_____
_____

For example—would career counseling help? How about going back to school? Can you admit that you might need some kind of therapy or counseling to help you break through uncomfortable barriers you may have found?

If you've really focused here, it's likely you can already feel some changes in your life (and even more likely that your children, friends, and family have noticed some positive changes, too) just from thinking about your special dreams.

Wise Words
"I got so beat down by life that I never realized how much I could make good things happen just by thinking positively about them. It really worked!"
—A 40-year-old divorced Dad

Part 1 ➤ You Are NOT Alone

> **Expert-Ease**
> Act your way into right thinking. Feeling blue? Take a walk. Feeling you can't do anything right? Try doing one small thing you enjoy. Finish it to your satisfaction. Little by little, these actions will put you in a positive space.

Counselors remind us that parents who feel good about their lives have more to give their children. So balance is not only possible but necessary: Psychological studies show, not surprisingly, that single parents who are happy in their own lives deal better with their children.

Kids are also more comfortable with parents who are comfortable with themselves—and need to see that contentment is possible after a trauma.

So you've learned some "hard" facts about the numbers of single-parent families, and taken some close looks at who and where you are, toward thinking—already—about where you could go.

The rest this book will show you how to get there.

The Least You Need to Know

- ➤ You are entitled to a life of your own—and living a full life will help your kids, too.
- ➤ Even while under stress, take care of yourself. Eat right, exercise, and practice positive thinking.
- ➤ A written inventory of your attributes and goals can clarify your life.
- ➤ Your own positive outlook can improve your children's lives. It can't hurt to try!

Part 2
Keeping an Eye on the Kids

Do you sometimes feel guilty for raising your kids alone? Do you think they miss living with another parent? Do you ever wonder how your single parent status will affect them as they grow?

The good news is, given enough love, support, and stability, the children of single parents can develop as fully and healthfully as kids from two-parent families.

This part will show you what to expect as your children work through different stages of development. It will show you how to handle trying times with kids at any age, from the terrible twos to teenagers and beyond. You'll also learn how to make critical decisions about childcare, custody, and visitation.

Chapter 4

Growing Patterns

In This Chapter

➤ How children develop

➤ Special problems faced by single-parent children

➤ The key to single-parent success

➤ The importance of listening to your kids

OK—so maybe "everybody" gets divorced these days. And maybe it is true that so many kids are raised by single parents that it's almost the norm. Does that mean that single-parent kids should have no problems? Of course not. The fact that single-parent living is statistically significant doesn't make it personally insignificant.

Rather, single-parent kids have in most cases endured the trauma associated with family upheaval, in many cases the loss of a loved one. And in all cases they struggle with a sense of being different, and with some fears and insecurities that are inevitable when faced with the reality of relying on one, rather than two, adults.

But with a little knowledge, you can protect your kids and help them grow stronger.

Child Psychology 101

To understand how children in single-parent families think and sometimes act, you first need to know a little about human development in general.

In some ways, the basic "job" we all face as humans is to discover who we are and what our relationship is to the world. As part of this, we all need a steady influx of acceptance, affection, stimulation, and security (different psychological schools have different labels for these terms, but the concepts are pretty well agreed upon).

The way we go about our life task depends upon the level of physical, emotional, and *cognitive* (learning) involvement we are capable of.

Kids start off in a very small world—the womb, their crib, a parent's lap—and gradually grow into a bigger one. At first we hold them in our bodies, then our arms, then our homes. And little by little we open our arms, let go of their hands, and see them off into the wide world. It is a parent's job, in other words, to become obsolete. If you want to create healthy, happy humans who can function in any life situation, you need to let your kids go—in the right way and at the right time.

First, you must build a solid base of trust and security for your kids, and they must *internalize* that base; that is, they must carry those feelings of trust and security within them as they march through an often scary adult world.

All children, no matter what their culture or background, follow a broadly similar pattern of development as they move from dependence to independence. They need to accomplish what psychologists call *developmental tasks*.

Not all children attempt and accomplish each developmental task at exactly the same age, but nearly all children do develop in the same sequence. (If they miss a stage, they're likely either to get "stuck" later in life—or come back to repeat it.) Every child develops differently, of course, but the pattern is one you can come to know.

> **Meaning?**
> *Cognitive development* refers to the ability to learn, beginning with an infant's exploration of his environment with his senses (like a baby sticking anything he can find into his mouth), to the adolescent's ability to grasp and manipulate complex concepts (like a teenager cleverly lobbying for use of the family car).

> **Meaning?**
> *Internalizing* a feeling or state of mind refers to taking the love, comfort, protection, and security that a parent or early caretaker provides externally to an infant or toddler, and developing a solid sense of that affection and support to strengthen the child as he or she grows.

> **Meaning?**
> A *developmental task* is a behavioral achievement appropriate to a given stage or age: grasping is one of the developmental tasks of early infancy; walking, of early toddlerhood. Developmental tasks tend to follow in sequence; for example, a baby has to learn how to crawl before it learns how to walk.

Climbing the Developmental Ladder

Here's a brief outline of the development process through which we all travel from birth to adulthood.

➤ Infants need to develop enough trust in their world to be willing to step out and explore it as toddlers.

➤ Toddlers need enough approval and security to literally taste, poke, and play with everything in their environment—and to learn to talk about it, too.

➤ Pre-schoolers need to gain the confidence necessary to explore and learn independently, so that by school age they are ready to get busy with learning.

➤ In the school-age years, kids become capable of learning more intellectually; they also step out into the social world while their bodies develop steadily but quietly.

➤ Adolescence is a time for kids to discover who they are—and develop a good feeling about their identity so that they can go out into the world as young adults and form close relationships with others.

> **Expert-Ease**
> If you haven't already, try to find expert guidance on child and adolescent development—either in a book or a class—from a source that can lay out the route of the journey you and your kids are on. (Resources are listed in Appendix A.)

Whatever stage your kids are going through, one of the most important pieces of information you need to know is that all children—from toddlers to teens—tend to think that the world revolves around them. Therefore, when anything goes wrong in their world, they are much more likely than adults to take blame for it. They are both powerful and powerless at the same time.

Possible Problems

So how do single parent kids develop into successful adults? As I mentioned in Chapter 1, not all single-parent kids are doomed to emotional and psychological failure. With the right support, in fact, single kids are as healthy as (or sometimes even healthier than) kids from intact families. But psychologists do express concern about some typical patterns found in the children of single-parent families. I'll look at some of those patterns in more detail over the following pages.

Expressing Themselves

One of the most common traits that counselors see in single-parent kids is that the kids don't, can't, or won't express their feelings. Often, kids won't tell you truthfully how they're feeling because they want to protect you. They may try to blame their other parent, but that makes them uncomfortable too. Even in the closest parent-child relationships, a child may well be reluctant to say: "I know Mom has enough on her mind," or, "I don't want to worry Dad by making him think anything is wrong." The child may think, "If I show I have problems, maybe I'll be out, too."

Fear and sadness are the most common negative emotions, psychological experts say. Psychiatrist Taylor Sachs refers to the "abandonment injury" caused by divorce or death, which can be compounded by a succession of caretakers who are also "lost," in his words, when they leave the child's life.

One of the greatest challenges of single parenting, then, is to be able to help your children identify and deal with feelings that you might rather not admit to. If you can meet the challenge and deal with those feelings openly, you're way ahead of the game. "If the situation, whatever it is (divorce, unwed parents, death of a parent), is dealt with openly at a level the child is capable of comprehending," says social worker Mary-Alice Olson, "the child can actually grow and mature a great deal. The child's feelings about these issues should be addressed and children should always have the opportunity to express their emotions."

Acting Out

The good news is some kids *will* tell you what's going on with them—the bad news is, they won't tell you directly.

> **Meaning?**
> *Acting out* refers to behavior (usually negative) that children and teens use to express feelings they can't explain verbally. Anger might be too scary to admit to a parent, for example, but letting the air out of a neighbor's tires sends the same message. While acting out is related to what a previous generation might have called *acting up* (causing problems), the difference is that children who are acting out are acting outside of their normal behavior patterns.

As a parent, you alone have the best opportunity to know your children's unique qualities and character. This is important, because when children are in a crisis they are most likely to show it by *acting out* of their own personal norm.

Social worker Mary-Alice Olson notes, "Things to be aware of with children of single parents (and with all children) are any kind of acting out behavior. If a child who was normally obedient suddenly becomes defiant or begins inappropriate behaviors in school or at home (for example, bed wetting, striking out at other children, biting, setting fires), this may be a sign that the child is having some difficulty with the situation.

"Also if a normally social child begins to withdraw and isolate, this could be a response to family stresses."

As you observe your child, watch for any behavior that is different from the norm: A happy child who cries a lot, a noisy child who is silent, a gregarious girl who starts holing up in her room, a loner who suddenly is wild with his friends, a good student whose grades plummet. These are all a child's ways of telling you that something is going on.

Role Reversal

Some children of single parents may become "little adults"—they develop into the "other parent" and take over chores like babysitting and housekeeping. In some ways, they actually become a partner to the parent. Taken to an extreme, these children may actually become the caretakers of their parents, a situation known as *role reversal*.

While having the child help out can bring added support to a single parent struggling with many demands, it can be unhealthy for the child, who then loses his sense of being a child and becomes an adult before he is emotionally or developmentally prepared to deal with adult issues.

A therapist comments, "I generally recommend that clients who are struggling with single-parent issues become involved in a support group, either an organization such as Parent's Without Partners or even something less formal. Many churches offer groups for single or divorced parents. Broadening the parent's support system and increasing their emotional support system will decrease their emotional reliance on the children."

On the flip side, you may observe *regression*, in which a child of any age goes back to the previous phase of development: A nursery-school child starts bedwetting again; a school age child restarts thumbsucking; a teen spends all weekend watching cartoons.

If your child exhibits signs of regression, you may be annoyed and even alarmed, unless you understand what's happening and see it as part of a broader picture.

Regression shouldn't be seen as a problem in itself, but as a symptom of a child's inner conflicts or hidden worries. Trying to control or correct the "babyish" behavior is likely to be frustrating and ineffective. For example, if your child who has been dry at night starts bed-wetting again after a family breakup, punishing or mocking the bed-wetting behavior may only make it worse. Instead, try to understand and eliminate the underlying worry. If at home approaches don't help, professional guidance is a good idea.

> **Meaning?**
> *Role reversal* occurs when a child takes over some (or all) of the functions normally expected of a parent, even to the point of becoming in some sense a parent or caretaker of the adult.

> **Meaning?**
> *Regression* refers to returning to more babyish patterns in one or more areas of behavior (for example, when a school-age child reverts to thumb-sucking).

Sexual Identity Crisis

Some child psychologists and sociologists fear that single-parent life may adversely affect the development of children's sexual identities as well as how they feel about members of their same sex.

What this means is that boys need to identify with men, and girls need to identify and imitate women, in order to develop appropriate gender roles and behavior. If one adult "gender model" is missing from the family, this is harder for kids to do. If one adult has deserted or abandoned the family, the child may feel anger and disappointment that make identification with that parent difficult.

You can overcome or offset this difficulty by including both men and women in your circle of close companions to serve as role models for your kids. You can also explore organizations, such as Big Brothers/Big Sisters of America, that provide one-on-one companionship for your kids (see Chapter 17). A recent in-depth study demonstrated that one-on-one mentoring between adults and single-parent kids has provable positive results.

Stress Proofing

While you and your kids may indeed face some tough times and tough situations, those very challenges offer benefits that more mainstream families may miss. Many others who have lived through these life experiences know firsthand the truth of the old saying, "What doesn't kill you makes you strong."

In fact, one of the characteristics common to many single-parent kids is what counselors call "stress proofing." If you have been through bad situations and come out the other side learning that you're still OK, you can deal with many more highly stressful situations in life with less suffering.

> **Parent Pitfalls**
> Some might say success comes from always putting the kids first—but kids in two-parent households who feel they always come first are at risk of serious spoilage. Instead, successful single parents say they always keep in mind that they are parents first—they have their own social, business, and intellectual lives, but always within the context of their parental role.

The Secrets of Successful Single Parents

So how do you help your children survive—and thrive? The most important key to single parenting is something both counselors and parents agree on: *Be a parent first*. This is one pattern that most successful single parents seem to follow.

What does being a parent first mean? You may have a career or a busy social life, but you don't lose touch with your children and their needs. You don't have to sacrifice your adult self just because you are a parent, as long as you make your children know they are number one in your life as a parent.

Jane Mattes, a therapist with 30 years experience specializing in single-parent families, mentions her biggest concern: "I don't think people are taught in any way today to be parents—and when they become single parents, it's even tougher. They veer toward either being a pal afraid to make any demand on their kids, or toward being totally authoritarian, instead of finding a balance: being an adult, neither a wimp nor a general. Kids really want to feel they have a parent."

> **Expert-Ease**
> "I recommend parenting classes for most of my clients, both single parents and couples. These classes offer opportunities to learn healthy limit setting, appropriate consequences and a venue to address specific issues."
> —Therapist Mary-Alice Olson

Focus on Your Family

Of course, one of the toughest jobs for a parent is really seeing your own kids clearly. However you became a single parent, you may have fear, shame, or guilt about what you might have "done to" your kids. You might be so engrossed in handling your own situation that you can't afford to admit any difficulties on the part of your kids. That's what it means to be a parent first: To be able to keep your head and heart clear enough to keep your kids on an even keel even when you feel like your own boat is rocking.

But it's well worth the effort to take a look at some of the expert references listed in Appendix A and thinking about how your kids stack up. Run through the checklist at the end of this chapter, too. An honest appraisal is always the first step toward making any positive change.

> **Parent Pitfalls**
> "Denial is not a river in Egypt." Psychological denial comes into play when we want so badly NOT to see or know something that we simply don't. We don't want to believe that our children are hurt or in trouble, so we simply don't see it. That's why outside help, from friends and family as well as professionals, can be crucial.

Listen to Your Kids

As noted in this chapter, your kids may not be able to tell you directly what's going on or how they're feeling. So use the following checklist to see if yours may be trying to get a message across to you.

39

Part 2 ➤ *Keeping an Eye on the Kids*

Watching the Kids Worksheet

If your single-parent status is new, list three behaviors of your child/children that are different than previously.

1. _____

2. _____

3. _____

Have others—family, teachers, neighbors—commented on changes in your children's behavior? What are they? _____
_____

If you've been a single parent for a while, has any change in status occurred that might cause reaction in kids? _____
_____

My child wants most from me as a parent:

_____ Unconditional Love   _____ Caring firmness

_____ Consistency   _____ Understanding of his/her needs

_____ Respect   _____ All of the above

_____ My presence

Your responses to this worksheet should give you a pretty good idea what's going on with your children. In the following chapters, you'll learn more about how to understand and help your children cope with single-parent family life.

The Least You Need to Know

➤ Your children develop according to a predictable, learnable pattern.

➤ Your children have to face special challenges and develop special strengths because of their single-parent status.

➤ You can optimize those strengths by always being a parent first.

Chapter 5

Dealing with Discipline

In This Chapter

- ➤ Discipline is not a dirty word
- ➤ When "misbehavior" is okay
- ➤ Deciding when to enforce the rules—and when to let go
- ➤ Handling discipline with your ex
- ➤ Tested tips to keep the peace

Discipline is a word and a concept that moves in and out of favor even faster than hairstyles. So maybe it's simpler and safer to think of discipline as *structure*. It's important to create structures—for behavior, for communication, and for living—within which everyone in your family can grow, live together, and feel both safe and comfortable.

A positive, active approach to creating this kind of framework for behavior is also especially important for single-parent families because it provides the extra dollop of security single-parent kids need. It'll help you, too, with the extra-strength backbone you need to resist the higher-powered parent-tests single-parent kids are prone to.

> **Meaning?**
> *Discipline* means teaching, not punishment, which is only a limited part of behavior management. The word is related to *disciple*, or one who follows a teacher or teaching. Remember that being an example is better than being a boss.

Many parents are uncomfortable with enforcing discipline. It may help to remember that the point of discipline is to meet goals. Long-term goals will help your child be the kind of person you want your child to be; on-going goals will establish a sense of stability in your home; and short-term goals will help you accomplish whatever you want to at the moment. Discipline also provides your child with security; the ability to know what to expect and the consequences.

In this chapter, you'll see ways to approach the difficult area of discipline.

Tracking Trouble

Parents (especially, perhaps, single parents—and even more so, recently single parents) tend toward one of two extremes: They either can't see anything wrong with their kids, or they're looking so hard for problems that they view simple normal development as troublesome.

The former situation can result in discipline that's too lax (or, if you prefer, structure that's too loose); the latter often leads to a grip that's too tight. Both can be self-defeating. The key phrase here is realistic expectations.

Of course, discipline is a tricky part of parenting even in two-parent families. Think about it: In a two-parent family (ideally, at least), both parents agree on a consistent philosophy and pattern of the kind of discipline they feel would best socialize their children. One parent can back the other parent up; or the two can take turns being good cop and bad cop. There is twice as much attention available for all the kids.

When only one parent is in charge, though, not only does that parent have a handful to handle, but may also have to share the kids with another parent who has an entirely different disciplinary approach.

If it sounds difficult, it is! The rest of this chapter, and the references in Appendix A, will hopefully help you set up consistent, fair, and realistic expectations for your children.

The Ages and Stages of Discipline

In Chapter 4, you read a brief overview of the developmental stages all kids go through. Unfortunately, each stage brings its own struggles and issues as your kids strain to "push the envelope"—to grow to the next stage.

Chapter 5 ➤ *Dealing with Discipline*

The child development books listed in Appendix A are valuable guides to the normal nuttiness of child growth and development. Let me give you some brief examples of the disciplinary issues you may face as your child grows.

➤ Infants often tend to get fussy as they approach a developmental dividing line—struggling in their determined effort to sit up, perhaps, or grasp something firmly.

➤ Toddlers tend to get pushy—to be on the move and to poke into places you'd really prefer they not—as part of the learning process.

➤ Pre-schoolers may make you nuts with their constant noise and questions—but that's only the normal outgrowth of their experiments with language and learning, and with being sure they're still connected to you.

➤ Your middle-year-school child is venturing into the social world with early efforts that may be awkward—and maddening to you—but necessary.

➤ Teens are famous for "bad" behavior—but they are struggling to break away from the family and need some workable channels for declaring their independence.

> **Parent Pitfalls**
> Underestimating your child's level of maturity or readiness for certain behavior can create more work for you—and less challenge for your child. On the other hand, overestimating your child's ability leads to frustration all around. Understand development and tune in to your child's abilities for optimal growth.

In other words, some behavior that drives you crazy is perfectly normal, and trying to impose unrealistic expectations at a given stage will only result in frustration all around.

Is Your Kid "Normal?"

Sometimes, though, you may be right to question your child's behavior. Sometimes (sometimes?!) kids in a particular stage carry their developmentally predictable behavior to the extreme and beyond. How can you tell when your kids' stretch is more than "normal"? Here are some stage-by-stage guidelines to behavior that is out of control.

Even your littlest children may feel the stress associated with your single-parent status. Infants and toddlers understand a lot more than we often give them credit for, so they may sense when there's tension or upheaval and it can make them fussy or worse:

➤ Troubled infants may revert to more babyish behavior. (They may need to be allowed to, temporarily.) When a baby spends more time crying than not, has persistent trouble sleeping, or is listless and wants to sleep too much, there's cause for concern.

> Toddlers may also regress. They may stop wanting to go to nursery school or daycare, or to play with friends. A toddler who runs nonstop and won't be distracted, or throws intense tantrums at the drop of a "no," may be showing signs of trouble.

Of course, distress over the family situation may be one explanation for extreme behavior in older children, too. But with older kids, there can be other, more complex causes for behavior problems—as well as external influences like school trouble, peer problems, relationship difficulties, or even drugs or other addictions. Behavior to look out for includes:

> School-age kids and young teens may resist going to school, or start doing poorly in school. It's typical for kids at this stage to seem to withdraw from their families in favor of their new-found world of friends, but if they also seem to isolate themselves from their peers, there may be cause for concern. They also may regress to babyish behavior, such as bed-wetting (see Chapter 4).

> Teens are trickier to check out; they tend to withdraw and appear to "act out" anyway. It's especially important to pay attention to their friends, the hours they keep, their eating patterns, and their physical symptoms. Also take note if your teen's (normal) isolation from the family becomes virtually absolute.

There are certain evergreen signs of trouble that may emerge at any stage in your child's development. They include:

> Trouble with peers

> Trouble in school

> Insomnia or nightmares

> Overeating or undereating

> Too much sleeping

> Retreat into fantasy (or obsessive TV, computer, books)

One final sign that all is not well: If you find yourself losing your cool more often than not—no matter what your child's behavior—or if you feel uncomfortable living in your own house, you need to look at what's going on.

Whether extreme or normal, your kids (indeed, all kids) can benefit from the establishment and maintenance of rules and expectations and from talking with them about how they feel.

Why Kids Misbehave

Why do your kids behave this way? Often, they're testing you. How firm is the structure you've created for their lives? How far will you let them go? They may not think about this consciously, of course. But on some level, they are putting you to the test.

Children of all ages want and need structure and stability in their lives—especially children who may be anxious because they are living with only one parent. Thus, as a single parent, you may find that your children test you often.

Unfortunately, many single parents often feel the urge to overindulge their kids—out of guilt, perhaps, or pity. It's a mistake because what the kids need (and what will benefit them in the long run) is a structure that makes them feel solid, not pitiful or babied.

The important thing to remember—even when your preschooler is screaming or your teenager is slamming the door—is that your child's behavior is not directed at you. When a toddler seems to "misbehave," for instance, it's not because he is basically nasty or just trying to make your life miserable; he's just growing and becoming independent.

> **Expert-Ease**
> Try to determine the cause behind your child's misbehavior. If your six-year-old insists on throwing food, for example, you might ask yourself, "Why is she acting up at the supper table? Because she doesn't know any better? Or because she's testing me?" You may choose to warn your child that she's only getting the food on her plate—if she chooses to throw it, that's all she gets. This gives her a consequence and makes her feel like she has some power. Kids often act out because they feel they have no control and are angry. Their responses are very primitive and should not be ignored.

Discipline as They Grow

So for whatever reason, your child is misbehaving. Whether you're dealing with a squalling child or an obstinate pre-teen or a moody adolescent (or some combination thereof), the appropriate method of discipline may be difficult to determine—and even more difficult to impose. Luckily, childraising experts have identified a number of disciplinary measures that work for children of different ages. Over the following pages, I'll discuss the most effective tools of discipline.

Discipline for Young Ones

Infants need as much physical and emotional protection as possible. They need a framework that keeps them safe. Your discipline should teach them that they have an impact on their world and that it is a safe and friendly place. A regular routine (feeding them at the same times every day, for example) and lots of gentle physical contact can accomplish that.

The mythical screaming toddler is feared by most parents. If your toddler is throwing tantrums, time-outs will separate him from the setting that has set him off and will allow him to sit down and cool off until he regains his composure. When you call a time-out, have your child sit quietly in a chair for up to two minutes while he calms down.

> **Expert-Ease**
> One of the most valuable tools for discipline is the time-out—have your child sit quietly in a chair for up to two minutes while he calms down from a tantrum. The teenage version is grounding. And remember that parents can take time-outs, too—excuse yourself and go to your room when you feel you are about to blow. Once you've calmed down, you can come back to discuss the issue more calmly with your child.

Never give in to demands when your child has a tantrum; you will only reinforce his behavior. Just wait out the tantrum as calmly as you can; if necessary, remove yourself and/or your toddler to a safer (and saner) distance. Punishing the anger is not the point—helping your child learn to express the anger less violently is.

Sometimes all of a toddler's behavior may seem like misbehavior, but it's not: it's normal exploring. Putting dangerous or delicate items out of temptation's way is the best way to keep your toddler out of trouble. Try not to be too strict with your toddler. Let him explore your home freely (after a thorough babyproofing, of course) with a minimum of restrictions and "no's."

Often kids in this age group learn limits best when those limits are set by other kids, which is one way in which placing your child in a daycare or playgroup setting can be invaluable. See chapter eight for more information on daycare.

Discipline for Pre-Teens

Pre-teens or children in middle school appreciate making rules to play by and make good use of rules that you set, especially if limitations are balanced by freedoms. For example, you might say, "You may not play outside after dark, but if you are quiet, you can play in the hall."

In addition, children of this age may need a script to help them deal with peers, so if your kids are having a hard time saying "no" to peer pressure, help them practice reasonable rebuttals, like "My parents would kill me if I did that," or "I can't smoke if I want to stay on the track team."

Be sure your kids know their friends are most welcome in your home when you are there, but not if you aren't. (You can enforce this rule without sounding like you don't trust your kid to stay on good behavior when you aren't home. Instead, say that you can't be responsible for other children when you're not around.)

Discipline for Teens

Teens are notorious for rebellion and bad behavior. Teens in single-parent families may have an even stronger need than most adolescents to test your parental strength: For as independent or even swaggering as they seem, they are also acutely aware of their vulnerability and the need to be sure they're safe.

One reason teens tend to challenge the rules is that they need to discover the consequences for themselves. Teens are not that different from toddlers in their persistent need to explore, test, and find their own way. Trouble is, teens are bigger and their "playpens" extend far beyond your living room. So, just as a toddler needs to learn by doing, a teenager needs to test the boundaries for himself: Why can't I stay out all night in a bad neighborhood? Why not drive over 65 miles an hour on the freeway? What will happen if I do?

Needless to say, this kind of testing can be difficult for a parent to accept. How can you reign your teenager in without pushing him away? Give him choices; help him come to a compromise without backing him into a corner. For example, if your kid wants to stay out all night, don't lock him in his room. Instead, say, "You want to stay at that party all night? OK—but let's figure out a way to do it so you don't get arrested." If you've got a speed demon on your hands, tell her if you catch her speeding, she'll be grounded; but offer to take her to an empty parking lot where she can enjoy a harmless joyride if she wants.

Teenagers also need healthy alternatives to bad behaviors. Just as a toddler needs to be distracted from sticking his finger in the electric socket, a teen may need to be subtly pointed toward an activity (playing music? sports? getting a part-time job?) that's healthier for him than hanging out with the corner gang.

> **Wise Words**
> "But everybody does that," says the teen—usually about hanging out, drinking beer, or staying alone in the house. The wise parent replies, "But *we* don't."

Teens are more likely to cooperate with rules they help make themselves. Discuss your rules with them—and the reasons behind those rules. Try to work out a compromise. Then don't bend those rules!

When you set your rules, make sure there are clear consequences for breaking them. For instance, make sure your child knows that if she breaks her curfew the first time, she'll get a warning. If she breaks it a second time, she's grounded. And be sure the consequences are imposed.

All that theory is well and good, but if you have a teen who repeatedly breaks your rules, whose behavior is too intense to handle, who is flailing (literally and figuratively), you

Part 2 ➤ Keeping an Eye on the Kids

> **Expert-Ease**
> Positive after-school activities are a great way to keep kids connected to safe activities that make them feel good, and give them contact with helpful role models. On the other hand, keep an eye on the friends your kids are hanging out with. If they seem troubled, they're likely to get your kids in trouble, too. If that's the case, try to divert your children from them, or limit their contact.

need help. Find a counseling center, therapist, or even a friendly third party to step in and help get some of that negative energy under control before your child's behavior has dangerous consequences.

A lot of the danger to teens these days, of course, comes from the use of alcohol and other drugs, and involvement with unsafe sexual activities. The first step to dealing with these very real threats is to admit that they are threats, even to your kids. The "not my child" attitude of denial has probably destroyed as many kids as the behaviors themselves.

It's also important to admit that single-parent kids may be more susceptible to these hazards than other kids: Rebellious behaviors are one way of acting out anger, for example. They are also a distraction from fear and other bad feelings that may plague your kids.

So assume that these are real dangers and start talking to your kids about them seriously by the time your kids are 11. Be sure your kids' schools have drugs and sex information programs, or that there are other sources available (teachers, friends of yours) for informing your kids, because they will most likely respond favorably to this information from someone who isn't their parent.

While keeping a watchful eye out for these dangerous behaviors, try not to approach them as punishable offenses, but as hazards you are protecting your children from (just as you wouldn't let your kids play in the street when they were little). "You're too important to me to let you hurt yourself," you could say. If you suspect you're children are already involved in dangerous activities, find professional help.

> **Singular Successes**
>
> The divorced mother of a teen-aged son found a positive, non-threatening way to discuss sex with him: "When he was just entering puberty, I made sure to talk with him about AIDS as a health threat. I was able to have his father talk more about the nitty gritty of sex, which was more comfortable for all of us. But at both my house and his father's house, we had condoms in the bathroom closet and we both told him, "These are here for you if you need them. No questions asked. And if the box gets empty, we'll get more. No questions asked. Just use them if you need them." So far, so good.

Disciplinary Tools for Any Age

Regardless of your child's age, there are time-tested, expert-approved methods and strategies you can use to implement discipline without being unnecessarily hurtful. The following sections will highlight some of the most useful disciplinary techniques.

Positive Consequences

Childraising experts suggest establishing well-explained guidelines for your child's behavior. A wide range of psychological and educational expertise on discipline can be distilled into one idea: model a *positive demonstration of the consequences of behavior.*

What does that mean? Let me give you an example. Let's say you tell your nine-year-old not to throw his baseball in his room. He throws the baseball anyway. It hits his beloved fishtank. He wails over his endangered fish while you point out the consequences: He must use his allowance to buy a new tank. Chances are he won't throw the baseball inside ever again.

Notice that expressing pity over his fish loss (while a normal reaction) won't teach him anything about not throwing the baseball. Neither will yelling or hitting him. Making him pay for the damage, however, is a positive action that reinforces the consequences of throwing the ball indoors.

You could empathize and at some point later relate that you understand how he feels. Empathizing with him, though, doesn't mean the consequences change; it just lets him know that he's still okay even though he's in trouble temporarily.

Corporal Punishment?

Few advisors recommend physical punishment, except in situations in which the child is in immediate, grave physical danger (or is endangering others).

For example: You and your toddler are out in town. You instruct your toddler to wait at the corner. She runs into the street instead. You grab her, yell, and swat her bottom; then you hold her tight and kiss her, saying, "You mustn't! You could get hurt. I was very frightened. I love you. Don't hurt yourself!" While the brief spank shows your daughter the consequences of her actions, the hug is still positive.

Often, discipline is delivered in anger; but unfortunately, if you are hysterical, you won't be effective. The old count-to-ten ploy works—if you feel yourself losing it, take a deep breath or a time-out. Reflect on what you really want for yourself and your child. Only when you are calm will you be able to discuss your expectations and goals with your child.

The use of physical punishment causes a great deal of controversy. In some families, communities, or cultural groups, it's accepted; in others, it's viewed with horror. Does it work? Would some other approach work better? It's an important question for you to answer for yourself.

> **Parent Pitfalls**
> Single parenting is stressful. If it feels so stressful that you are taking out your fears and frustrations out on your kids—if you get so angry you can't control yourself—help is available. Check your phone book for child abuse prevention support services, or contact the national office of Parents Anonymous at 909-621-6184.

Some parents try spanking and find that it's too painful all around; others wouldn't even think about it. If you do decide to spank your child, explain your actions to your kids: "You know there are some things that are so dangerous that I might have to hit you to remind you not to do them. Let's try to avoid that."

This is very different from angry, reactive hitting. Probably every exasperated parent has struck out at a child at least once (maybe more). What to do if you slap your child in anger? The best response is to apologize. When calmness has returned, you can talk about the upsetting behavior and work out ways to avoid it in the future.

The books on childraising and discipline listed in Appendix A can be very helpful, as can the experts in your community.

"I" Messages

Many professionals suggest that you use "I" messages. Use language that attacks the behavior, not the child. For example: Say your teenager once again fails to clean the kitchen as promised, and is gabbing on the phone when you arrive home from your job exhausted. You explain your feelings: "I don't ask you to do too much, but I was looking forward to not having to cook after the day I had. I'm very disappointed."

Your teen replies, "OK, can we get pizza?"

You say: "No. I'm taking a shower while you clean the kitchen and cook something—anything—as you have agreed to do. AND—You will not get on the telephone OR the computer for the rest of the evening." Your teen whines, "But MOM!" And you say: "Cook or starve—you promised."

Notice how you said, "I'm very disappointed," referring not to your child in general, but to the fact that dinner wasn't made as promised. This is a far better response than, "Can't you do anything right? Why are you so lazy?" or other negative you-messages.

Picking Battles

Do you ALWAYS have to be on the case? Of course not. Sometimes single parents get stuck on the idea of strength or perfection because it's so important for them to feel sturdy. But if you find that you're ALWAYS doing battle over rules, you're missing the point of discipline—which is to keep things comfortable and peaceful. Maybe it's time to ease up a bit where it doesn't really matter.

Ask yourself why do you have this rule? If it doesn't make life easier or teach your child an important lesson, why are you going nuts enforcing it?

Rules are always subject to revision. Review the following list to determine which rules matter to you and which don't:

- Respectful speech and tone
- Not making too much noise
- Obeying curfew
- Keeping room clean
- Performing household chores
- Doing homework on time
- Doing well in school
- Joining the family at the dinner table
- Dressing a certain way

If you feel that some of your rules aren't necessary, then involve the kids in a discussion to lay out new rules.

Advice from the Frontlines

No one understands the problems of single-handedly disciplining a child better than other single parents. Here, a few pieces of advice from others who've been there:

- Begin by making sure that your children understand, by your words and your actions, that you are concerned about them and love them even when you are away from them. Enforce your guidelines for behavior firmly, and praise good behavior and independence.

> **Wise Words**
> "My son and I used to battle constantly about his horribly messy room. Then I decided how he lived was his business. I told him, 'Just don't let that mess ooze into the rest of the house.' He was surprised. 'And if you can't find anything, including clean clothes, that's your problem.' It worked!"
> —Divorced mother of new grandson

> **Expert-Ease**
> On issues that aren't life threatening, many parents have discovered (often by accident) the power of inaction. Dirty clothes on the floor? Don't do the laundry. Bike left out in the rain? Let it rust. Sometimes when we show that we're ready to give up (which is not the same as giving in) the kids will pick up the ball.

- Try to spend quality time with your children. Set aside a period of each day when, no matter how tired or overworked you feel, you concentrate on your children. Talk, play, listen; ask questions; share news. This needn't be a big event; just being together or sharing chores can make everyone feel closer.

- Make sure your child's discipline problem isn't a physical one. A constantly cranky preschooler may just need extra quiet time or a few more snacks, for example.

- Don't contribute to the problem. If you want to calm a hysterical child, you have to be calm yourself.

- Pick your battles—remember, not everything matters.

- Emphasize that you and your children are in this together. Teach your kids that rules help keep the household running.

- Remember, you can use time-outs, too. If you feel yourself getting angry or upset, take a breather.

- Agree on the bottom-line issues with your kids, and then clearly communicate them. Post the rules of the house where everyone can see them.

You and Your Ex: Discipline Duo

When you're a single parent, it's not enough for you to work out disciplinary rules of your own and get your kids to stick with them. You also have to make sure that your child's other parent enforces the same rules you do. When two parents are separated, both should try to agree on discipline styles and rules for the children so that one parent is not undermining the other.

The best solution to discipline conflicts is to be able to work them out with the other parent (or caregiver, daycare provider, and so on). If you can, negotiate discipline rules and put them in writing.

That may not be possible, of course. If you cannot come to an agreement, make it clear to your kids that dad has his rules for his house, and mom has hers. If the kids try to wheedle ("But Mom always lets me stay up to 11:00!), your answer is easy: "You're not in Mom's house right now, you're in mine."

HELP! And How to Find It

Sometimes, of course, common sense, goodwill, and personal support just aren't enough. Kids are troubled—maybe more so in single-parent homes, maybe not.

How can you tell if your child's problems are more than you can solve alone? Here are a few signs:

- ➤ Your child's behavior is extreme or persistent.
- ➤ Your child doesn't respond to careful discipline.
- ➤ Others comment to you about your child's behavior.

What can therapy do for you and your family? What kind is best suited to you?

Therapists, whether psychiatrists, psychologists, social workers, or lay counselors, can work separately with parents and children and then bring them together to help both sides see things in a new perspective.

Choosing a Therapist

Here's what you should look for if you decide to find a therapist:

- ➤ A referral or recommendation by a friend or relative whom you trust, by a doctor or other professional, or by a recognized organization or agency.
- ➤ Your therapist should be licensed or certified by the state, a professional association, or both.
- ➤ Full membership in a recognized society or association for his or her specialty—the American Psychological Association, for example.
- ➤ A postgraduate degree in the specialty, plus evidence of additional, supervised training.
- ➤ An ability to make both your child and you feel comfortable.
- ➤ A willingness to answer fully any questions concerning training, credentials, or therapeutic techniques.

Here are some questions to ask a potential therapist to further determine whether he or she is right for you and your family:

- ➤ "What experience have you had in working with single parents?"
- ➤ "What experience have you had in dealing with my kind of problem or situation?"
- ➤ "About how long do you think therapy will take?"
- ➤ "How often would you want me (and/or my child) to come?"
- ➤ "How much will it cost? Can extended payments or reduced fees be arranged?"

- "Are your services eligible for insurance coverage?"
- "What therapeutic theory or school do you follow?"
- "How will the process work? Individually? In a group? By talking only, or with other activities?"
- "Is there any reading on the topic I can or should do?"
- "How much will my family be involved with therapy sessions?"
- What of what my child says is confidential even from parents? Most therapists have a policy on this and it needs to be clear to the parent.
- "Can I get in touch with you between sessions?"

If you feel confident and comfortable with a therapist's ability to understand you and your child, it can't hurt to try a couple of sessions. If you—or the child's teachers—notice no changes in behavior after a few weeks, meet with the therapist to discuss the situation. If the therapist won't meet with you, consider another therapist.

Other Sources for Extra Support

Paying a professional is not the only way to get outside help. Your community is probably filled with organizations—Big Brothers/Big Sisters, the community service society, the mental health association—geared to provide information and guidance. More informally, you can ask your child's teacher, scout leader, pediatrician, or religious counselor for extra support or feedback.

The library has books and videos on parenting, and the Internet support groups offer advice as well (see Appendix A). Check local bulletin boards and newspaper listings of workshops where you can hear the experience of other parents.

The Least You Need to Know

- Structure is especially important for kids in single-parent families.
- Discipline is not a dirty word; it is the way you guide your children to living in society successfully.
- Discipline is more likely to be successful if it includes realistic expectations, clarity, consistency, and respect.
- Make sure your children understand that actions have consequences.

Chapter 6

Your Children, Yourself?

> **In This Chapter**
>
> ➤ Self-esteem is not a buzzword
> ➤ The importance of practicing praise
> ➤ Why helping your children means helping yourself
> ➤ Get a life—and how!

So far, you've been exploring feelings—yours and your kids. Hopefully, you've come to accept and understand the feelings of fear and frustration that affect all single-parent families from time to time.

Understanding your feelings is, of course, only the first step toward dealing effectively with them. Behavior is a result of those feelings. Awareness of negative feelings isn't worth much unless it leads to positive actions. In this chapter, you'll learn the steps to take that turn bad feelings into a good life—for your kids AND you.

The Importance of Self-Esteem

One of the best ways to deal with negative feelings is to counteract them with positive feelings. The good drives out the bad. It can be that simple.

Good feelings begin with *self-esteem*—yours and your children's. Self-esteem is such a buzzword that it's easy to forget how vital it is to healthy development, as demonstrated by the massive amount of articles and studies produced on the subject.

Psychologists explain that children—like all of us—need to feel that they deserve success if they are to succeed; they need to feel valued by the important people in their lives if they are to value themselves and their own activities. They need to know that they are loved and valued unconditionally—that mistakes and imperfections don't diminish their worth.

> **Meaning?**
> *Self-esteem* is defined by the experts as a combination of how we feel about ourselves and how we believe others perceive us. It's also defined as a sense of being both capable and worthy of love.

This ego-building process can be organized into three steps:

1. Erase your child's sense of blame.
2. Steadily support your child's sense of worth.
3. Encourage hobbies and activities that make your child feel good about himself.

Each of these steps will be explained in more detail over the following pages.

Building Self-Esteem in Your Kids

Low self-esteem is one characteristic that is common to both many single-parent kids and their parents. Here's why: Children whose families are divided through divorce, death, or abandonment have a hard time esteeming (valuing) themselves because they think the family troubles are their fault. (Remember that kids of any age tend more than adults to consider themselves the center of the universe—and therefore the cause of all that goes wrong.)

The thought process of a child in a single-parent family can lead to lowered self-esteem in his mind and heart. Take a look at the following examples. Notice that these thoughts are completely unrelated to the child's IQ or to the reasons why a family has been divided:

- My family isn't whole.
- I acted bad.
- I broke my family.
- So I must be no good.
- If I'm no good, I can't do anything good.

If your child can't or won't tell you how bad the pain is, it's because he won't risk hearing an answer he doesn't like, such as "Yes, you're right, you're no good, it's all your fault." He also may be afraid of hurting your feelings (and maybe driving *you* away, too).

Chapter 6 ➤ Your Children, Yourself?

Hence, Step One: Erase the blame. The first and most important building block for your child's self-esteem is his thorough understanding that he is not the cause of any family disruption—or in fact of any adult difficulty. So talk about it! Say it out loud. Put it on the table so that your kid knows he can talk about it if he wants to.

You'll want to use "language" that's appropriate for each age-stage: Infants need to be held, stroked, and cooed so that they literally feel that an important adult cares about them. And why not make up a song or a story about how great they are? It's good practice for talking later—and you never know how much your baby may understand.

With young children, the indirect approach may work best. Say, "Some children who are living just with their Mom or just with their Dad sometimes get the idea that something they did make the other parent go away. Well, that's not true…"

As kids get older, they're increasingly able to hear "the whole story" and to be directly encouraged to discuss their feelings. You can even support them if they look for other sources of advice: "If you'd be more comfortable talking to someone else about this, just let me know and we'll find someone."

Once your child is over blaming himself for the family breakup, you can begin with Step 2: Steadily support his sense of worth. Experts note that worth is that combination of competence and lovableness that kids need to feel.

It's important to note here that feeling worthy is different than feeling merely competent. Experts say that many single-parent children feel competent because they feel they have to manage situations that are beyond their years. But the feeling of being worthy of love is more tenuous.

Here are a collection of suggestions from parents and professionals on how to channel a steady stream of positive support to your children:

➤ Show respect for your kids—their space, their ideas, their opinions, their decisions, their taste. Don't be afraid to tell them what is special about them.

> **Parent Pitfalls**
> You may not encourage your kids to talk about painful fears and feelings—because, frankly, you don't want to believe that your kids are hurting. But communication is crucial! It's your kids' first step toward believing they aren't to blame.

> **Wise Words**
> Self-esteem building advice: "Hug your kids three times more than you think they need." —A single Dad with joint custody

> **Wise Words**
> "When my son has a problem at school, instead of assuming he did something wrong (as I used to), I assume he's right and try to figure out how to work out the problem with his teacher." —A single Mom in the Midwest

> Show an interest in what they enjoy—and involve them in activities of yours that they express interest in. Help them find things to do that they love.

> Share with them one-on-one your own experiences and outlook—in a conversation, not a lecture.

> Praise them! Just as you may forget that your kids blame themselves, you may also neglect to praise their good deeds. You assume they know you appreciate them. Childraising specialists suggest that you praise all positive behavior—even things your child is "supposed to do."

There are plenty of things you can praise about your kids: things they already do well; improvements in their behavior; even their attempts to do new things. Remember, it's not the finished product that matters, but the effort.

> **Expert-Ease**
> Childraising professionals at Boys Town, a home for children that has become a center for parenting expertise, have what is called the "4-to-1" rule: For every negative behavior exhibited by a child, they find four positive behaviors or reasons to praise the child.

To be effective, praise needs to be specific. Describe exactly what you value in your child ("I love the way you take the time to help your little brother with his math homework." "I think it's great that you practice the clarinet every day.") You can praise your child with a detailed statement—or just a simple hug and "That's wonderful!"

Praising has some surprising side effects. The more you positively communicate with your child (with both language and presentation), the more positive you'll find yourself feeling in general. (Don't believe it? Try it!)

Something else remarkable happens when you help your kids feel good about themselves. You feel better about yourself as a good parent!

Building Your Own Self-Esteem

As a single parent, you may be struggling with self-esteem. It's not just your kids that suffer loss through a death or divorce, and that may be even harder to admit. Your deepest secret thoughts and feelings may well run like this:

> I "failed" at marriage; or

> My spouse "deserted me" either literally or by death (irrational as this is); or

> I wasn't "good enough" to attract a mate, so I must raise this child alone.

It's not so different from the child-like thought process outlined earlier. Yes, it's irrational—but feelings aren't meant to be rational. And with feelings like that eating away at the soul, "feeling good about ourselves"—good enough to have our own successes and happiness in life—is not a light-hearted matter for either your kids or you.

So it's not only important for your children that you be a good parent—but for yourself as well. The same steps I mentioned earlier for kids will work on building up your sense of self-worth, so let's back over the suggestions offered so far and try applying them to you.

Step One: Erase the blame. Don't blame yourself for your current situation or for feeling like an inadequate parent. Research repeatedly shows that single parents are competent and successful in their family lives and that single-parent homes are capable of producing healthy children. No single parent should face life feeling "less-than." (Suggestions for attitude adjustment in this area can be found in Chapter 21.)

Time for Step Two—Support for your sense of worth. Go back to the inventory in Chapter 3: How are you doing in YOUR life? Take a hard look at every negative idea and focus on turning it into a positive. Polish up the positives. You deserve it—and so do your children. Children will learn from your example of a high self-esteem and a positive outlook.

Little by little, your actions more than your words can convince your children of their own worth. And little by little, by taking actions that make you feel good about yourself, you will eventually come to believe in your own self worth.

> **Wise Words**
> "After years of therapy," says a 42-year-old non-custodial mother, "I came to understand that I felt to blame for my Daddy's 'leaving me' at the age of 2. If I was that bad, nothing I ever did could be good enough. Right down to where I believed I couldn't be a good enough parent, so I left. Now I understand how bad I felt about myself and why—but it's a bit late. "

Getting a Life

Now let's move on to the third step in the self-esteem process for both you and your kids: Encourage hobbies and activities that make your child feel good about himself.

Often the simplest way to let go of a painful idea is to focus attention on a positive one. So help your children discover activities they enjoy—and let them find successes there.

Creating Success

Emphasize your child's talents. Is she good in art but not sports? Then praise her artwork, and watch the feeling of confidence expand into other areas of her life.

It's VERY important that kids at every age get involved with people and activities outside of the family. They need contact with both other kids (whom they can relate to) and a variety of reliable adults (whom they can model themselves after). You'll find specific suggestions for activities in Chapter 16.

59

Part 2 ➤ *Keeping an Eye on the Kids*

> **Wise Words**
> "Keep your needs to a minimum... Of course, maintain self-esteem and stay in good physical and emotional health or you can't put the kids first. Where dating and vacations are concerned, remember that you'll have years—nearly a lifetime—without them when they've flown the coop. Spend time with your kids, go camping, go to dance rehearsals, and drop in at camp." —A divorced mother of 4 adolescents

> **Expert-Ease**
> Stay close to your kids, no matter what! Get off work early for soccer games, if you can. Help organize music for the church youth choir. Volunteer at the high school library at night if you have a job and can't come during the day. Do what you can to share your child's activities.

> **Meaning?**
> *Co-dependent* describes an unhealthy, overly close relationship in which each party is made to live for the other and feels incapable of freedom.

Many single parents also find it valuable to develop activities the whole family can do together. For example, many single-parent groups offer opportunities for kids. Group sports are a great example: Single Moms and Dads can socialize while supporting their kids and enjoying themselves.

The people who seem to have the most success as single parents are those who don't focus on (and bemoan) their single-parent status—they focus on their lives. In other words, the more you can focus on life, on living it and enjoying it, the more likely you are to have a life to share with your children.

Separate Togetherness

As in any relationship—there are some things we share and want to share: Perhaps you and your kids enjoy certain sports or hobbies together. That's great! But each of us at any age needs to have our own special interests as well.

There is an important part of family life where each member goes off on his/her own and comes back with a richer piece to share.

The Good, the Bad, and the Co-Dependent

Let's talk about boundaries. Where does healthy supportive togetherness cross the line and become role confusion? In psychological parlance, when do you and your child risk becoming *co-dependent*?

Where's the line? The key is motivation. Ask yourself, who's the activity for? Do you spend all your free time with the children's activities because you want to support them while staying close? Or are you afraid to let them go too far—or to find grown-up activities for yourself? Co-dependency is about trying to live another person's life—or trying to live one's own life for another person. A healthy dependency fosters growth and independence. Unhealthy dependencies hinder growth and maintain dependency.

If it seems your kids are devoting a lot of their time and energy to doing things with you or for you, try encouraging them to detach. Use a pattern of "praise and release." For example: "You know, you do a great job of keeping the house clean, but I think we should find some new ways of doing this stuff so you have more time on your own. What do you think?"

Observe other families in your community who have kids the same age as your own. What activities do kids engage in on their own? How much freedom do they have? How much time seems to be shared by parents and children? What kinds of activities do parents do themselves? Compare these patterns with your own. Think about encouraging your kids to participate in their own activities. Try carving out a little more time for your own hobbies.

> **Expert-Ease**
> Here's powerful evidence for the importance of social connections for your kids: Research demonstrates that single-parent children who participated in the Big Brothers/Big Sisters program are 46 percent less likely to begin using illegal drugs, 27 percent less likely to begin using alcohol, 53 percent less likely to skip school, and 37 percent less likely to skip a class. They are also more confident of their performance in schoolwork, less likely to hit someone, and they get along better with their families.

Feelings or Facts?

You may have feelings that actually get in the way of getting a life for yourself or helping your kids find one. For example, you may think, "If I enjoy myself I'm cheating my kids"—but the fact is, they'll be proud of an independent parent.

You may also worry, "If my kids enjoy themselves, they'll leave me, and I'll really be alone. If I let someone else into their lives there won't be room for me." But the fact is, kids need more than one person to look up to. They are capable of learning to love a lot of people and need to exercise that capability to grow strong.

Parent or Pal?

A parent helps a child find activities he enjoys. A pal wants to engage in all those activities together. What's wrong with that?

A pal wants to play the game with the kids; a parent socializes with the other parents who sponsor the team.

A parent includes an interested child in his or her normal activities; a pal wants to always be included in the child's play.

A pal gets involved with a child's disputes; a parent helps the child work through difficulties with peers.

See the difference? Single-parent children often get closer to their parent than two-parent kids. This can be good when it enhances positive identification without blurring roles. On the other hand, it often happens that single-parent children develop into the "other parent"—a partner or pal. This is often found when the parent uses the child as a peer or a pal, and it's inappropriate.

One way you can maintain closeness with your child while remaining a parent is to establish what family psychologists call an *executive structure* within the family, that is, every family member is drawn into the decision-making process—often in a formal manner—and it's clear their input is valued. But the *parent* is in charge.

Setting Priorities

If you are feeling confused by shared activities and roles, it may help to keep in mind the goal of single parenting that says, "go beyond 'survive' to 'thrive.'" Remember you want to raise children who are competent, happy, and successful at their chosen activities—while optimally developing yourself as well.

In other words—get a life, and help your children get their own.

Putting Kids First

Should you put your kids first? Of course—but what does that mean? It means helping them find their own way.

Here's what single parents erroneously believe putting a child first means:

➤ Not taking a job that would cause more upheaval in the household.

➤ Not going away for the weekend.

If putting kids first means always putting your own life aside, you risk eroding your own self-esteem so far that you will be not be successful at parenting.

Being a Parent First

You should remember the advice to "Be a parent first" from Chapter 4. Does being a parent first mean putting yourself second? No—it just means that, whether you are the custodial or non-custodial parent, your focus is on what's good for the kids.

Being a parent first means that in any situation, you first ask yourself, "How will this affect my children?"

It doesn't mean always forgoing your own needs and wants; it means finding ways to adapt to fit everyone's needs. If a job is offered across the country, for example, you don't

Chapter 6 ➤ *Your Children, Yourself?*

automatically take it—but you might see if relatives could stay with your older children if you had a temporary opportunity elsewhere.

If you have a chance to go away for a weekend when it's your turn to have the kids, being a parent first means you'd go away another time.

Now that you see the importance of spending time with your kids and helping build their self-esteem, the following checklist will help you brainstorm activities and events you all can share.

> **Expert-Ease**
> Psychologist Gayle Peterson refers to being a "good enough" parent: "A parent who does the best he or she can with the best of intentions. Nobody is perfect; we all can be good enough."

Checklist: What's Fun?

Three activities my kids really enjoy (away from me) are:
_____
_____
_____

Three activities I really enjoy away from my kids are:
_____
_____
_____

Three activities I can plan now to share with my kids are:
_____
_____
_____

If you have a very hard time answering those questions, something's missing. So step back and evaluate:

My kids and I (check one):

_____ work well together

_____ play well together

_____ seem to always be in each other's way

_____ should spend more time together

_____ should spend less time together

This checklist should give you an idea of how you can better spend time with your kids. Single parents must be creative with their time because they don't have a lot of it. In the next few chapters, I'll show you how to organize your time with your children so you all can make the most of it.

The Least You Need to Know

- ➤ Self-esteem is not some vague concept or passing fad. It's critical to healthy growth.
- ➤ Self-esteem tends to sink in single-parent children—and their parents.
- ➤ Self-esteem in both parents and children can be boosted by some positive activities that bring rewards.
- ➤ Self-esteem can bloom simply by letting go of pain, negativity, and harsh self-criticism and embracing fun and positive activities.

Chapter 7

Whose Rights? What's Right? Support and Custody

In This Chapter

➤ Who should get custody of your children?

➤ How are support decisions made?

➤ Working out legal issues—without battling in court

➤ Arranging care for your children after you're gone

By whatever means you became a parent, at least one other person was involved. Perhaps you did it the old-fashioned way: got married, got pregnant, got divorced. Even if you're a more modern, single parent by choice, you still required a partner to make a baby. And once there are two individuals involved, there is the potential for conflict (that's why crowds line up these days to enroll in law school).

There are common legal issues that single parents in every situation need to be aware of: custody, support, and mobility; or, in other words, childcare, money, and freedom. (These issues arise for all single parents, even those who have become single parents by means other than divorce.) This chapter will help you to focus on the issues that you may need legal help with—and show you where to get that help.

While this book is not a legal guide, this chapter will help you to focus on the issues where you may need legal help...and will show you where to get that help. You'll find some excellent sources of specific legal advice and information in Appendix A.

Ignorance of the Law

Back when you were making those babies, of course, you didn't think about law or conflict; you had other things on your mind (or perhaps your other body parts). But ignorance of the law is no excuse, as the saying goes—and what you don't know about it can hurt not only you, but also your children. So consider the legal questions raised by your specific life situation.

> **Meaning?**
> *Custody* means the right and duty to guard and care for someone or something. *Legal custody* of a child is the right and obligation to make decisions about the child's care. *Physical custody* refers to a parent's right to have a child live with him or her. *Joint custody* means both parents share in legal custody, physical custody, or both. The *custodial parent* is the parent who holds kids in custody; the *noncustodial parent* is without such custody. The noncustodial parent usually (although not always) is granted *visitation*, which means the right to visit the child according to a certain schedule.

Depending on how you came to be a single parent, you likely have a slightly different take on legal matters. Widows and widowers, for example, may face entanglements due to wills and estates—or the absence thereof—while needing to be aware of social security, public support such as veteran's benefits, and other available resources.

Divorced, *custodial* patterns may feel continually uptight about getting support, while for divorced, *non-custodial* parents, the battle for visitation may seem endless.

Unmarried opposite-sex partners may have conflicts over their shared children similar to those of divorced ex-married parents; live-in partners may pose roadblocks to a parent's legal settlements and practical visitation issues.

Unmarried same-sex partners, even when they live together, must always consider the "other" actual birth parent (male or female) who may have claim to the child. If same-sex partners separate, there are potentially complex legal situations depending on whether or not the child was adopted by the non-birth parent.

Then there's the never-married mother, who may feel completely out in the cold if she is one of the many who have no support or recognition from the child's father or extended family, while contending with a shrinking public-support safety net.

> **Meaning?**
> *Parent* comes from the Latin word for giving birth—as if that were the end of it. Any idiot knows that *to parent* is to care for, defend, and take responsibility for a child into adulthood, no matter who gave birth to it.

Single mothers by choice have the legal matter of paternity to deal with also. If they have planned ahead, however, they may have worked out these issues formally before the baby was even conceived.

And so it goes... Sometimes we get so caught up in the tangle of circumstantial details that we forget what is or should be central to it all: However you felt or now feel about your

Chapter 7 ➤ Whose Rights? What's Right? Support and Custody

partner, no matter how angry you may be at him or her, and no matter how independent you would like to be, you are called on to be a parent first. At the heart of the matter are the kids.

Protecting Your Kids

Children need fiscal and physical protection. They rely on their parents to provide that. At its core, parenthood is that simple. If we could focus on the kids, we'd avoid a lot of the conflict and heartache we experience and inflict. For example, if you think of spousal support as a way of protecting your children rather than as a means of punishment or revenge against your ex, you and your kids would be free of a lot of conflict and stress.

Repeated studies of single-parent kids of various backgrounds come to similar conclusions: A child in a divorced family develops the same emotional and psychological profile as one in a two-parent, nondivorced family *if* the conflict that caused the divorce does not continue after the split.

And IF a child living with a single parent feels a sense of security similar to one living with two parents, the trauma of loss is greatly reduced.

In other words, however you came by your single-parent status (as a widow/er, divorcee, unmarried parent, or never-married parent), the less you expose your kids to any conflicts that might arise, the better off your kids will be—now and later.

> **Wise Words**
> "I HATE to hear them fight on the phone... They never stop! It makes me want to disappear." —Kevin, 9, a child whose parents have separated

The Best Interests...

Based on the courtroom dramas on TV and in the tabloids, you might assume that "law" means court-fight. Yes, the law covers our family relationships and our children's lives, but that doesn't necessarily mean we have to go to court to fight about it. It means being aware of what the rules are.

The laws relating to parenthood always put "the child's best interests" first. At all levels (federal, state, and local) the government has a legally justifiable, active interest in your child's life. Trouble is—once you take your child-raising issues into court, it's the court that's going to tell you what those best interests are.

So that's one reason to work out your living arrangements out of court.

> **Expert-Ease**
> Sources for help that might keep you and your kids out of court include the following: Family Service Association, the American Arbitration Association, the Child Welfare League of America, and others. See Appendix A for contact information.

67

> **Parent Pitfalls**
>
> Parents who fight tooth and nail for custody—either during a divorce or separation, or with other relatives after the death of a spouse—often don't think the matter through to its outcome. Remember, when you "win" a custody battle, you then have the ongoing responsibility of raising children—and you may not be fully prepared for the task. Before you begin arguing for custody, you should think of it in terms beyond the "victory" in court.

It's also appropriate that you do your best to protect your kids from your legal hassles. This is not to say that you shouldn't fight for what's rightfully yours and your children's. But sometimes your "rights" aren't what's right.

So here, I'll outline some of the basic issues—custody, support, and flexibility—in a way that you may find useful to avoid becoming (or leaving) emotional roadkill on the road to single parenthood.

Custody: Who Decides?

As experts point out, custody is not ownership. Custody means simply caring for. It applies to all children—not just those of divorced parents. The U.S. court system has devised detailed procedures for making this caring possible. They seem like pretty good suggestions for anyone trying to come to terms—even outside of a court—with how to best care for their children.

Custody is always a major issue to be resolved during negotiations for a separation agreement or divorce decree. Custody and child support are also matters for negotiation between unmarried couples. Whatever the case, these negotiations almost always require the professional assistance of a mediator or lawyer in order to make sure required forms are followed, even when there is no fight over custody.

If parents are able to make amicable agreements at this stage, there is no need for a court fight; the court is simply required to formalize the agreement made by the parents. In the case of disagreement over who should get custody or how visitation arrangements should be made, the conflict is taken into the appropriate court. After hearing arguments from both sides, and in accordance with governmental guidelines, a judge decides on who gets what rights regarding custody and visitation.

The Rules

All 50 states and Washington, D.C. rely on the Uniform Child Custody Jurisdiction Act, which lets a court determine how to arrange custody, even in contexts of decisions made in other states.

Physical custody refers to the actual caretaking of the children. *Legal custody* concerns making decisions (such as those regarding education or religious instruction) that affect their interests. *Joint custody* is now widely accepted—and even preferred—in every state by statute or by legal rulings.

Joint custody usually takes at least one of these forms:

➤ Joint physical custody (the child spends equal time with each parent).

➤ Joint legal custody (decisions regarding the child's health, education, religious instruction, and other issues are shared between the parents).

➤ Both joint legal and joint physical custody.

How Custody Decisions Are Made

How do the courts decide which type of custody arrangement is best for the child? Here are the factors that are considered:

➤ The child's age, gender, and mental and physical health

➤ The mental and physical health of the parents

➤ The parents' lifestyle and other social factors

➤ The emotional ties between the parent and child

➤ The parent's ability to give guidance and provide food, shelter, clothing, and medical care

➤ The child's established living pattern (school, home, community, and religious institution)

➤ The child's preference, if the child is above a certain age (usually about 12)

In awarding physical custody to one parent, courts often grant *reasonable* visitation to the other. It's up to the parents—often with the courts' help—to define reasonable.

> **Parent Pitfalls**
> Once mothers almost always were given custody of their children, but today, gender is not always a guiding factor: rather, most states require that custody be awarded on the basis of the children's best interests without regard to the sex of the parent. If both parents seem equally fit to have custody of young children, the mother's gender may serve as a "tiebreaker." On the other hand, older children may be more likely to go with the parent of their gender, if both parents have equal standing.

What Works: Joint Custody

Joint custody seems like a good idea if both parents (or all adults involved) get along comfortably. More and more courts create even unwilling cooperation between parents by making them work out a fairly detailed parenting plan that sets the *visitation schedule* and outlines who has responsibility for decisions affecting the children. This is not only important to smooth any conflict between parents but is also vital for the children. A schedule is very important in that a child knows there are definite times they will see each parent. The schedule offers consistency and a sense of security.

At its most basic, a visitation schedule might look like this: "The child/ren is/are with the mother at all times except alternate weekends, and every Wednesday evening, when they are in their father's care. During school vacations, the children are in the charge of the father for four weeks; and in charge of the mother for the rest of the vacations, except and unless parents mutually agree to send children to camp or elsewhere for vacation. Children spend Christmas with their father in alternate years beginning 1999, and in those calendar years when this occurs, children are with their mother for Thanksgiving."

Parents can work out visitation schedules themselves, if possible, within guidelines of what the court considers reasonable: That is, visitation at reasonable times and places, leaving details up to the parents so they can work out a more precise schedule and allow for flexibility.

When parents can't work together reasonably, the court sets up a fixed visitation schedule, which establishes the times and places for visitation with the noncustodial parent. Such a fixed schedule serves to protect a child from constant conflict between the parents. Likewise, if a noncustodial parent has a record of being abusive, courts establish "supervised visitation," ordering an approved adult other than the custodial parent to be present at all times during the visit.

However it is derived, the final parenting agreement may cover points like the following:

- ➤ Who gets custody, and what kind of custody
- ➤ Support amounts and payment schedules
- ➤ Visitation schedules
- ➤ The child's residence, including any agreements about future moves
- ➤ Schools and schooling: which school the child will attend, parental participation in education decisions and school life
- ➤ Who provides what healthcare for the child, including "nonessentials" like braces
- ➤ Who provides "extras"—non-basic clothing, support for extracurricular activities
- ➤ What type of religious training the child will have
- ➤ Disciplinary goals and guides
- ➤ The child's scheduling needs (bedtime hours, homework times, and so on)
- ➤ Limits on parental behavior (dating, no badmouthing other parent, maintenance of visitation schedule, and so on)

Chapter 7 ➤ Whose Rights? What's Right? Support and Custody

Each family will have its own details to cover, so if you and your ex are working out a parenting plan, it's a good idea to brainstorm lists of everything that will affect your child: Should your child's pet come along on visitation visits? Are there daily religious practices that need to be maintained in both homes? Does your child require special equipment that should be on hand in both homes? The more items that can be covered in writing, the smoother daily life will be for all of you after the separation.

Whatever your plan, it needs to be submitted to the court (usually by a certain deadline) before the divorce or separation can be finalized. And your parenting agreement should be reviewed by an experienced professional (mediator, lawyer, or family court counselor).

The message: Any caring adults can work out ways to get along and to plan the parenting of the children in their lives—even without the aid of a court.

A parent who is denied custody can appeal the court's decision; many couples' custody fights go on for years (sometimes until the kids no longer require custody). This is a parent's right, of course, and it often greatly benefits the lawyers who get involved. The unfortunate side-effect is the fallout of tension experienced by the children. A more positive approach might be to negotiate a compromise: A parent who doesn't get custody is granted expanded visitation rights instead, for example, or the parents agree to review the custody agreement in a certain number of years. That way, the noncustodial parent has hope to change the agreement, but the fight is temporarily suspended.

> **Expert-Ease**
> What factors would you put into a parenting agreement? Why not try drafting one yourself, without the enforcement of a court order. It's a good test to find out what kind of child raising arrangement works best for you.

Custody agreements can be changed even if both parents do not agree. If the custody arrangements—or any substantial change in the living situation of the custodial parent—do not serve the best interest of the child, a court may agree to make changes. Any changes that seem detrimental to the child—if the custodial parent moves away from the child's customary environment for example, or is charged with substance abuse—can be grounds for a change in custody. The noncustodial parent seeking such a change needs to document his or her concerns and present them formally in court. Often however, it may be enough for the noncustodial parent to tell the custodial parent, "This situation is damaging, and if we can't work out some changes, I will take the matter back to court." See Chapter 12 for more on rearranging custody.

> **Singular Successes**
>
> In a classic situation, a teacher noticed that a child in her seventh grade class was always out sick for a day or two after spending the weekend with her Dad. She asked the girl, "When your Dad comes, does he bring his new wife?" The girl said yes, he did. "Do you like that? Do you think it might make your stomach upset?" The girl said maybe. "Would you like me to ask your Mom to talk to your Dad about it?" The girl did. The teacher spoke to the girl's mother as promised; and from then on, Dad saw the girl on his own.

Fund Fights: Support

Your child has a right to be cared for financially by both parents. In theory, this means that "custody" and "support" are separate issues, and whoever provides the daily care gets help from the other parent in the form of money. That's support at its simplest. But of course in real life it's usually not that simple.

> **Meaning?**
>
> *Child support* refers to the parental duty to provide sufficient funds for the care, protection, education, health, and well-being of his or her child. In the courts, this is usually the larger responsibility of the noncustodial parent, since it's assumed that the custodial parent share of support takes the form of daily care and supervision.

Check out the following figures from the U.S. Office of Child Support Enforcement:

- ➤ Of the 11.5 million families with one parent living elsewhere, only 6.2 million (54 percent) of the custodial parents had awards or agreements for child support.
- ➤ Of the total $17.7 billion owed for child support in 1991, $5.8 billion was not paid.
- ➤ Among those single parents due support, about half received the full amount, about a quarter received partial payment, and about a quarter received nothing.

Important social movements in the 1990s were geared toward everyday child-support rules to ensure children's financial security without reliance on government support.

Getting Support

If you can't work out your own child support arrangement, the government will do it for you. Here's how, under recent federal and state laws establishing support obligations:

Chapter 7 ➤ Whose Rights? What's Right? Support and Custody

States must have guidelines to establish how much a parent should pay for child support. Support agency staff can take child support cases to court, or to an administrative hearing process to establish the order. Health insurance coverage can also be ordered.

The amount of child support to be paid is calculated according to fairly rigid formulas that follow federally regulated state guidelines, administered by the Child Support Agency. If custody matters are presented to a court, the court follows these guidelines; if they are agreed to out of court, the agency administrators set the amount.

Here are some of the factors taken into consideration when support decisions are made:

➤ The regular expenses for food, clothing, and shelter

➤ Health and insurance costs

➤ Education costs

➤ Daycare costs

➤ The special needs of the child (special medical conditions, activities, or preferences that require additional support)

➤ The custodial parent's income and costs

➤ The noncustodial parent's income and costs

➤ The child's pre-separation standard of living

Courts usually require the paying parent to file financial papers, and the custodial parent must also be able to show actual costs and needs. Although courts are required to be fair in these determinations, they often do not seem fair; for instance, a paying parent's actual living expenses are often not considered; rather, reference is made to what those expenses should be.

Child support agreements may be adjusted by various means. Some agreements have a Cost of Living Adjustment (COLA). This clause requires payments to increase annually at a rate equal to the annual cost of living increase. Or, both parents may agree to vary the support amounts to meet changed circumstances (temporary or permanent).

Temporary changes might be made in the event of:

➤ The child's medical emergency

➤ The payer's temporary inability to pay

➤ Temporary economic or medical hardship of the recipient parent

Permanent changes might be made in the event of:

- An increase in income for either parent (from remarriage or other sources)
- Changes in the child support laws
- A job change of either parent
- A cost of living increase
- The disability of either parent
- Changed needs of the child

> **Wise Words**
> "After the confusion at the court I learned I couldn't count on getting the support I was due. So I took in a roomer and found other ways to make up the difference. The support money will either come through, or it won't. Meanwhile, I'm OK." —Divorced mother of a teen

Child support will not be changed in response to changes in the visitation schedule; that is a legally distinct issue, and must be addressed separately in the courts.

Finally, child-support payments change or end when the child reaches the age of majority (which differs in various states); the child is adopted by a stepparent; or the child is living independently and has been declared emancipated by the court.

Every parent has an obligation to support his or her children. When one parent has visitation rights (but not physical custody), he or she is usually ordered to pay some child support to the other parent. That's where so much of family conflict develops, but there is a reason for it: The parent with physical custody is considered to meet the support obligation through the custody itself.

Getting Help

There are such big bucks involved in parental support conflicts that the government has set up systems to facilitate their flow. In 1995, about $10.8 billion in child support payments was collected by the Child Support Enforcement (CSE) program, a federally mandated program usually run by state and local human services departments (often with the help of prosecuting attorneys, other law enforcement agencies, and officials of family or domestic relations courts).

What happens if a parent refuses to pay support? The parent can be required to pay child support by *income withholding* (having money withheld from paychecks). The new welfare reform legislation establishes state and federal registries of newly hired employees to speed the transfer of wage withholding orders. Overdue child support can also be collected from federal and state income tax refunds, or from savings accounts or property,

Chapter 7 ➤ *Whose Rights? What's Right? Support and Custody*

and the property itself may even be sold with the proceeds used to pay child support arrears.

Services like these were provided in over 19.2 million cases through the CSE Program: More than a million new child support orders were established through the Program in 1995.

The Federal government also is helpful in locating absent parents. Child support enforcement officials use local information and resources of State and Federal Parent Locator services to locate parents for child support enforcement, or to find a parent in parental kidnapping/custody disputes. About four million cases are processed annually by the Federal Parent Locator Service.

> **Parent Pitfalls**
> Surveys indicate that parents who have apparently disappeared from their children's lives are actually more often than not willing to participate in supporting the child-raising process if they're allowed to do more than pay the bills—and if they can see the kids more and be more included in their activities.

Establishing paternity (legally identifying a child's father) is a necessary first step for obtaining an order for child support when children are born out of wedlock. Establishing paternity also provides access to social security, pension, and retirement benefits; health insurance and information; and interaction with members of both parents' families.

Many fathers voluntarily acknowledge paternity. Otherwise, father, mother, and child can be required to submit to genetic tests, which are reported to be highly accurate. Paternity was established for hundreds of thousands of children through the CSE Program.

Not only can you get this kind of technical support through the Federal government, but each state has similar procedures.

Going Mobile: Can You Move?

Because both parents are supporting the child, whether physically or fiscally, both parents have a right and a need to spend time with the child. That means that the parent with custody does not necessarily have the right to move the child away from the other parent. (Doesn't that sound simple, too?)

Future freedom is not something you might think about when working out a custody agreement—but when it comes up, it can be a big issue, so it's a matter more and more parents are agreeing on ahead of time.

Moving On

If a parent wants to move, he or she may need to change the existing court order affecting custody or visitation. If the other parent won't agree to the change, he or she must file a motion requesting a modification of the order from the court that issued it, along with an argument based on grounds that include a geographic move. Some courts switch custody from one parent to the other, although the more common approach is work out a plan that accommodates both parents.

Staying Put

Courts take many factors into consideration in deciding where children should live. For instance, does the child have significant connections in the state with sources for care, protection, education, and personal relationships?

> **Wise Words**
> "When we had to make some geographic changes due to work and school demands, my children's Dad and I drew up a letter of agreement to amend to the separation agreement. We negotiated changes, had it notarized, and when the divorce was final, it was included. No point in fighting—if you don't go where the work is, who's going to pay the bills?"
> —A divorced Mom

Do You Have to Go to Court?

Be aware that you don't have to let a court decide custody or support issues for you! There are various other sources for advice.

Just remember, you need emotionally detached advice. You may not be able to rely on your family and friends, for example. It's not just that they aren't professionals—but they have their own axes to grind. Your mother may not want her grandchild to go live with "that woman." Your sister may be dying to help you raise your kids. Your friend may be acting out his own trauma.

Luckily, in addition to your own good judgment, you have some good nonpartisan resources to rely on. There are legal resources on the Internet and in the library, and many independent and government agencies can help, too. See Appendix A for more information.

Conflict Resolution

There are other alternatives to legal battling that can provide formal, recognized resolution to conflict and positive plans and solutions for potentially damaging family situations.

Many marriage and family counselors provide advice on legal steps to take—including *formal mediation*. In *mediation*, a neutral person meets with the disputing parties to help them settle the dispute. Mediators are trained and skilled at getting parents to cooperate

Chapter 7 ➤ Whose Rights? What's Right? Support and Custody

in parenting. When necessary, mediators can work with each parent separately until some minimal agreement is reached. Though the mediator does not have power to impose a solution on the parties, mediation is often helpful to a divorcing or divorced couple, and courts usually follow the mediator's recommendations when issuing judicial orders.

> **Meaning?**
> In *mediation*, a neutral person meets with disputing parties (such as a couple going through a divorce) to help them settle the dispute.

Several states require mediation in custody and visitation disputes; a number of others allow courts to order mediation and make a recommendation.

Doing It Yourself

Earlier in the chapter, you learned about the factors considered in custody decisions. Can you work out your own agreement based on these factors? Why not??

Many experts in family law agree… With rare exceptions, you can do a whole lot better crafting your own decisions, which fit your unique situation, rather than hiring lawyers and turning the ultimate decisions over to a judge. You and the other parent can negotiate a parenting plan that reflects the needs and best interests of your children and assures them the maximum possible contact with both of you.

Court intervention is crucial only if the children's safety or well-being is at risk, and if the parents cannot agree on a way to reduce that risk. It is far better, in experts' opinions, for parents to negotiate their own parenting agreement, with help from mediators, counselors, and lawyers as needed.

Battling It Out in Court

And when all those simple, theoretical scenarios don't play out smoothly in reality, what then? Well, remember all those people waiting in line to get into law school? There may come a point when you see no way to avoid a court fight.

Or, you may have been battling your heart out and losing every round. What now?

What do you do when there's nothing left to do? Obviously that's a highly individual decision. Some matters to keep in mind:

> **Wise Words**
> "Who 'wins?' Maybe you don't 'win' right now—but if your kids do, you're ahead. Take it from those who've lived through this and can look back: Whichever parent wins by making some nasty fight is the one who in the long run is likely to lose out on the kids' respect and affection."
> —A single Mom, 12 years after "giving up" custody

77

On the one hand, your children may need to have you "fight" for them—or they may need to know you tried. On the other hand, there's a lot of research that says that when a family fights, it's the children who suffer.

Remember, too, that you may win all the battles and come up with a decision entirely in your favor. But it may be worth nothing if the other parent ignores the ruling or just pays lipservice to it. (As the saying goes, "You can't legislate affection.") Surveys have shown that when one parent tries to cooperate with the other parent, rather than force him/her into parental compliance, that parent is more likely to be drawn into the parenting process.

> **Meaning?**
> *Interference with custody* is the legal term for the crime of parental kidnapping, or the taking of a child by a non-custodial parent.

When absent fathers, for example, have regular and frequent visitation, they are more likely to come through with their obligations for support. The less involved, the less readily they paid support. The worse the conflict, the more likely is parental kidnapping—or *interference with custody* as it's called. Not only do non-custodial parents commit this crime—grandparents and other family members are likely to, too. And it IS a crime. The kidnapper can be punished… but in the meantime, the kids suffer.

Your Kids Are Key

The bottom line: Those parents who can step back from their emotions, take a deep breath, and put their common sense into gear will find it valuable to work with the other parent (even if they dislike them) in the interest of the kids.

So what do YOU do when there's nothing else to do? First, think of your kids.

Take some time to be honest with yourself about where you might best strike the balance in arranging your single-parent life. Here's a checklist to help you focus on what feels right.

Chapter 7 ▶ *Whose Rights? What's Right? Support and Custody*

Legal Issues Worksheet

Why am I continuing my legal struggles?

_____ Because I need what I'm demanding

_____ Because I want to hurt my former partner

What do my children really want?

_____ To be with me alone

_____ To be with their other parent alone

_____ To have time with both of us

Do I know what they really want? _____Yes _____No

Have I ever used my children as bait to get something from their other parent?
_____Yes   _____No

Why do I want custody?

_____ Because I love the kids

_____ Because I hate their other parent

Am I truly willing to let go of the other parent—or struggling to NOT let go?
_____
_____

Am I comfortable letting my children go? _____Yes   _____No

Have I tried every non-confrontational procedural aid—or gone straight to court?
_____
_____

Do I always meet MY terms of the agreements in question?
_____
_____

Do I ever use any of our points of conflict to point the finger at my former spouse or other family members in front of the kids?
_____
_____

The Final Word: Your Will

While we're talking legal matters, let's not forget the final word: wills. What happens to your kid/s if something happens to you? If you die while your children are still minors (and this does happen, even though we don't like to think about it) who gets the kids? If you have no will containing a provision for this eventuality, your kids will go to whomever the laws of your particular state designate.

Therefore, do your own designating now! Get legal advice on how best to go about it, and do it. After all the effort you've gone through to have this child, raise it, and protect it, if you don't make provisions for what happens after you are gone, all your efforts were wasted.

And, though they may not say so, your kids are worried about this! Studies and surveys demonstrate that kids—and especially single-parent kids—do always worry about what's going to happen to them. So plan for them.

Pick and consult with the best surrogates you can think of. Make sure the people you select to raise your most precious products are ones whose values you share. If you get along with your ex, then you will probably be comfortable with him or her serving as the kids' guardian. (If not, godparents and the other traditional guardians established by various cultures and ethnic groups often serve this purpose.)

Write your choice into a legal document—and tell your kids about it. Tell them in as non-threatening a way as possible, but let them know. It will not only reassure them, but will be another reminder that you always keep them in mind.

Also, it's a good idea to legally appoint an official guardian or proxy to watch out for your kids even if you don't die prematurely but are unable to care for them.

> **Wise Words**
> "When I was a kid living alone with my mother, I always wondered what would happen to me if she died," says one single Mom. "I don't know where that idea came from, but it scared me—and I didn't want to go live with Dad. But I was too scared to say anything. So with my son, I've been careful to let him know exactly who will watch out for him if I'm not around for any reason."

> **Expert-Ease**
> You should pick a family member to leave in charge of your children in case of death. If you should die, your child's next of kin—that is, the other parent, or perhaps grandparents—will almost automatically get guardianship of them. If these aren't folks you would choose, then you should put your decisions in writing now.

Review you answers, think about them, and consider what changes in action or attitude you might want to take toward being a parent first.

Chapter 7 ➤ *Whose Rights? What's Right? Support and Custody*

The Least You Need to Know

- ➤ You should protect your rights and your children's rights. But if at all possible, consider working out custody issues without going to court.
- ➤ When deciding custody, support, and mobility issues with your ex, make sure you keep the children's welfare at the forefront of the discussion.
- ➤ You can get professional help from family service organizations in your community and the federally mandated child-support agencies.
- ➤ Make sure to make a will stating who will care for your children if something happens to you. Tell your children about it.

Chapter 8

Caring About Caretakers

> **In This Chapter**
> ➤ Is childcare good for your child?
> ➤ What are your childcare options?
> ➤ Affording childcare
> ➤ Choosing safe childcare

Finding safe, affordable, and reliable childcare is every working parent's worry. Concern over a sick child at home gets in the way of efficient work on the job for any parent, and more and more kids—in two-parent as well as single-parent families—are placed in daycare for at least some of their childhood years.

But when it comes to childcare, single parents face an even greater challenge than two-parent families (even those in which both parents work). Two-parent families don't have it easy, but when up against it there's always another parent who can act as some kind of childcare backup. Single parents don't have that option.

So how do you put together a reliable, affordable childcare service that's convenient for you and fun for your kid? In this chapter, you'll learn how.

Is Childcare Good for Children?

Whatever career you dream of or job you can manage, you have to see that your kids are cared for first.

Every parent who has to leave a child in the care of another feels an uncomfortable tug.

It's important to acknowledge those feelings and express them as needed. Even letting a baby or toddler know you're sad to leave is appropriate (as long as the child doesn't sense hysteria on your part). Talking to your child about what a wonderful day he or she will have can help you feel better about it.

One thing you probably *don't* have to feel badly about is the effect that competent daycare will have on your child. Child-development experts do recommend that very young infants stay with their parent or parents to develop emotional bonds that are needed for a sense of security. After the newborn period, though, other caretakers can be introduced, without apparently making much difference on the child's later development.

Lots of research is being done on how daycare affects young children, and the results of the studies are inconsistent except in one respect: Virtually all experts agree that consistency in childcare is critical. That is, a child who has the same regular caretaker/s over time is much better off than one whose caregivers change frequently. Once your child is placed, it's better to be able to stick with the same setting or person than to switch.

So you will do well to make a real effort from the beginning to find good daycare: safe, healthy and nurturing for your child; comfortable, convenient, and affordable for you.

Your Childcare Options

Your childcare options will vary based on where you live, what level of care you are looking for, and how much you can afford. Here's a brief list of the different kinds of childcare settings you may want to explore.

➤ **Childcare in a Home Setting.** Childcare workers who come to the home are often referred to as babysitters or nannies. They are usually not regulated or licensed by the state. Many parents hire babysitters or nannies who have been referred to them by other parents, neighbors, or relatives. There are also reputable agencies that can provide referrals.

Costs for home childcare are high, so this option, while perhaps the most comfortable for the child, is usually used by parents with high-paying jobs. Salaries are negotiated between the parents and the employee. They may also negotiate the job description, which may include some level of housework as well as childcare.

- **Family Daycare.** Family daycare is provided in the home of a childcare worker who may care for several children. This person may or may not require licensing. Family daycare is often the preferred type of out-of-home care for infants and very young children, because the groups tend to be smaller than in more formal settings, and there's more of a personal touch.

- **Group Family Care.** Group family care, like family daycare, is also provided in a caregiver's home. It is usually regulated by a government agency. It is less formal, more expensive, and possibly more trustworthy than less formal daycare.

- **Out-of-Home Care.** Out-of-home care is provided at public or private childcare centers and may be offered full- or part-time in licensed facilities. Workers in childcare centers usually must be trained in early childhood and child development before they are licensed. They provide age-appropriate activities for children and usually offer written care plans and policies.

- **School-Age Childcare.** This includes pre- and after-school activities for children ages 5 to approximately 12. It is often referred too as "before and after school care." School-age childcare is found in a variety of settings: schools; YMCA's; community, religious, or childcare centers; and family day-care homes. School-age childcare is often state licensed and formally programmed. Nonprofit groups charge fees (and usually have longer waiting lists than private organizations).

- **Part-Time Childcare Programs.** These programs include nursery school, temporary babysitting, play groups, and other services that may be part of a full-time childcare center or a separate nursery school or pre-school program. These are often held in community, childcare, religious, or cultural centers; schools; or other settings. These programs are usually subject to similar licensing requirements and standards as full-time programs.

In choosing the type of care, you will want to weigh costs versus services and licensing supervision (unfortunately, those services that offer the best level of childcare may not be affordable). Your child's age, and special needs, if any, must also be considered.

Affording Childcare

A big question with any kind of childcare: can you afford it?! Good childcare can be costly.

Fortunately, public or employer-sponsored programs are available to help pay childcare expenses in some cases. Your health department or local school can give you more information.

Childcare is also a major item to be negotiated with your child's other parent, as well as a benefit that you can negotiate with a current (or even prospective) employer. Many single mothers who erroneously feel that they can't make demands for themselves can push for benefits for their kids.

Refer to Chapter 15 to learn about employment options such as flex time, telecommuting, or on-site daycare.

The *Wall Street Journal* recently reported that of all the childcare options available, the system used by a majority of working parents is also the most affordable: care by a family member. If you live near an aunt, uncle, parent, or other family member who is willing to watch your child on a regular basis, it's probably the optimum solution. You know your kids will be safe, and the arrangement will serve to strengthen family bonds.

If this is not an option, you may consider forming a "baby-sitting coop" with other single parents you know and trust. When a child-sharing arrangement like this works well, the network of parents and kids may turn into a kind of extended family, as kids take turns staying in each others' homes. This only works if participating parents have different schedules, of course. And it may not be as reliable as a paid service: if the "mom for the day" backs out, you've got to scramble for another option. Still it's worth looking into.

Getting Quality Childcare

No matter what type of childcare you choose for your child, you should check it carefully. The following list summarizes the basics. But you'll also want to use your own intuition to judge.

1. Check references of the caregiver and program.
2. Check the licensing and accreditation of the worker or program; different states, counties, and localities have various ways of licensing childcare.
3. Check that all staff are certified by whatever agency your county or state requires.
4. Make sure all staff members have the appropriate training for their jobs and clearances regarding character and fitness.
5. Check the staffing history. Is there low turnover, or do staff members come and go frequently?
6. Are children assigned to the same child workers for consistency of care?
7. What's the child-to-staff ratio? How many workers are looking after how many children?
8. Does the center hold current liability insurance coverage?

9. Get the philosophy, policies, fees, and schedules of the worker or center stated in writing.

Finally, spend time on-site, watching the childcare worker or center in action. Take note of the following:

➤ Is the environment clean?

➤ Is it child-proofed? Are there plenty of exits? Are toys safe for kids to play with?

➤ Does it have enough of the appropriate toys for all children? Are there a variety of toys? Are they stimulating enough for the children?

➤ Are snacks given regularly? Are they healthy?

➤ Are parents welcome and encouraged to visit?

➤ Do the children seem happy?

➤ Are the workers at the center good with children? Do they seem comfortable with children? Do they keep the children's interest? How do they handle temper tantrums or tears?

While your preliminary assessment of a childcare center is crucial, you'll of course want to stay in touch after you've enrolled your child to make sure your child is getting good care.

Checking Up on Childcare

After you've chosen a childcare center or worker, keep in touch! Spend time there and talk with the caregivers regularly.

Stay aware of indirect signs of childcare problems. If your child consistently shows signs of being unhappy—moodiness, frequent upsets, an unwillingness to go to daycare—take it seriously! Drop in unexpectedly for a visit at the center. Ask other parents how their kids seem to be doing. Talk to the daycare provider to gain cooperation in dealing with any problem your child may be having. If you continue to sense any problem or any reluctance on the part of the staff to talk with you, best look for another provider.

Also, if your child seems to be getting sick a lot, check out conditions at the center. It's normal for kids to pick up germs from other kids, but if your child seems to be constantly sick, the center may not be adequately protecting the kids or cleaning the premises.

Childcare Through The Ages

Leaving babies and small children with strangers can be nerve-wracking—but the childcare challenge doesn't end when your kids are in school. Use the same suggestions in this chapter when it comes time to evaluate after-school programs or other arrangements for your school-age or teenage child.

In sum, whatever the age of your child, you will feel more comfortable and confident when you know you've found the most appropriate kind of care for your child while you work.

The Least You Need to Know

- ➤ When choosing childcare, pick the option that best fits your budget, your schedule, and your child's age and needs.
- ➤ Children need stability and consistency, so choose a childcare setting and provider you know you can stick with.
- ➤ If money is tight, consider creating a "baby-sitting coop" with other single parents.
- ➤ Screen any childcare worker or center carefully before signing up, and continually monitor the center to make sure your child is getting good care.

Part 3
Finding Space and Time

If you're a new single parent, arranging your living space can be a great way to start "arranging" your new life. If you and the kids have been on your own for a while, rearrangements can help you create some fresh new patterns.

As for time—no single parent ever has enough of it. But if you can focus on managing time, the rest of your complicated life may calm down.

In this part, you'll find opportunities to be creative about every aspect of your life—and to include your kids in the planning, too. The goal: A household in which you all stay secure and comfortable and yet still have room to grow.

Chapter 9

Designs for Living

In This Chapter

- ➤ Your home: More than four walls and a roof
- ➤ Feeling at home—wherever it is
- ➤ Creating space—inner and outer
- ➤ The importance of privacy
- ➤ Finding room to grow

Our homes are said to be expressions of ourselves. It's certainly true that, when it comes to single parenting, "home design" is about a lot more than fashion or even self-expression.

Arranging a (usually limited) amount of space to optimize both privacy and connection—and to accommodate even those who may not live there full-time—is no easy trick. The very fact that you try sends an important message to each member of your family—a message about the value of both privacy and connection, about the value of each individual, and the interest in creating a family unit that respects every member. How you manage it says even more.

Part 3 ➤ *Finding Space and Time*

As in other single-parenting matters, the baseline is safety and comfort—in the physical, psychological, and all other senses. In this chapter, you'll learn how to create a safe haven for your family.

> **Singular Successes**
>
> "My son was not with me full-time during his teen years. I had a small studio-plus apartment with barely enough room for myself and my work, and like most single parents, barely enough cash flow to cover one set of costs.
>
> "But by the creative use of freestanding bookcases, curtains, screens, and storage boxes, and a sofa bed for me, it was possible to make a space that became his alone when he was there. In that way, just as he had two parents in separate places, he had two real homes where he could be himself. Whether your kids have two parents or one, that experience sums up the issues involved in creating living space for your unique family."
>
> —Divorced mother of now-grown son

Relax: Make Yourselves Comfortable

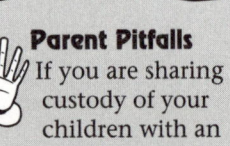

> **Parent Pitfalls**
> If you are sharing custody of your children with an ex, making a comfortable home the kids enjoy staying at should not be a contest between the two of you! One parent may have a bigger household budget than the other, and try to "buy" loyalty with fancy decor. Or, a single parent against a financial wall may hang on to miserable housing rather than ask for help. Nobody wins in such a competition—and no matter what, it's the kids who lose.

Parent or child, large space or small, it's important, for more than superficial reasons, to feel good about where you are. Each family member—whether a full- or part-time resident in your house—needs a safe space, and it's important that that space be comfortable.

Life may not be as easy as you'd like it. OK, so what? You can still make your living space a place that you, your kids, and their friends want to be, whether they live with you full-time or visit on weekends.

We all need to feel safe, in a space to call our own. Even if it's not grand, the fact that you go out of your way to make (or help your kids make) a space that's theirs alone says something important to them.

Even if your children don't live with you full-time, it's important that they know they have a space that's only theirs to come "home" to. Remember, this is your home. It's where your kids are growing up, at least part of the time, and where you're living your life. So make a space you all like to be in. (And don't forget that you need space to retreat to, too.)

Approached with care, household arrangements can become vehicles for expressing the needs of each family member and the value you place on both the individuals and the family unit.

Stretching Space and Money

Single-parent families tend to live in smaller spaces than intact families. A single parent may not have the kids full time. A blended family may have to stretch to accommodate more kids (and adults) at least part of the time. How do you make room for everything?

The more creatively you furnish and decorate, the easier it is to keep even a filled-to-the gills home fairly tidy—which in turn leads to more space.

Fortunately, there are ways to carve a liveable niche for everyone, even if space is at a premium and money is tight. Here are some small, inexpensive decorating ideas to try:

> **Expert-Ease**
> Environmental stability keeps kids in balance even under stress; so when other living arrangements are in disorder, try to keep your kids' space orderly and filled with their important objects.

For sleeping space:

- Futons
- Cushions
- Captain's beds
- Indoor sleeping bags that double as bedspreads or bolsters

For storage space:

- Trunks
- Building-board shelves
- Decorative storage boxes
- Baskets
- Clothes peg boards
- Corner drawers

93

Expert-Ease
One final thought about home. Kids don't care about material things if what they have instead is your love and attention. That's a trade off most kids will readily make. Also, even a tiny one-room apartment can be a home if your love and support permeates the atmosphere. Home is about heart space, not floor space.

Expert-Ease
Kids of any age need and appreciate a space that's theirs to decorate and arrange as they please. Whether they have an entire bedroom to themselves or if they're camping out in a corner of the living room, if it's their own to decorate and control, they'll be more willing to cooperate in "your" part of the house. Get the kids involved in designing their space, picking paint and fabric, and using it to decorate.

For privacy:

➤ Freestanding screens

In the kitchen:

➤ Folding or partially folding chairs and tables
➤ A microwave
➤ A slow cooker
➤ "Real" plates and dishes

The corner drawers, trunk, and shelves can hold personal possessions as well as clothing. Shelves made from crates and boards (or cardboard cartons spray-painted or covered in contact paper) cost almost nothing but demonstrate an interest in creating a special place for everyone's things—and can make the place look cheerful.

An inexpensive rug, curtains made from (nicely patterned) bed sheets, a futon and cushion, and baskets for storage can create a pleasant, comfortable room in an instant.

In the kitchen, a microwave and a slow cooker are a busy family's lifelines to fast home-cooked food. "Real" china and utensils are cheaper in the long run than paper goods—and feel better too. Items like these are worth finding the money for.

Whatever the design or furnishings you choose, make sure everything you have is easy to clean and straighten! Also, try to stick with light furniture that's easy to move around; use the heavy bookcases or Goodwill dressers as room dividers, because you won't be able to move them on a whim. Think about making it easy to manage and keep in order.

Chapter 9 ➤ *Designs for Living*

Private Space, Private Time

If you're lucky, you have a separate room for every person. Fewer and fewer people have this kind of space, but we all need privacy. Experts say psychosocial boundaries are important to all of us.

Here are a few ways you can carve out a special "room" for every person in your household, even if space and money are tight:

➤ Arranging screens and furniture dividers can carve separate rooms out of an open space.

➤ Loft bed arrangements are good, too. They allow each child a self-contained bed, clothing, and work space, so that each child has a "room" within a room.

➤ Create an individualized work area for each student in your household made with desks and bookcases painted to match.

Even if separate spaces don't have doors that close, by adding dividers you establish real privacy demarcations, so that each person's space is protected, doors or no doors.

Then respect those boundaries! Kids should knock before going into your room—and you shouldn't go into your kids' space without an invitation or at least making an announcement.

As for sharing space more closely—sharing beds creates a lot of controversy among professional counselors. In single-parent homes, it may be tempting to share a bed for company—but probably not a good idea, given the single-parent family tendency to role-reversals that can create trouble later for the kids.

Creating private time for each family member is as important as carving out private space. Even in a hectic household, you can find ways to make sure that each individual has private time:

> **Meaning?**
> *Psychosocial boundaries* define who we are as separate from each other. They are critical for healthy development, especially as children separate from parents.

> **Expert-Ease**
> Environmental stability keeps kids in balance even under stress; so when other living arrangements are in disorder, try to keep kids' space orderly and filled with their important objects.

> **Wise Words**
> "After her Mom died, my daughter had trouble sleeping. So I would go into her room and hold her, then stretch out on the floor by her bed to sleep. It seemed like a better idea than letting her come to bed with me—though we did curl up together in the daytime to read or watch TV."
> —A widower on his young daughter

95

- Schedule bathroom time—not just to survive the morning rush, but for longer, private, bubble baths to enjoy without feeling guilty.
- Sharing a telephone can be a real pain for a teen or pre-teen. Set aside some time when it's hers alone—and maybe a space (even in a closet) where she can use it in privacy.
- If every family member has small a tape player/radio and earphones, you can all listen to your own music—even in a small space—without driving each other crazy! And why not? As long as the earphones come off the young ears every now and then!

Time for Togetherness

A sense of "separate togetherness" (the idea that there's a connection for security but a separateness for individuality) is probably more important in single-parent families than in more traditional ones because of the greater difficulties in maintaining boundaries.

Just as you each need space for yourself, your family needs space to be together. Maybe it's not sit-down suppers every night, but some place—the kitchen, the sofa, wherever—where all can gather and do things together on a regular basis.

Maybe you have some time each evening when the TV is turned off, and you all get together to play a game or just talk about your day. Maybe you have some times each week when a TV show you all enjoy is turned on.

Today's kids sometimes act so sophisticated, at even young ages, that you may be surprised by how much these family rituals mean to them—especially in single-parent families where routines often tend to be in perpetual flux.

But in less literal ways, you and your kids need connection when one family member is "missing."

Many single-parent kids are separated from important members of their family (at least part time) so it's important to have connection with them. Think about always having family-related items wherever your child is—a photo of the other parent, pets that come with a visiting child, or anything else that gives your child a feeling of solidity and support.

Chapter 9 ➤ *Designs for Living*

Safety First

Even if money is no object, be sure your space is safe, literally and figuratively, for each member. Your "design for living" must be grounded in some hard-and-fast attitudes about health and safety, which are especially important if your kids stay at home for any amount of time by themselves.

Parents who must leave their children at home alone understandably have a lot of worries. You will feel better about the situation if, first of all, you do everything you can to make sure your kids are safe.

You will want to talk about safety in a way that will not frighten your children too much (you know best your own kids' fears and needs), but a little healthy respect for danger is not a bad thing.

Your children will probably feel more secure if you establish firm rules for safety, geared to each child's age, personality, and skills. These rules should cover every possible hazard—fire, accident, strangers at the door, and any special dangers posed by your home or neighborhood. Even children who complain about rules really appreciate the concern they demonstrate.

Here are a few safety rules you should set:

➤ Wherever you and your kids are, they must always know how to be in touch with you. This way, even when you have to leave them you can remain in touch by setting up contact systems.

➤ If you place emergency telephone numbers as well as numbers of dependable neighbors next to the phone, you can make certain your kids will be able to get help in a crisis.

➤ You can be sure they'll know how to get out of the house or apartment fast in an emergency if you go over escape routes and plan with them carefully. Practice these plans with fire and safety drills.

➤ Smoke alarms and good locks can be installed at very low cost.

➤ Any neighbor or nearby relative who acts as an emergency back-up for you should know the name and number of your pediatrician and where to reach you. They should also have a medical authorization note signed by you that gives permission for emergency hospital care. Many doctors will not offer treatment beyond basic first aid without such permission.

Part 3 ➤ *Finding Space and Time*

Don't feel that you are being overly fearful or nervous taking precautions like these. You are simply being sensible. And think how you would feel if an emergency did arise and you hadn't prepared for it! When you are confident that your children can handle any problem, you will feel less anxious about leaving them home alone.

Wish Lists

Important as the basics are, they are, of course, never enough. Rather than think of extras (a car, a vacation, or a new house) as impossible luxuries, why not focus on what could be possible if you all worked toward it together?

Go through the following checklist with your kids—the ones who live with you and the ones who visit regularly. Anyone else who's in your home on a regular basis could participate, too. That way, even if things aren't perfect on a day-to-day basis everyone will feel less discontented because they've been able to provide their input.

Wish List Worksheet

If you could arrange our living space any way you wanted, what would you wish for?

_____

_____

_____

If we could furnish our living space anyway we wanted, what would you wish for?

_____

_____

_____

_____

Now for each wish think of a do-able step to take toward it: (For example, "Someday I'd like to re-decorate the whole place." OK, go to a paint store and pick out some paint colors and wallpaper patterns to play with.)

_____

_____

_____

_____

Chapter 9 ➤ *Designs for Living*

List 5 household items we NEED:

What we need	What it costs	How do we get it?
1. _____	_____	_____
2. _____	_____	_____
3. _____	_____	_____
4. _____	_____	_____
5. _____	_____	_____

List 5 household items we WANT:

What we want	What it costs	How do we get it?
1. _____	_____	_____
2. _____	_____	_____
3. _____	_____	_____
4. _____	_____	_____
5. _____	_____	_____

Wishes turn into goals. If we can dream of what we want and take real steps toward those dreams, we can get there. In the meantime, we have something to look forward to and work together for.

The Least You Need to Know

- ➤ Living space is just that—space for living—so making it pleasant is a necessity, not a luxury.
- ➤ The baseline for creating your space is safety and comfort.
- ➤ A little creativity goes a long way toward making any environment a place that allows for both privacy and connection between family members.
- ➤ Build in flexibility to leave room to grow.

Chapter 10

First Things First: Getting Organized

In This Chapter

- ➤ What's the point of getting organized?
- ➤ The simplest way to organize anything
- ➤ How to cut through clutter in your life
- ➤ The smart way to set organizational goals
- ➤ How (and why) to get everyone involved

"I don't have time to get organized!" is a common single-parent complaint. But think of this: If you take the time to organize your household, you will have more time and space for the rest of your life.

Plus—a *big* plus—your kids feel better and act better when their lives and environment aren't in chaos.

The key is creating a structure for things you have to do, such as laundry, shopping, and cooking—and to do it in a way that's simple to deal with, one that doesn't add another layer of complication. The whole point is to make life manageable, not more complicated by rules. In this chapter, you'll learn how it's done.

Part 3 ➤ *Finding Space and Time*

> **Meaning?**
> Management experts call it *sequential organization*, but most of us know it as doing first things first. "First things first" means putting on your pants before your shoes; knowing why dessert comes after meatloaf; and finding facts and facing them. It means taking care of the most urgent business first and working hardest toward the most important goals. It also means focusing on what you can do and not on what you can't.

Getting Organized

To organize anything, you have to ask yourself two questions: What do you want to accomplish and what's the simplest way to do it?

You'll have your own answer to those questions, but as a single parent, they are likely to be along these lines: To make your life as manageable as possible so that you and your kids can be comfortable.

To a custodial parent, that means finding ways to make being a working parent in sole charge of children possible to manage.

To a non-custodial parent, it means planning ahead to be able to spend uncluttered time with your kids when you do see them.

Goal-Setting Checklist

Good organization serves the purpose of helping us to achieve goals in various aspects of our lives. But how do you set achievable goals? Management consultants say that goals should be "smart"—that is:

➤ **Specific:** You should be able to accomplish them through well defined steps and procedures. "To become an astronaut" is not a specific enough goal, but "To visit a career counselor and discuss the possibilities of becoming an astronaut" is a specific first step.

➤ **Measurable:** You should know when you've reached your goals. "To lose weight" is not a measurable goal. "To lose five pounds in the next month" is.

> **Expert-Ease**
> Time-management books and household-organization manuals can be a help—you'll find some listed in Appendix A.

➤ **Accountable:** There is a point to your goals. They have genuine value; they are more than "busy work." Light weekly cleaning to keep your home safe and pleasant is a worthwhile goal; cleaning your house to the point of perfection is probably not necessary.

➤ **Realistic:** You can reasonably expect to achieve your goals, given adequate effort. Aiming to clean out the hall closet on a Saturday afternoon is a realistic goal; expecting to revamp the attic, garage, and basement in that time is not.

➤ **Timed:** You've set a practical deadline for your goals. "We're going to finish cleaning this room by 4:00 today" is a lot more practical than, "We've got to clean this room sometime."

Setting small goals—to clean the house or handle everyday projects and chores—is great practice for setting (and meeting) grander life goals. And when your kids see how the process works, they will have an easier time setting goals for themselves.

Organization: A Family Affair

Get your entire family involved in your quest for organization. Ask everyone to think about your family's purpose: What are your goals? Is there a specific standard of living you want? An educational or life-achievement goal you aim for? Anything else?

More immediately, you all probably want life to go smoothly enough so that you can do more of what you want to and less of what you hate.

Life-management specialists suggest meeting with your family members to get their insight into what important goals need to be accomplished in your household. That way, everyone has a say in what's important, and you can make sure you've got time for work, time for play, time for the family to be together, and personal time for everyone. The suggestions you receive should be made into a master calendar or list.

This is an especially valuable technique in single-parent families because it involves each family member and strengthens family bonds while keeping the domestic structure in place.

Make it clear that this list is not just a regimented set of rules about daily living; it's a way of attaining and maintaining your mutual purpose.

> **Wise Words**
> "I didn't think I could insist that my kids keep their things in order when my drawers and files were a total mess"!
> —Working mother of 2

One advantage of working together as a family on this organization stuff is that you adapt systems to fit your family's style. What and how you organize is an expression of your family's values. Is it more important to focus on saving money so you can buy a big-screen TV or order pizzas twice a week? Is it more important to be on time for everything, or to lay back and savor every experience? Only your family can say.

Your organization needs to come out of your own family personality rather than out of a book. But creating some kind of structure for your family life will make it easier to live the life you all want.

By the very process of working out organizational systems, you help your household develop into a family. Each person gets a better sense of the strengths—and limitations—of the others.

What Needs To Be Organized?

What kinds of issues should you and your kids discuss when you attempt to create your own family schedule? Here are some suggestions:

- Homemaking
- Storage
- Meals
- Social life
- Finances
- Holidays and vacations
- Time and scheduling
- Personal interests

For example, what kind of stuff gets in your way? Look around your place. You and your kids have probably accumulated lots of stuff:

- Clothes (old and new, clean and dirty)
- Books
- Paperwork, bills, and receipts (current and ancient)
- Mail
- Magazines, newspapers, and catalogs
- Sports equipment (balls, shoes, uniforms)
- Music equipment (tapes, CDs, instruments)
- Household odds and ends, from puzzle pieces to hair rollers
- Cosmetics or other personal-care items
- Tools and parts
- Appliances, broken and functioning
- Projects in process

Chapter 10 ➤ *First Things First: Getting Organized*

So much stuff, it seems impossible to sort out, let alone staighten. But if you and your kids can get this in order, your life is going to feel better. It's simple if you go step by step:

1. First, target a specific area, such as the kitchen closets. (Keep your area small and specific so you don't overwhelm yourself.)
2. Then, prioritize: which closets come first?
3. Set a strategy. Where do you put the stuff when it comes out?
4. Decide what to keep and what to toss (take a vote).
5. Get down to dirty work. Empty the closet, sort the stuff, clean the closet, and replace what's going back (neatly).

This system will work for all parts of your house, whether you're trying to organize the clothes in your closet, the parts of a project, or all the paperwork your kids need for school.

Simplify Your Life

Need a few more tips on how to organize and cut through clutter? Here are a few suggestions:

➤ Consolidate your money into one bank.

➤ Keep all your bill-paying necessities (bills, envelopes, stamps) in one desk, drawer, or file basket. Pay your bills and balance your checkbook twice a month at most.

➤ File all your paperwork in the simplest way. If you're very tidy, fine, but if not, who cares? As long as all the items you need to keep together are together, you will feel organized.

➤ Once you've cleared out a space, set up simple filing systems to keep things from getting jumbled again. Your files don't have to be fancy—just big envelopes or small boxes for records and information by topic that are easy to put stuff in and simple to stash neatly.

➤ The same "basket" approach applies to laundry, make-up, holiday projects, gift wrap—anything you want to keep together to streamline projects and chores.

> **Wise Words**
> A time-management expert who's also a Mom says, "Put your clean little ones to bed in the clothes they'll wear to daycare in the morning. It's one less piece of hysteria to deal with at dawn."

105

> **Singular Successes**
>
> My grandmother had a mending basket. (Does anyone mend anymore?) In it, she kept all the family clothes that needed minor repairs. In odd moments, she would have it handy to sew on a button or two. Even when she was resting, she kept busy. I'm that way, too: I keep various baskets filled with projects (bills to pay, notes to write, and so forth) that I can work on while we're all watching TV, or while I'm waiting for the kids.

➤ The cheapest and easiest organizational tool is a list. Lists provide the simple, orderly, step-by-step way to organize anything you want, from your plan of how to live happily ever after to every color sock you want to buy. Lists work especially well for managing matters of immediate concern, like what to buy at the grocery store and what you need to do for your child's birthday party.

You should realize by now that organization is about more than just cleaning closets and making to-do lists. An organized, streamlined household is one in which every family member gets the time and space to pursue his or her interests; a cooperative household is one in which the entire family as a unit decides what its goals are and how it will achieve them. Plus, if you teach your children how to set and achieve goals now, they will benefit for the rest of their lives.

The Least You Need to Know

➤ You can apply the principles of good organization to every aspect of your personal and family life.

➤ Good organization makes family life less work and more fun.

➤ Good organization helps single-parent kids feel more secure and helps them learn to apply techniques to their own lives.

➤ Set goals as a family, and make sure your goals are smart: Specific, measurable, accountable, realistic, and timed.

Chapter 11

Handling Housework

In This Chapter

➤ Making a home in more ways than one

➤ Creating a clean team

➤ Getting help with chores

➤ Helpful household hints

➤ Hiring outside help

TV-commercial cleanliness (gleaming floors, sparkling windows, full-course dinner set out on fine china) may be out of the range of most single working parents.

You Don't Have to Eat Off the Floor was the title of a book leading the backlash to the superclean homes of the 1950s. Yet the families of the 1990s seem to expect everything polished, too—because the tools and chemicals are available to keep everything shiny, it's thought that today's homes have to be TV-perfect.

Do they? How messy a home are you comfortable with? Maybe you really do value a shining home. Great. Then it gives you pleasure to clean it. But if you're a single parent coping with childraising, breadwinning, and housekeeping, smiling faces may have more value than shining windows.

You shouldn't beat yourself up if you can't attain any media-imposed ideal, but there is a point to housekeeping. Done right, it can underscore the sense of teamwork and family stability in your family. It can, in a real sense, make a home.

In thinking about what matters and what doesn't to you and your home, here are some broader issues you might want to consider.

In Praise of Housework

No, you needn't be a Felix Unger in your tidiness, but yes, your kids (and you) need a sense of clarity and order as part of a developing sense of stability. So whatever you can do to keep your family space organized and functioning, the more organized and functioning your family life will feel.

Surprising as it may seem, housework is an excellent arena for getting practice in dealing with all the issues that can make single-parent life less than joyous.

Tackling housecleaning as a team effort can strengthen family bonds and foster positive discipline. (Doesn't that make scrubbing the toilet more interesting?)

And housecleaning can also offer a big plus in boosting your child's self-esteem: by fostering a sense of self-confidence and competence, cleaning skills can boost your kid's positive outlook. If your child knows that he can feed himself, keep his own clothes clean, and care for things that matter to him, he's going to feel more sure of himself in the world beyond the front door. Feeling like an important part of the family can only boost his sense of self.

The practical skills that your kids will learn from home-maintenance are things we tend to take for granted—until we spend time with people who literally can't boil water, sew a button, or run the dishwasher.

> **Expert-Ease**
> A family counselor says that by doing housework, many children develop a positive sense of responsibility and are able to identify with a parent's healthy responses to life's daily needs.

If you do everything for your kids, or allow them to ignore group needs completely, you'll raise human beings who are going to have a tough time living in the world with other people. Beyond that, kids who help around the house learn reliability, responsibility, and respect for the people and things that provide their livelihood.

There are gender issues at stake, too. Surveys of children of single-parent working families indicate that both sons and daughters see both sexes as having the ability to be equally competent at almost any task, including housework and employment.

Particularly in single parent-families headed by females, daughters can learn how to challenge historically defined roles by seeing women as the heads of households, and sons can learn a respect for women and their traditional and non-traditional roles. In addition, sons of working mothers are more apt to acquire independent living skills for daily living, like cooking and doing laundry.

Besides all that philosophical stuff, having a clean environment, clean sheets, and clean clothes just feels good. And makes us feel good inside and out.

What Kids Can't Do

So helping around the house is good for kids, right?

Within the context of boundaries and role-reversal (discussed in Part 2), it may seem that having kids "keep house" might be taboo. Not so! Properly handled, according to the experts, having kids help out can be a psychological boost! It can make them feel a part of the family, as long as limits are placed on how much caretaking is asked of them.

To sum up the research: Kids can be involved in keeping house as long as they don't overstep their boundaries—which is good news, because everybody HAS to help.

However, keep in mind that kids cannot be expected to:

> **Wise Words**
> "It's not brain surgery: We each have to clean our bedroom and bathroom. We get together to clean the living room and kitchen. We try to do this first thing Saturday morning—and most of the time it works." —Widowed father of two boys

- ➤ Have full responsibility for much younger siblings.

- ➤ Do physical work that's beyond their strength and developmental capabilities.

- ➤ Cook or use chemicals in ways that could be dangerous—especially when they are alone.

- ➤ Clean with substances that are toxic. (It won't hurt you, either, to use vinegar and water instead of killer chemicals.)

- ➤ Be physically entrusted with large sums of money for shopping.

- ➤ Have the sole responsibility for maintaining the home. If your work schedule keeps you from handling any kind of domestic work, then you need to make other arrangements (covered later in this chapter).

- ➤ Do tasks that they insist, strongly and repeatedly, they cannot or do not want to do. You can't expect them to do a good job of tasks they really hate. Respect that and work around it.

Part 3 ➤ *Finding Space and Time*

➤ Be blamed if home maintenance is not perfect.

➤ Be asked to do household work in preference to schoolwork.

Getting the Kids Involved

The easiest way to get housework done is to make it a team effort. Get the family together to review the tentative list of to-do's. Talk about who can do what—and listen to opinions about what needs doing and what can be skipped. Then come up with an assignment list of who does what when. The checklist at the end of this chapter may help: It gets everyone in on the delegations and lets everyone see that the nasty jobs—like changing the cat litter—really do get rotated.

> **Expert-Ease**
> If you're going to reward your child's household work with an allowance or extra money, be extra specific about your child's responsibilities and rewards. Many child-rearing specialists feel that some household participation should be done for free; that some allowance be granted with no strings attached; and that pay be offered, if at all, for beyond-the-call duties.
>
> In this way, your child might be expected to keep her room tidy no matter what, and to do the trash or the dishes as part of the team effort. She'll know that she will always be given enough pocket money to cover her needs, and that she may be able to earn extra cash for taking on special projects (shoveling snow or mowing the lawn).

Depending on your household routine, the best schedule for cleaning might be a couple of concentrated hours each week (say, Saturday morning clean-up). You'll get best results if you focus on one big job each week, and simple maintenance in the rest of the house. Don't let cleaning time drag on, or you'll turn your kids off to helping out.

It's important when assigning duties to give thorough instructions about how to do each chore. For instance, tell kids to put paper on the floor before they start defrosting the fridge, or to wipe the walls from top to bottom so they don't spread the dirt around. Instructions like these may seem obvious to you, but they may not be to your kids. So give them clear directions beforehand, rather then criticizing them afterwards.

Once you've got your list, write it up and post it on the fridge, in each room, or wherever your family communication centers are.

While you're meeting, come to terms on matters of rewards and consequences. Agree ahead of time what will happen if a chore doesn't get done. Come up with a formula: "No washed dishes, no TV." "A messy room means no time on the computer." Or whatever sets of carrots and sticks works for your family.

Schedule a brief time each week when you go over the upcoming days' lists of what needs to be done and when.

Keep the chore schedule subject to review. Every day, do a quick check; did the day's jobs get done? If not, why not? And if not, who skips TV or loses other privileges?

If one task never gets done, or one team member always seems to lag, find out why before cracking the whip.

Getting Organized

Some parents complain that delegating and overseeing the household tasks is as difficult as doing the chores themselves. How do you make sure that chores are done and done right? Simple—you organize. Here are a few suggestions:

> ➤ In the same place where you keep your weekly chores list, keep detailed how-to's: menus for the week, a never-ending grocery list, a list of errands that must be done.

> ➤ On the dishwasher, keep a step-by-step how-to guide so everyone knows how to run it (no broken fine china). Same for the washing machine and dryer.

> ➤ Keep a jar of coins for the laundromat handy.

> ➤ In the broom closet, post a how-to guide to using the equipment (vacuum, Dustbuster, and so on).

> ➤ Spend time once or twice a week to prepare meals ahead of time, and have everyone help. You can prepare your own foods and save money while getting better nutrition. For instance, French toast or pancakes can be made ahead of time and frozen in individual plastic bags. Then your kid can heat them in the microwave and toaster for a really nutritious breakfast. Same with hamburgers; you can cook them, freeze them, and then let the kids microwave them for a fast meal or snack.

Expert-Ease
Family management experts offer these suggestions to keep housework easy:

➤ Have everyone add to the grocery lists as you run out of items.

➤ Place all items that need repairing in one box or basket.

➤ Set up meal preparation so everyone can participate according to ability.

➤ Always keep things as tidy and uncluttered as possible, but tackle in-depth wiping and mopping weekly, with only one major cleaning task a month.

Making the Most of It

How can you get the best participation from your kids? By making chores fun!

No, mopping the kitchen floor is not going to be a gas, no matter what. But you CAN add interest to housework. For instance, depending on the size and style of your family, make

Part 3 ➤ *Finding Space and Time*

> **Parent Pitfalls**
> Parents who take for granted that their kids will help forget to praise their kids for their efforts—and lose all the benefits of housekeeping as a family activity. Make sure to praise your kids when you see them making efforts and improvements.

> **Wise Words**
> "My Mom seemed to think we were all there to work all weekend. It was a real drag." —An 11-year-old boy

it a contest. Give Olympic points for outstanding achievements in each task area. Plan a regular special event to follow the day when chores are done, such as a Saturday evening pizza.

Chores should NOT be a serious matter! If your kids want to make a race of dumping trash, or use tossing clothes in the laundry as basketball practice—why not? If the child with cooking duty wants to make a kidney bean omelet—well, it's nutritious (and creative).

Another way to encourage cheerful participation is to offer a financial benefit for work that goes above and beyond the call of duty. If it saves money to do a project in-house rather than outsourcing it, for example, you might want to spend the savings on something fun for you and your child. If your child helps you launder shirts, for instance, or paint the porch, then take that savings and spend it on, say, an extra movie for the month.

Although household duties rank (probably far) behind schoolwork and personal growth in terms of their importance in your child's life, they can provide character benefits that outstrip simple dust-free living.

Housekeeping How-To

Once upon a time, housekeeping tips were passed on from mother to daughter, aunt to niece. Today, that doesn't happen anymore. So how do you know what to do? Well, there are some simple how-to rules that make housekeeping simple and streamlined. Here are a few suggestions:

➤ Focus on one small area when straightening. This prevents you from feeling overwhelmed. For example, clean one small shelf or drawer a day. By the end of the year, you will have cleared 365 of them!

➤ Follow the "down and out" rule for cleaning: Start at the top of whatever you are cleaning (a wall, a refrigerator, an oven), and work down. Do walls before floors. Dust the top shelf before the bottom. (Why? Because the dirt falls downward, so you want to finish cleaning at its last stop.) If you have tall kids and short ones, older and younger, why not have the taller or older ones do the "ups," and the little ones focus on the "downs"?

> As for the "out" rule: If you want to clean a closet, do that before you clean the room. Your natural instinct may be to stuff everything in the closet, but that only delays things. Also, if you are washing a floor, start from the inner corner and work toward the door—not as much fun as leaving footprints in the floorwax, but more efficient.

There are also lots of helpful books on housecleaning hints. Consumer Reports has a good one, and Mary Ellen and Heloise are full of tips. See Appendix A for more suggestions.

Hiring Help

Think household help is a luxury you can't afford? Maybe not. Household help need not be a luxury. It might even be a cost-saver if used appropriately. What if you hired a cleaning service once or twice a year to come in and do one big, in-depth cleaning? Then you've got a clean base from which maintenance will be easier for the rest of the year.

To afford it, suggest taking one week's allowance from each family member, or some other system to allow for a cleaning fund.

You may also be able to hire someone who can do double duty. A childcare worker might be willing to do light housework. (She may be even more willing if you allow her to bring her own child or children to your house.) It's something to consider when you look for folks who can help you out.

Here's another idea: Hire a teenage baby sitter to watch your kids while you tackle the tough jobs undisturbed. Do that once or twice a week and see how much easier housework gets.

Sharing Chores

You may not have to pay for household help if you can share it with freinds, family members, neighbors, or other single parents you trust who live nearby.

Let's say your neighbor works near a huge discount store. Great! They she can help with your big monthly shopping. In return, you can offer to do her laundry.

Consider an organized barter system to divvy up big jobs: If your neighbor washes your windows, you'll offer to mow his or her lawn.

Or follow the old barn-raising model. If you and another single-parent family you know have a big project to do (painting a room, cleaning out a basement, holding a yard sale), then joining together can halve the effort—or better. And it can even be fun.

Part 3 ➤ *Finding Space and Time*

Chores Checklists

Inventory your own household needs and make a list of what projects need to be done, who is responsible for them, and when they will be done.

Chores To Do:

Yearly: _____
_____
_____
_____

Semi annually _____
_____
_____
_____

Monthly: _____
_____
_____
_____

Weekly: _____
_____
_____
_____

Daily: _____
_____
_____
_____

Chapter 11 ➤ *Handling Housework*

Weekly Assignment List

Chore	Who Does It	When It Gets Done

Organizing the housework this way has several benefits: things get done, and people feel life is more orderly; chores get done when they need to be done; and everyone sees that everyone else is sharing the burden.

The Least You Need to Know

- ➤ The benefits of housekeeping together are greater than simply enjoying a clean house.
- ➤ Kids can and should be part of the "clean team" to the extent of their age and ability.
- ➤ Learn good techniques to make cleaning easier.
- ➤ It's OK and possible to hire cleaning help, or share housekeeping duties with others.

Chapter 12

Making Time

> **In This Chapter**
> - Making the most of your time through better organization
> - Rescheduling for the long term
> - Creating a family to-do list
> - Learning how to beat burnout

Time is tough enough to manage by itself. If you doubt that, take a look at all the time management and organizational systems on the market: They take up miles of bookstore shelf-space.

When you then plug in children and their schedules—school, after-school activities, hobbies, homework—it's enough to make you want to unplug. And when there's only you to manage your time and your children's time, well...

This chapter will help you learn how to make more efficient use of your time, show you ways to simplify your schedule, and help you ease the labor of managing your kids' lives.

Divide Time to Double It

Efficiency experts have recently created a new buzzword to describe doing more than one thing at a time: they call it *multitasking*. Where have they been?! You've probably been multitasking for years. A parent who can't is in trouble. And a single parent who can't diaper a baby, check math homework, make supper, talk on the phone, add the fabric softener, and check the e-mail—all at the same time—is in *big* trouble.

Yes, doubling up on time can be efficient, but it can also lead to burnout if you overdo it. If that sounds like you—always ultrabusy yet never getting ahead—you can take some steps to divide your time.

Where Does Your Time Go?

> **Meaning?**
> *Multitasking* is doing many things at once.

The first step toward making more time is to list all the things you do in a day or a week that involve time:

If you're like most single parents, your total probably adds up to 30 hours a day, nine days a week.

Now, let's find ways to eliminate unnecessary activities and combine the rest.

Timely Tips

Too-busy working parents have figured out lots of ways to get it ALL done with time to spare. Here's their advice:

To handle errands:

- Share errands with your neighbors if you can. If your neighbor works near a big grocery store, for example, maybe she can help with your shopping—in return for which you take her clothes to the dry cleaner. Or whatever. Be creative!

- Double up on errands by planning in advance all the things you can do in one particular neighborhood. If there's a cleaner or other specialty store near your kid's school or your office, for example, then you can swing by on the way without making a special trip.

- Think of three other ways you can cut down on repeated errands: Find the closest post office and bank near your kids' karate center, for instance, so you can run errands while the kids are in class.

- When shopping, go for bulk: If the cash flow permits, buy a lot of non-perishables at once. It's cheaper and it will save you time.

- If you can't buy or store a lot of food at once, at least cook a lot at once. Make double or triple the chili, soup, or casserole and store individual portions in separate containers in the freezer for meals later.

To take care of your kids:

- The next time you pass a card store, stock up on a supply of "thank you," "I love you," and "great job" cards. You'll always have a card on hand when you want to give your kid a special note. Buy birthday and anniversary cards in advance, too, so you always have them on hand.

- Use TV time wisely. This can be fun. If you're watching TV with your kids (which you should do, for bonding as well as for keeping an eye on what they're watching) keep busy: write notes, update your calendar. Hey—do some mending!

- Set up every routine activity in advance—especially the stuff you need to do in the morning, like get your kids dressed, have breakfast, and hand out lunches. All your and your kids' things for the day should be by the door—and always keep your keys in the same place so you don't waste time searching. Write notes to your kids in advance, ready to stick in their lunch bags (when you make them the night before).

- Keep a standard checklist prepared for every time you have a babysitter or someone else in to watch your kids. Then you don't need to make a new one each time.

- Find another member or two of your single-parent community who can help you with childcare. Maybe there's a nearby Mom who can take the kids to school. Maybe there's an at-home Dad who can host the kids after school in return for evenings off.

To make housework easy:

- Get rid of clutter—things are easier to find when you don't have to dig.

- Keep a master list of household tasks that need doing—so you don't reinvent the wheel each cleaning day.

- Keep everything together that goes together. Keep cleaning stuff in one container with a handle. Stash laundry supplies by the washer, bathroom supplies in the bathroom. File bills and other financial papers in one drawer or basket. Then, if you keep putting stuff back where you got it, you'll never lose it.

- Time your tasks. Put a load of wash in before you go to the grocery store, for example, so it'll be ready to dry when you're back, and ready to fold as soon as you put the groceries away.

Part 3 ➤ *Finding Space and Time*

- ➤ Create "time capsules:" Set aside one morning for cleaning, one evening for bill paying, and so forth. Decide that you will spend a given amount of time on a project like ironing—and when the time is up, stop.

- ➤ Keep a timer handy and set it so you know when the dryer is done, or when the kids have filled their TV quota, or when you've done enough of a particular task. This will help you begin to get a realistic sense of how you spend your time.

- ➤ Once a week (perhaps while you all watch Sunday evening TV?) review your calendar and go over your to-do lists. Make one big list for the week, and use individual sticky-notes to break down your errands and deadlines day by day.

The most important tip: create an overall time structure for all your activities and keep it posted where everyone in the family can keep an eye on it. The fridge is ideal (just arrange the kids' artwork around it).

sKIDules

There are fancy ways, fancy words, and fancy tools for making a schedule. Here's the very simplest:

1. Photocopy a blank calendar page and enlarge it with a photocopier.

2. Get a big notepad, and gather your kids around. Write down everything that you have to do in a typical month. In addition to the basics (soccer practice, ballet lessons, tutoring sessions, the monthly meeting of your single-parent group), don't forget special activities: deadlines for big projects (yours and theirs), school trips, athletic events, social events, parties, birthdays, and anything else.

3. Write in all the regular events on the calendar in (erasable) colored pencils.

4. In a different color, write down the special activities for that month.

5. To make the calendar clear (and colorful), use a different colored pencil for each family member, and have each person write in his or her activities with the right color.

6. To make the calendar useful, it must be easy to maintain. Keep the colored pencils handy by attaching them to a string next to it. Keep a set of small sticky notes next there for things that require special attention.

> **Wise Words**
> "I've learned that if I have a big project, I need to start early and commit myself to doing a little bit of it every day. Even with just a little bit each day, it always gets done. I'm trying to convince my kids to do their term papers that way." —A single father of teens

7. Keep a master list of activities and chores that must be done every week by the calendar, too.

At the beginning of every week, review the upcoming activities with your kids. Figure out the best way to get them all done.

For instance, review your chart of how you spend your time, as well as to your to-do lists for the week and month. Which activities can be combined? Use a colored pencil to match up, say, trips that can be carpooled or errands that can be multitasked.

Suggest some rearrangements. If Jenny wants to go to basketball practice Tuesdays and Thursdays after school, see if older brother Jeff can find a place to do his homework early and pick her up.

Get the idea? Do as much as you can toward fitting everyone's arrangements into the week—but do what you can to make it as easy as possible. Let your kids know that they are responsible for marking their activities on the calendar, and that if they don't, last-minute arrangements may be impossible.

Keeping a steady, regular schedule goes a long way toward making single-parent kids of any age feel secure. So post a daily timetable near your calendar, and pick a regular time for the kids to check in by phone after school, start heating the pre-cooked meals, and expecting you home.

In making individual and family plans, helping your kids to prioritize is valuable both for practical reasons and for their own long-term experience with self-management. By actually helping to plan, your kids see how they have to fit the things they want to do in with the things they have to do, like homework. They may become more willing to help around the house if they realize that may make more time for their special events. It's a good learning experience for them.

> **Parent Pitfalls**
> Parents who are always at the beck and call of their kids not only wear themselves out, but keep their kids from developing some sense of being responsible for themselves.

Who Gets to See the Kids?

If you're sharing custody of the kids with your ex, you may find it useful to establish a visitation calendar a year at a time so there aren't any quibbles about who does what when. Of course, you'll want to review it regularly, and one hopes you've gotten to the stage where you can do that in a friendly fashion.

Maybe there's even more that needs reviewing as well?

When you need time for yourself is when you're likely to be most grateful that you have either an "ex" or other family members around who can watch the kids. Admitting that you need a break—a day or a weekend of doing nothing, just to re-kindle your energy—can do wonders for your multi-tasking self. You surely have family who will be happy for a visit from the kids. And if you're burning out too often, maybe it's time to talk with your ex about rearranging that custody/visitation schedule that seemed so perfect once.

> **Wise Words**
> "We wrote into our initial custody agreement an overall schedule, including when our son would be with whom for major holidays. We also wrote in that when he reached a certain age, he could decide on with whom he wanted to live. Both eliminated a lot of tension."
> —Divorced Mom of now-grown son

Rearranging Custody

Your toddler has turned into a teen. Your emergency job has turned into a major career. It's occurred to you that maybe your child's other parent could parent as well as you could at this point. Why not? It's something to consider and discuss with everyone involved. It's a very real possibility if you've been keeping your ex-partner up to date on your child's progress by regular meetings, open communication, and shared time.

Rearranging Visitation

A less drastic but also valuable solution to your time crunch might be to fiddle with the visitation schedule. This is called for when it seems that visitation with the other parent is interfering with your child's schedule. So rather than fight it and make everyone unhappy, try to rearrange time with your ex.

Likewise, maybe you can take over more responsibilities by keeping your children for longer spells at a time.

Rearranging custody or visitation agreements may not be the right answer for your family. But it's worth talking about, and it sends a good message for your kids about not being too rigid.

Beating Burnout

When you look at the chart of how you spend your time, or the lists and calendars of things to do, who in your household benefits most or least from all the activities? In all likelihood, it's you who puts the most in—and who gets the least out. To a certain extent that's appropriate: it's your job to do for your kids.

But if you don't carve out time for yourself, you're in danger of burning out from exhaustion and resentment. So it's important to carve out some significant time for yourself.

And the most likely way to do that is to eliminate some of your to-do's. Here are a few suggestions:

If you're too physically tired to do something—don't. Unless it's absolutely necessary, you'll do it (whatever it is) better after you've had some rest. Fatigue causes screw-ups that can sometimes be dangerous. So put it off till tomorrow.

If it's all too much, it's all too much. Look at your schedule and see what can be cut out. Be ruthless—like cleaning a closet. The goal: Simplify!

In your review, there are two very important words to use: "NOW" and " NO."

Like this: In considering an activity or a request for your time, review it this way:

> Must it be done?
>
> Must it be done now?
>
> Must it be done now by me?

The simplest way to prioritize your schedule—to decide what comes first—is to ask, "What must be done now?"

> **Meaning?**
> *Prioritize* is a big word for doing first things first, when the first thing is the most important, most urgent, or even the things that you're just bored of thinking about.

Here's another simple, but revolutionary concept in time management: "NO" is a complete sentence. It's the best sentence to use when you're about to go into terminal overload and you get asked to do just one more thing.

The Least You Need to Know

> ➤ Time management is as important for busy single-parent households as it is for major corporations.
>
> ➤ The principles of time management are to prioritize tasks and to simplify as much as possible.
>
> ➤ Learn to multitask. Group errands together in order to cut down on the time it takes to do things.
>
> ➤ If every family member has input into the daily, weekly, and monthly planning process, everyone will feel and act more responsibly.
>
> ➤ Schedules not only make single-parent households function better, they make everyone feel better and more secure, too.

Part 4
Money Matters

Life, it's said, can be seen as a two-ring circus: in one ring, "love"; in the other, "work." To put it another way, the major drama of most lives takes place in the arenas of romance and finance.

Romance you can avoid, if you like (more on that later). But finance, you can't. For many people, money raises almost as many mixed emotions as love—especially for single parents with children who depend on them.

The facts of finance can be truly frightening, but they get less scary as they're faced. So the chapters in this part will help you break the money monster down into smaller, more tame-able pieces.

It's simple, really—the key to money management is to take in more than you spend. Simple. Now, let's try to make it easy.

Chapter 13

Facing Your Financial Facts

In This Chapter

➤ The special money challenges faced by single parents

➤ Understanding alimony and child support agreements

➤ Exploring other sources of support

➤ Using credit carefully

➤ Learning to rely on yourself

How often do you count the days till payday, wondering how you'll make it? How often have you scraped the last spoonfuls from a generic-brand peanut butter jar, hoping to postpone another grocery bill? How many times have you said to your kids, "We can't afford that"?

Financial facts of life like these apply to many families, of course. But for single-parent families, financing is almost always even tougher. Government statistics show that 45 percent of single-parent families headed by a woman (and 19 percent of single-parent families headed by a man) live in poverty. In contrast, only eight percent of married couples with children under the age of 18 live in poverty.

The weekly earnings of married couples ($783) continued to be about 25 percent higher than those of single parent-families maintained by men ($520) and twice as much as the earnings of single-parent families maintained by women ($385).

If you are struggling to make ends meet, this chapter will give you an overview of the steps you need to take to organize and improve your finances.

Steps to Financial Freedom

What do you and your kids really need—and how are you going to pay for it? That's really all you need to know to manage your money. To answer these questions, follow these four steps:

1. Calculate your expenses.
2. Add up your assets (income *and* property).
3. Figure the difference between what you have and what you need.
4. Decide how to make up the difference.

Steps 1 and 2 are covered in this chapter; Steps 3 and 4 are discussed in the next.

If you're a divorced or separated parent, this figuring should have been done before you signed any agreements with your ex. It's still important to do it now, though, because you can adjust your settlements if necessary—and because you may qualify for special aid based on your need.

Calculating Your Expenses

Begin by carefully estimating and adding up all your monthly expenses. The following worksheet will help you do this.

List *fixed* and *variable* monthly expenses. Fixed expenses are those that stay the same every month: your rent or mortgage payment, for example. Variable expenses are those that vary with use: your phone and gas bills, for example, may not be the same from month to month. In the case of variable expenses, try to look back over the past year's bills (if you save them) and come up with a realistic average.

Calculate annual, semi-annual, and quarterly expenses, like insurance, on a monthly basis by dividing the total amount you have to pay by the number of months you have in which to pay it and putting aside the average amount every month. For example, if you pay $1,500 in car insurance annually, your monthly payment would be $125.

When you figure your expenses, write down the actual amounts—not a guess, or the amount you wish or hope to spend. If you haven't been keeping financial records, look at

Chapter 13 ➤ Facing Your Financial Facts

your checkbook or charge account bills to get an idea of what you spend. The closer you can get to an actual figure, the better; it's worth the effort.

Where Does Your Money Go?

Living Expenses	Monthly Payment
Housing	
Rent or Mortgage	_____
2nd Mortgage	_____
Condo/Co-op Fee	_____
Utilities	
Gas/Heating Oil	_____
Electric	_____
Water	_____
Telephone	_____
Cable	_____
Food	
Groceries	_____
Household Supplies	_____
Dining Out	_____
Transportation	
Auto payment	_____
Auto maintenance	_____
Gas/Oil	_____
Parking	_____
Commuter fares	_____
*Alimony/Child Support	
Childcare	
Sitter	_____
Tuition, school fees	_____
Daycare/After-school fees	_____
Transportation	_____
Lunches, snacks	_____

continues

129

Part 4 ➤ *Money Matters*

continued

Living Expenses	Monthly Payment
Personal	
Cosmetics/Hair Care	_____
Tobacco/Alcohol	_____
Books/Papers/Magazines	_____
Clothing	_____
Your clothing	_____
Your children's clothing	_____
Laundry/Dry Cleaning	_____
Other	_____
Recreation	
Entertainment	_____
Membership fees (i.e. gym)	_____
Other	_____
Periodic Expenses (divide into monthly amounts)	
*Insurance**	
Life	_____
Health	_____
Disability	_____
Homeowners/Renters	_____
Auto	_____
***Taxes**	
Personal Property	_____
Income Taxes	_____
Other local taxes	_____
Emergencies/Repairs	_____
Vacations	_____
***Medical Expenses**	
General medical visits	_____
Dental/Eye Care	_____
Medications	_____

Chapter 13 ➤ *Facing Your Financial Facts*

Other	_____
Miscellaneous	
Gifts	_____
Dues	_____
Contributions	_____
Other items not listed here:	_____
TOTAL Monthly Expenses:	_____

*Don't include amounts that already may be deducted from your paycheck.

Adding Up Your Assets

Now, take a look at the monthly money you currently have available. Use the following checklist to help you figure it out.

Where Does Your Money Come From?

Source	Amount
Paycheck (from first job, less deductions)	_____
Paycheck (from second job, less deductions)	_____
Alimony	_____
Child Support	_____
Social Security	_____
Insurance Settlement	_____
Dividend Income	_____
V.A. Benefits	_____
Rental Income	_____
Interest Income	_____
Unemployment Income	_____
Freelance Income	_____
Other	_____
TOTAL	_____

131

Part 4 ➤ *Money Matters*

(Note that if you cannot absolutely count on any of these items, you're better off leaving them out of the equation, and treating them as a bonus if you do get them.)

Now compare your total from the first worksheet with your total from the second worksheet. The likelihood is, your income doesn't match your outgo, unless you're on the higher rungs of the economic ladder. For those of us without dividends, annuities, or trust funds, it's iffy, to say the least. But you may not be getting all that you are due.

Collecting Child Support and Alimony

If you are separated or divorced from your partner, you may be eligible for *alimony* (a regular payment your partner agrees to pay you).

> **Meaning?**
> *Child support* is money owed by the non-custodial parent to pay expenses for the children. Child support is collectible by public agencies if necessary.
>
> *Alimony* is a payment to former spouse or partner agreed to at separation. Alimony is not usually collectible by public agency.

Alimony is more rarely granted in today's legal system, and its amount and method of payment are determined on a case-by-case basis by the court granting the separation or the divorce.

As the custodial parent, you may also be eligible for *child support* (as described in Chapter 7) to help you pay for your children's educational, medical, and living expenses.

Accepting the reality of how hard it may be to get alimony and child support is important, so you can clear up any unrealistic expectations that might create a financial crisis. Remember, you can't spend your separation agreement or benefits letter at the grocery store. As discussed earlier, court decrees determine these payments and enforce compliance when necessary.

Desperately Seeking Support

Of the 11.5 million single-parent (non-widowed) families, only 6.2 million (54 percent) of the custodial parents had awards or agreements for child support. Of the total $17.7 billion owed for child support in 1991, $5.8 billion was not paid.

To break it down more specifically, among those custodial parents due support,

➤ about half received the full amount due,

➤ about a quarter received partial payment, and

➤ about a quarter received nothing.

For this reason, the Child Support Enforcement (CSE) Program has a mandate at the federal, state, and local level to locate parents who owe child support. The CSE Program attempts to establish paternity and establish and enforce child support orders.

Chapter 13 ➤ *Facing Your Financial Facts*

Parents who do not cooperate and pay child support may be forced to do so in a number of ways. Part of their income may be garnished, for example. Overdue child support can also be collected from federal and state income tax refunds. Liens can be put on their property, and the property itself may even be sold so the proceeds can be used to pay child support arrears. Finally, parents who do not pay support as required may find their professional licenses or even their drivers' licenses suspended.

Under laws passed in the late 1980s, child support is automatically deducted from a parent's pay; and so-called "deadbeat dad" regulations since then have made it even easier to track down and gain compliance from parents who ignore their child support obligations. If your former spouse is not paying child support as required, take action immediately: contact the Office of Child Support Enforcement (www.acf.dhhs.gov/programs/cse).

> **Wise Words**
> Joyce went through all the steps of separation, negotiation, and divorce and worked out support agreements with her ex—who rarely paid. Liens against his salary were useless once he lost his job. So Joyce stopped figuring him into her financial figuring. "I decided to count on myself instead," she says.

Improving Your Support

Even if you do receive support, however, it may not be all that you need. The Census Bureau reports that the average amount of child support received is slightly over $3000 a year per child.

When you worked out a financial arrangement with your children's other parent, you hadn't lived the single-parent life yet; you may not have fully realized the extent of your expenses. Your kids' needs change over time, too. So, even if you're not friendly with your children's other parent, are you stuck with what you agreed on back then? No. You can go back to the court that provided the divorce or go to court to argue for additional support.

An official in your local family court can tell you how best to go about it, as can the Child Support Enforcement program. (The CSE can also request special medical support for your child if needed.) If you need special help, at low cost, go to the Legal Aid Society; lawyers there can help you negotiate in or out of court.

> **Expert-Ease**
> If you're widowed, be sure your kids get the social security support they're entitled to, as well as veterans' benefits or pension benefits from employers of a now deceased parent.

133

Part 4 ➤ *Money Matters*

> **Expert-Ease**
> If you seek government benefits, remember that not all benefits are strictly financial in nature. If you qualify, you may be eligible for job training, a significant opportunity.

> **Parent Pitfalls**
> As you search for other governmental sources of support, avoid any individual or organization who promises to find this information for you for a fee. There's no need to pay for this free information.

> **Wise Words**
> "If your family wants to help—say yes!" says a divorced mother of four. "My family is big but not rich, so even when they couldn't give money directly, they were great about helping with tuition, car maintenance, and even a computer."

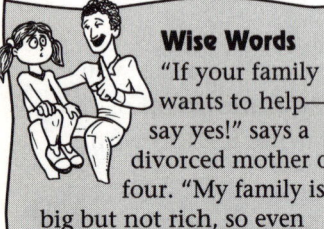

Other Sources of Support

From similar government sources, you can get detailed information about funds that you may be entitled to if you're NOT a divorced single parent. You and your children may be entitled to special help from public agencies: The Veteran's Administration, for instance, or the Social Security Administration.

To find out about other payments you may be eligible for, check directly with your state or local office of social services, the social security administration, and the office of veterans' affairs. All these agencies are listed in the government pages of your local phone book (or call the toll-free directory at 1-800-555-1212) or on the World Wide Web.

One word of warning: If you're thinking of turning to the government for last-ditch help, better start digging now. Public assistance is not as widely available today as it used to be.

Your family may be yet another source of financial support. If you have family that can help, don't let pride stand in your way. Some family members automatically take stray or troubled members under their wing; others don't. Some will give money generously, others prefer to make loans. Whatever way your family tends to operate, you may be able to negotiate support for your kids.

If a family member does offer to give you money, you may feel more comfortable making a formal arrangement, complete with a signed letter of agreement, as you would have with any lender. Or you can agree with them more informally that they will provide the "extras." But you're still better off if you continue to act on the assumption that you *are* on your own.

Charge It! Using Credit Carefully

A good credit rating is a tremendously valuable asset. If you use credit wisely and make payments promptly, you will build a good credit rating, with which you can buy a new car, new furniture, or take your family on vacation. Further down the road, a good credit rating will help you take out larger loans, which you can use to buy a house, start a business, or send your kids to college. Without good credit, however, it will be difficult (or even impossible) to do any of these things.

Americans suffer a fundamental conflict over debt. Historically we think that buying items on credit is wrong, or a kind of vice. Yet advertisements and commercials constantly entice us to use credit to purchase all kinds of things we might want.

Credit, used wisely, can be a very valuable asset when your cash flow is tight. On the other hand, misuse of credit can take your whole family down the tubes. So how do you know what is healthy credit use and what's not?

Charge cards can help with cash flow at times when money is tight. If you use credit wisely, you don't maintain balances that balloon.

On the other hand, overuse of credit can make you literally sick with worry and tension, and large monthly payments can tie you down rather than freeing you up.

You may be slipping into a credit "pit" if you experience these danger signs:

- You pay only the minimum, or less, on credit cards each month.
- You juggle other bills to keep up the minimum monthly payments on your credit cards.
- You've reached the credit limit on your credit cards.
- You use credit cards to pay for items you once bought with cash (groceries, sundries, and so on).
- You repeatedly pay late fees on overdue bills.

> **Wise Words**
> "The separation was nasty but before the divorce was even final, I figured that, with the kids at this stage and the income as expected, within eight years I'd be $40,000 in debt. So I took out a second mortgage on the house and put that money in the bank. In eight years, I was $40,000 in debt, but I had that in the bank to cover it." —A financially savvy divorced mother

If you have gotten in debt over your head, there are ways to dig yourself out:

- The first step toward getting out is to stop digging the hole—cut up those cards and go on a cash-only basis. This can be tough and requires careful budgeting. See the next chapter for more help.
- Consolidate debts where you can.
- Beware of come-ons from finance companies.
- Be careful about home-equity loans that can threaten the roof over your head if you have more problems. (Your home is used as collateral for the loan. If you can't make the payments, you lose your house.)

Part 4 ➤ Money Matters

> ➤ If it's impossible to make even minimum payments each month, work out a realistic payment schedule with your credit card companies.

> ➤ Once you've gotten your monthly payments in line, don't start eating into your new credit availability!

> ➤ If you need more help, go to Debtors Anonymous, the CCCS, or other local credit counselling agencies for advice.

If all this makes sense but you still can't get a handle on your spending, don't be surprised. Money is more than just dollars and cents; it has an emotional effect as well.

Your Money and Your Life

As if managing your finances wasn't complicated enough, money also has emotional strings attached.

> **Wise Words**
> "I thought I had to keep buying over my limit to keep my kids attached to me—then my daughter told me that I was more important to her than the things I bought."
> —A non-custodial mother of a teen

> **Wise Words**
> "Mom uses the divorce as an excuse. Anything we want, she says, 'We don't have the money for that—but we would if it weren't for your Dad.' It gets sickening!"
> —A single-parent teen

When it comes to money, people are either afraid of failure or afraid of success. Messages we carry from the past tell us our money equals our value, so if we have no money (or have too much debt) we feel of no value ourselves. Before you fall into the trap of letting your money determine your worth, here are some points to consider:

➤ You are not your money. How much you make or spend does not add to your value—as debt does not diminish your value.

➤ On the other hand, if you believe you're worth feeling financially secure, you have a better chance of getting there.

➤ Do you find yourself buying things you don't need simply to make yourself feel better? Or buying things for your kids when they're out of sorts? Try exploring other ways to boost your self-esteem that do not involve spending money.

➤ Do you find that you always keep yourself close to the financial edge even when you don't have to? What do you gain from that?

➤ Do you ignore money in the belief that you'll be taken care of? Realize that you can't depend on anyone else helping you out of your financial problems. You need to solve them yourself.

Chapter 13 ➤ *Facing Your Financial Facts*

If you're having a constant struggle with bad spending habits, chances are good you have some emotional issues that are expressing themselves through your misuse of money. Do what you can to clear that away, with help if necessary. Some of the guides in Appendix A can help you uncover some of these self-defeating attitudes.

If you are worried about money, you may pass that fear on to your children without meaning to. Your kids probably worry about money more than you realize—most single-parent kids do, especially if you're constantly telling them, "We can't afford that."

Better to be as honest as possible within limits. Tell your children, "We have enough money to pay for what we need, but we have to be careful about our spending."

The best thing to do—for both you and your kids—is to allay your own worries.

> **Expert-Ease**
> One important way that single parents can provide security, according to both experts *and* kids, is not to provide all the money that kids want, but to show care and fairness in handling the money that is available.

Your Assets and Liabilities Checklist

In addition to any cash you may have in the bank, you have other assets: your car and all household items (appliances, electronic equipment, for example). Check throughout your home and list all your possessions (this is a good idea for insurance purposes, too). You may be pleasantly surprised as you begin to tally the value of your possessions; most people are worth more than they think they are. And whatever your status, the better your picture of yourself is, the better off you are.

Among your liabilities, list not only current debts but long-term bills (such as tuition for this year) that are due.

From this and other inventory lists in this chapter, you know what you have, what you spend—and how you feel about it. You may even have an idea of how and why your attitudes block your ease with money.

At least, as a practical matter, when you compare what you have with what you need, you know how much more cash you have to take in on a regular basis to make ends at least meet. The next chapters will help you with that.

Part 4 ➤ *Money Matters*

The Least You Need to Know

- ➤ To manage your money successfully, you must first tally up your income and expenditures.
- ➤ You can get help if you are not collecting all the alimony and child support that is due you.
- ➤ If your expenditures change significantly, you may be able to negotiate a change in your alimony or child support payments.
- ➤ Beware of the high costs of credit. Use credit cards wisely.
- ➤ Don't let your financial state affect your sense of self-worth. Raise your kids to be aware of—but not overly worried about—your financial situation.

Chapter 14

Balancing Your Budget

In This Chapter

- ➤ Determining what you want—and what you need
- ➤ Setting a workable budget
- ➤ Clever ways to boost your income
- ➤ Easy suggestions to lower your expenses
- ➤ The importance of saving and investing

Do you find it nearly impossible to run a household on one income? If things are tight, don't be embarrassed. You aren't alone!

Surveys show that all parties in a divorce usually suffer a diminished lifestyle and income. If you're widowed, you suddenly have to get used to living on only one income instead of two. And if you've always been single, remember that you're now a single parent in a society of double-income, two-parent families who have more spendable cash.

Your finances don't have to be frightening—there are actions you can take to flex your financial muscles and build fiscal strength. It's just a matter of matching out-go to income by keeping careful track of both. This chapter will show you how.

Getting What You Want—and What You Need

It may seem like your kids want something more—a new toy, more clothes, the latest video game—every week. Do you give in to all their demands? Of course not.

Parents want things, too. You probably desire all kinds of things for yourself and your kids. We all want more than we have—it's what makes the economy go 'round. A new suit, a dishwasher, a better car... How do you decide what to get, and what not to get? Should you always say "no" to the things you and your children really desire?

Not necessarily. Some of your "wants" really are "needs"; for example, a new suit that will help you land your dream job, a reliable car that gets you around safely, a new pair of shoes that will help your kid feel comfortable in school.

So how do you sort it out?

Some single parents overcompensate for the absence of a second parent by buying things for their kids to assuage their own guilt. But that's not the best way to raise your kids—or manage your money. It's your job to walk the line between making your kids feel insecure and worried about money, and being too indulgent.

> **Wise Words**
> "I wish my Dad would get it that I don't need to have him buying me presents all the time—it's okay to just spend time with him!" —A 14-year-old boy

Instead, get together with your kids and say, "We have enough money to meet our needs—to keep us warm and fed and safe. We don't have a lot of extra money. So if we want to get more than that, we have to think about how."

Here's how you can help your kids learn the difference between wants and needs.

First, go over the list of expenses you created in Chapter 13 with them. Ask them if you've left out any "needs."

Once they understand how much money is needed to cover your basic expenses, you can have them help figure your *discretionary* expenses (your wants).

> **Meaning?**
> *Discretionary income* is the money left over after your necessary living expenses are paid. It's what's left for the things you want (dining out, entertainment, clothing, and so on).

Sometimes a want and a need overlap, and each family has to figure out which takes priority.

A computer with multimedia capability and Internet access is a good example of a "want" that could be a "need" that could actually save you money. Such computers are available for under $1,000 and can be a source of entertainment *and* education for you and your children. They can help you save money on research your kids need to do for school projects. Plus, the computer can serve as a moneymaking source—and keep you connected to others like you. So a computer could be a highly profitable expenditure (if you carefully control your modem and phone-line costs, and supervise your children's access).

Likewise, a decent, reliable car fills a need for most American families. You may not be in the market for a new, fully equipped Range Rover, but a cheap old clunker in constant need of repairs can cost you more than it saves.

Everybody's money needs are different. We all need to spend money on fun, for instance, but that's a different expense for each family. Your kids may need more pocket money than those in another area of the country. Maybe they insist on buying their lunch; OK, then let them earn some money to pay for that extra cost. See what works best for you. Planning ahead and keeping tabs on what's actually going out is key.

Budgeting Basics

As a single parent, you have to budget extra carefully and plan ahead for expenses because you have less margin for error than a dual-income family. By following a close budget and spending plan, you can survive financially without denying your children's needs (and some wants, too). How? By setting a budget.

The first tip that financial experts offer on budgeting is not to call it a budget. Call it "money management," or "life financing," or a "spending plan" instead. "Budget" is a word like "diet"—an enforced discipline you eventually break rather than a healthy habit you keep.

So how much do you have available for your spending plan? First, carefully list all your income. Then take your total income and subtract all of your necessary payments (as determined in the previous chapter).

Not sure which payments are most important to make? Set up a first-things-first financial system. Pay priority items before you spend money on something else.

> **Wise Words**
> "When I started thinking of it as a spending plan, I could finally stick to a budget."—Single mother by choice, struggling with childcare bills

First, pay yourself; put money toward your cash reserve, periodic (quarterly) large expenses, and long-term goals. (You'll learn more about savings later in the chapter.)

Then continue to prioritize, in the following order:

1. Food and shelter
2. Utilities

3. Medical/Insurance

4. Childcare

5. Other payments (credit cards, for instance)

6. Special items

Sticking to Your Budget

So you've come up with a workable budget. You know how every penny you earn needs to be spent (or saved). Now comes the tough part—living within those allotments, every month. It sounds difficult—and it can be. Luckily, experts have loads of tips on how to manage.

(For those of you whose expenses actually exceed your total income, don't worry. There are ways you can boost your total income or lower your necessary expenses. I'll give you some ideas on how to do both later in this chapter.)

Here are some ways to stick to a bust-proof budget:

➤ When you withdraw cash, take at least a week's worth of cash at a time; don't visit a cash machine in between except in an emergency, and carry only a minimum amount of cash on you.

➤ Put aside five percent or more of your take-home earnings as savings.

➤ Keep a cushion: the unexpected can (and usually does) happen. If you have money set aside, you won't have to rely on credit cards or loans. Experts recommend saving enough cash to cover 3–6 months worth of expenses. Even if you can't swing that much, do keep some emergency money on hand.

> **Expert-Ease**
> Financial advisers sum up a good money-management system as one that is a planned approach to spending, saving, and investing to help you achieve your dreams and goals in the real world.

➤ Try to pay your bills in one sitting (or two at most) per month. Balance your checkbook at the same time. Also, try to take time to review your spending pattern and cash flow for the month in time to cut back if you're going to go over budget.

➤ Keep your records simple: Don't overdo your ledgers. Just keep a month-by-month list of income and expenses.

➤ Your credit payments should not exceed 15 percent of your monthly income, so let your budget determine whether another purchase is worth adding to your credit card debt.

Chapter 14 ➤ *Balancing Your Budget*

No matter how you choose to manage your finances, you'll find that simply the act of monitoring your saving and spending habits will curb your tendency to overspend: Simply paying attention can help keep you on track.

More Money

So what if, in Chapter 13, you determined that your necessary expenses actually exceed the money you're taking in each month? As you already know, you're in dangerous financial territory. You need to get to a place where you take more money in than you spend out. Over the following pages, I'll show you what you can do to improve your financial situation.

Boosting Your Income

There are big ways and small ways to take more money in. You can try everything from refinancing your mortgage and other loans to always redeeming your soda cans. Here are some suggestions:

➤ Make sure you are getting all the alimony, child support, and so on, due to you (as noted in Chapter 13).

➤ Upgrade your job. Start by studying to improve your qualifications for the job you currently hold. Your employer may offer tuition reimbursement or on-the-job training.

➤ Take on a less demanding part-time job. (Or, if possible, try to hold down two local jobs that keep you close to home and your kids.)

➤ If another job outside the home sounds too exhausting or unworkable, follow some of the suggestions in Chapter 15 for at-home work: from babysitting and cleaning to yardwork and doing others' errands for a fee. Look around your community to see what needs doing and fill that gap. (Bonus: You get to meet the neighbors you never knew!)

➤ Hold garage or yard sales on a regular basis—and manage other people's yard or garage sales for a percentage of the take.

➤ Can you have your kids contribute without committing the sin of role reversal? Yes—especially if they want to. Older kids can work toward covering their basic expenses if necessary (and if

> **Parent Pitfalls**
> Some single parents try so hard to protect their children from being overburdened that they don't get the kids to help out financially. Of course if your kids are old enough, they can help make a financial contribution.

143

> **Parent Pitfalls**
> If you run a family business, there are strict rules governing salary paid to your kids. Check with a tax professional for details.

a part-time job doesn't interfere with school or homework). And kids of any age who want something special—a car, a videogame, new boots—can work toward that and save money in a special fund.

You'll find that taking a positive approach to money matters helps: Always think in terms of what you can do, and don't dwell on what you can't do.

Decreasing Your Outgo

If you can't find ways to boost your income, you can still balance your budget by slashing your expenses. Where can you cut? Review your list of expenses from Chapter 13 and see where things could be pared down. Start saving up pennies, and soon you'll have a whole lot of bucks per month to save or spend on necessities. Here are a few ideas.

> **Parent Pitfalls**
> When you're paring down your budget, don't completely eliminate items like entertainment. If things are really tight, perhaps shave a bit off other areas to contribute to the entertainment fund. Just remember, entertainment is a necessary expense, because fun is a necessary part of life—even if it's a once-a-month movie.

To save money on your home and housing expenses:

➤ You may be eligible for some kind of housing support. Many states and localities offer rent subsidies for income-strapped families. Also, the Federal government offers low-interest and low-down payment mortgages for first-time, limited income buyers. Check it out! Contact the Federal Home Loan Mortgage Corporation (Freddie Mac) at 800-373-3343 for your regional mortgage provider.

➤ Handle simple repairs yourself, such as painting and decorating, rather than hiring others to do them.

➤ Instead of buying new, full-price furniture, shop at garage sales.

➤ Make your own cleaning supplies.

To save money on utilities:

➤ Lower the temperature at night to save money on heat.

➤ Conserve your use of lights and electric appliances to lower your electric bills.

➤ Limit your long-distance calls.

➤ Don't use call-waiting or other special phone services.

➤ Save heat with storm windows; seal all cracks in winter.

Chapter 14 ➤ *Balancing Your Budget*

To save money on meals:

- "Brown bag" your lunch as often as possible.
- Cut down on meals away from home.
- Only buy "specials" at the grocery store. Use coupons.
- If you've got the storage space, buy food and household supplies in bulk; it's usually cheaper.
- If you've got the space (and the talent), grow a garden.
- Limit food shopping to once a week.
- Plan menus in advance for your shopping trips—and use a list!

To save money on transportation expenses:

- Use public transportation.
- Only keep one small car. Make sure you keep up on maintenance to keep operating costs down.
- Arrange a carpool, if possible.

To save money on clothing and toiletries:

- Buy clothing that is washable and easy to coordinate with other clothes.
- Organize your laundry so that you only need to run a minimum number of loads.
- Mend clothes promptly.
- Have children change to old clothes for rough play.
- Select low-cost toiletries.
- Cut your own hair and your children's hair, if you have the talent for it.

> **Wise Words**
> "When I stopped smoking I got multiple bonuses, not just improving my health and getting my son to stop nagging me to quit. Everyday I put the money I saved in a jar—and we took a vacation! Every little bit isn't a little bit." —An ex-smoking single Mom

To save money on health care and medicine:

- Try to prevent the need for health care by eating well and living safely.
- Investigate services offered by the health department; public clinics provide vaccinations, blood pressure monitoring, weight control workshops, and a lot of other free opportunities.
- Use immunization clinics.

To lower costs on entertainment:

- Use the public library for books and magazines, computer usage, and videotapes.
- Eliminate your subscriptions to most magazines.
- Have potluck affairs at home.
- Use public parks and picnic areas.
- Eliminate cable TV premium channels.
- Share vacations with other single-parent families.
- Coordinate purchases of games and toys with the parents of your children's friends to avoid duplication.
- Plan ahead with other parents or other family members to share big expenses like education.

To reduce your credit card and loan debts:

- Financial advisers say you shouldn't spend more than 15 percent of your take-home pay on your debts. Try to get under that limit—and stay there.

> **Wise Words**
> "The bikes we got at a yard sale and fixed and painted ourselves have been more fun for all of us than we could have thought," a New England single-parent family reports.

> **Parent Pitfalls**
> Using plastic to pay for luxuries, like fancy shoes, should become less tempting when you remember that you can use credit to leverage your child's college education.

- Do all you can to consolidate debt into one or two low-interest rate credit cards so that you can pay the lowest possible monthly amount.
- Those come-ons from the credit card companies can actually be good for you if you treat them with care. Transfer your high-interest balances onto cards with lower interest rates. Just make sure you can pay them off before the special low-interest rate offer ends.
- Close and destroy all credit lines and cards but one that you'll use for emergencies.
- Don't charge if you don't absolutely have to.
- If you *do* have to, make it a practice to pay off your balances right away.
- If you're having trouble paying off your debts, don't wait to get help! A record of missed or late payments can destroy your credit report. Nonprofit counseling services such as the Consumer Credit Counseling Service (CCCS) provide free budget guidance to help you.

Chapter 14 ➤ *Balancing Your Budget*

There are plenty of other practical tips on how to spend less. See the Consumer Credit Counseling Service Web page, the *Consumer Reports* guides, or the *Penny Pinchers* books, all listed in Appendix A.

Keeping Records

Record keeping is crucial for keeping costs down—and so is keeping it simple. Otherwise you won't do it.

Here's an example of an easy way to keep your books. In a small notebook or expense record notebook, write your allotted amounts for each category (transportation, clothing, utilities, and so on). As you spend money, record the amount spent in the appropriate category. Then deduct the amount from the total available.

At the end of the month, you can simply photocopy the page and put it in a large binder or notebook. Then you'll have an accurate "snapshot" of all the expenses you've paid for the month.

A budget sheet like the following is useful—and if you keep it in small form that you can carry with you, you can keep track of how much money you have left as you go along. That pocket record can also be filed, to avoid extra accounting work.

Budget Sheet

Expense Item	Planned Cost	Actual Cost
Household costs	_____	_____
Utilities	_____	_____
Food	_____	_____
Transportation	_____	_____
Childcare/Support	_____	_____
Insurance	_____	_____
Credit cards	_____	_____
Other	_____	_____
	_____	_____
	_____	_____

Keep a running expense sheet each month. Carry it with you to note purchases and keep a tally of how much you've spent. That way, you'll stay informed on how much you have left.

At least twice a month, review and total your expenditures, seeing if you're within your allotted amount. In your tally, include all charges and checks as well as cash payments. Be sure to keep your checkbook balanced—and if your bank offers a toll-free phone number you can call to get automated updates, check on your account status between bank statements as well.

The Big Picture: Setting Goals

Once you've got a handle on your monthly income and outflow, you can begin to think about what you hope to accomplish with your money in the long run.

As in other aspects of single-parent life, when it comes to money management, goals are important. One goal is making it through the week. A careful budget will help you do that. But you'll also want to establish specific longer-term goals. For example:

Long-Term Goals

- Real estate purchases
- Future education
- Retirement

Mid-Term Goals:

- Getting out of debt

Short-Term Goals:

- Home improvements
- Buying a new car
- Travel
- Investing (stocks, bonds, mutual funds)

Only you and your kids can set your individual financial goals. Goals are great motivators for the careful management of money. If you and your kids are working together toward something important—a house, a big vacation, an education—it will be easier to put off immediate wants.

Get the kids in on family goal-setting. And let them choose their own goals to save for, too.

Chapter 14 ➤ *Balancing Your Budget*

Building Your Savings

Once you and your kids have made a list of goals, determine how much you need to save monthly by dividing the total amount of money you need to meet each goal by the amount of time you have to save.

You should also begin a savings account for meeting predictable but unexpected expenses: a major car repair, for example, or a new washing machine when the old one breaks down. That's what set asides are for.

Setting aside money for saving can be hard; it may be difficult to put money away when you have so many immediate needs and wants to take care of. These savings tips can help:

- ➤ Determine your saving goals.
- ➤ Be willing to compromise: Put off a present "want" for a long-term "need."
- ➤ If your employer offers automatic payroll deductions for savings, take advantage.
- ➤ Save any bonus income you earn.
- ➤ Keep your loose change for savings. Store it in a container, and when the container is full, roll it and take it to the bank. Either deposit it in your savings account or use it for special treats, like Saturday night videos and pizza. It will make you feel luxurious.
- ➤ Save on a regular basis: pay yourself first!
- ➤ Alter your spending habits, using the suggestions above, to leave more money for savings.
- ➤ Use savings for emergencies only.
- ➤ Explore savings bonds and IRAs: These can help you invest for your children's education—or toward the purchase of a home.
- ➤ Invest something. Take even the tiniest amount to buy into a sound investment, such as a mutual fund. Keep adding and don't take any money out. The compound interest will build into quite a nest egg—that's why they call it the "magic of compounding."

Not only will saving even small amounts regularly add up to a lot in time—but it will make you feel better and more in control of your money—and your life.

The Least You Need to Know

- ➤ No matter how much or little your income, you can get more out of your money by setting a careful budget and watching where your money goes.
- ➤ Explore ways to boost your income, such as training for a new job, taking a second job, or working out of your home.
- ➤ Use cost-saving tips to decrease your expenses on food, clothes, furniture, health care, and transportation.
- ➤ No matter how tight your budget is, set aside money for savings.
- ➤ By setting saving and spending goals together, your family can feel like a team.

Chapter 15

What Works

In This Chapter

- ➤ Choosing the career that's right for you
- ➤ Exploring flex-time options to make your job fit your life
- ➤ Should you go back to school?
- ➤ Is working at home right for you?

As recently as two decades ago, single parents were a rarity in this country; families headed by two working parents were almost nonexistent. Today, most married or single American parents work, and 64 percent of all mothers have jobs.

Now, that may be a recipe for constant fatigue, but it's also good news for single parents: It means that society and the workplace are becoming accustomed (and, in many cases, legally required) to accommodating to the needs of single parents and our kids.

In this chapter, you'll learn how to juggle your professional life with caring for your kids.

Finding a Job That Fits

Single parents face a number of trade-offs when it comes to juggling family and work. Some single parents, faced with the need to earn a living for the kids who depend on them (whether their kids live with them or not) feel pressured into taking on work that they hate or that isn't good enough. Other single parents have careers they love, yet are still timid about seeking concessions that would make the work/family balance easier.

There's good news. You *can* be a parent first and still seek an "ideal" job, one that best challenges and rewards you. You may think that working checkout on the night shift in your local grocery is the best you can manage, but that may not be true.

You owe it to yourself to at least try for something rewarding and creative. Searching for a fulfilling job is not only about climbing the career ladder; being satisfied in your work will make you a happier parent—and will set a good example for your kids about how to give their goals their best shot.

To find the perfect job, you first need to focus on your goals and dreams. Review the checklists in Chapter 3 to discover your strongest passions and interests.

Finding a job that fits your life and your goals may not be easy. Here are some of the details you need to think about:

> Dreams: What do you want to do?
> Income: How much do you need to make?
> Schedule: How many hours can you work—and on what schedule?
> Possibilities: What are the jobs that meet all these criteria?
> Actions: What steps can you take to go after these jobs?

You'll begin to examine each of these factors over the following pages.

Wise Words
"I started out in theater, but when I chose to become a mother, I realized I needed to adapt to my son's needs. So I took a good look at my skills and the possibilities, and went back to school for a teaching certificate. Now I teach drama, love it, and my schedule fits his." —A single Mom by choice from Connecticut

Expert-Ease
John Crystal, one of the gurus of modern-day career planning, offers this sage advice: "Be yourself—nobody else is qualified."

Dare to Dream

If you could do anything at all in life, could just follow your desire, what would you do? Take some deep breaths, close your eyes, and let your mind wander a bit. Ask yourself these questions:

> - What do you do in your free time? Note what kinds of activities you most enjoy watching and reading about. What kinds of activities send you into daydreaming?
> - When you visualize yourself happily working, what do you see yourself doing, and where?

Single parents are likely to be so focused (and with reason) on their present needs, that it's hard to look ahead. But if you can, you'll have a much better chance for success and satisfaction.

Earning Income

Now that you've got a clear sense of what you want, it's time to figure what you need in terms of money. Here's how:

> - Determine your necessary income by looking over those budget sheets from Chapters 13 and 14.
> - In addition to income, make a list of all benefits (like health insurance, childcare, and 401(K) accounts) that are important to you.
> - Multiply your necessary income figure by 150 percent to calculate the salary you'll need to produce the take-home pay to cover your costs.

Now start to figure how you're going to earn the money you need. Can you do it on your current job alone? Would you be able to do it if you got a promotion or an upgrade? Would a second job help? Or would you be better off looking for a new job entirely?

Exploring the Possibilities

Career counselors say that to turn all those ingredients into a satisfying mix of life and work, you need to make goals—to set goals that are smart.

Now, maybe you can't pursue your dreams—yet. Maybe the career you'd love is too demanding to allow for parenting—or maybe it doesn't pay enough to support you and your kids.

> **Expert-Ease**
> When you're thinking about what you need and want from a job, don't think in terms of "I can't"... If you know what you want and focus on getting it, you have a better chance than you can imagine. In fact, imagination can be powerful: Visualization is a tool recommended by counselors in various fields. Visualize the work you want. It works for many people, and it can't hurt.

> **Parent Pitfalls**
> Single parents who assume they must sacrifice their career goals to their children's needs are likely to be just as mistaken as those who relentlessly pursue personal career goals despite their children. Success at both work and home comes from "negotiating" with yourself to find the win-win solution to your own career/parenting conflict.

Part 4 ➤ *Money Matters*

But you might be wise to keep it as a goal—and to find work that's in the same line since people who are happy in their work make happier parents.

> **Singular Successes**
>
> Many working parents piece together jobs that fill both their dreams and their needs. For example, computer specialists do local freelance consulting and take in word processing as well. Artists of every kind take on mundane jobs and make time for their art after the children's bedtime. Aspiring lawyers work as paralegals and postpone law school for the years when parenting becomes less demanding.
>
> Perhaps an option like this is possible for you, too?

Think of ways that you could combine your personal dreams with your practical realities to meet your whole family's needs.

Taking Action

To find the jobs that fit your dream-needs and real goals—and to get help in taking the actions necessary to get those jobs—you have plenty of helpful resources. Some of the most useful guides are listed in Appendix A.

Finding a Company That's Family Friendly

There's a revolution in progress in the way employers understand, and try to accommodate, working parents. Today's employers are offering policies and possibilities that would have been unheard-of 20 years ago.

> **Meaning?**
>
> A *family friendly employer* is one that provides benefits and options, such as on-site childcare to flextime—that make it comfortable to be both a parent and an employee.

Today, the majority of mothers (not just single mothers) work. Two-parent families seek dual careers out of preference or out of need. "Career women" want kids, and have them, over a longer period of years than ever before. Employers have come to accept these realities, and in adapting to these new patterns have found that job flexibility can bring success all around.

In sum, it's a great time to be a working mother—or a working single parent of any gender.

Since 1986, *Working Mother* magazine has evaluated employers in four key areas:

154

➤ Above-average pay for the industry

➤ Promotion opportunities for women

➤ Childcare assistance and other onsite daycare centers

➤ Flexibility of the workplace and other family-friendly benefits

Over time, this kind of scrutiny has inspired working parents to push for these benefits elsewhere in the workplace, encouraging businesses to follow the lead of these role models.

"Family friendliness" has also proved profitable, resulting in the creation of more workplaces that offer employees the opportunity to both advance in their careers and have a good family life.

The magazine's reports note that family-friendliness is becoming part of the culture, and workers at every level are more able to get what they need.

So what are the hallmarks of a family-friendly company? Here are a few:

➤ A sharp rise in the use of flexible work schedules, generally known as *flextime*.

➤ The opening of on-site childcare centers.

➤ Financial benefits paid to reimburse childcare costs or the down payment on a first home.

➤ A greater use of paid leaves for new Dads and adoptive parents.

In the following sections, you'll learn how to make some of these benefits work for you.

> **Parent Pitfalls**
> It's not an accident that the "best companies" list is promoted by *Working Mother* magazine. While family-friendliness should apply to both working mothers and fathers—legally, of course, any privilege granted to women should be available to men—many single fathers report it's harder to convince employers they need flexibility as much as single Moms.
>
> In 1996, *Business Week* started a similar survey indicative of the realization that this isn't just a "mommy" issue.

> **Meaning?**
> *Flextime* refers to an employer's ability to adapt employee's job schedules to fit their family demands, and can mean anything from shorter weeks of longer days to shared jobs to telecommuting.

Flextime

Telecommuting (working from home on a computer, modem, phone, and fax) works for some parents, at least part time. Even with e-mail, the Internet, faxes, and cellular phones, however, this option isn't for everyone.

It takes the right kind of job, for one thing: one that can be done at home. Sales, human resources, and customer service, for example, are all largely on-site jobs that would not be good candidates for at-home work. Editorial, telemarketing, and database management jobs are much better options. Telecommuting also requires a personality that's disciplined and self-starting.

> **Expert-Ease**
> The specific companies that make the *Working Mother* "100 best" list changes each year. But on its website (www.womanweb.com), the magazine offers a database where you can make your own evaluation of any company you are considering. (And although it's called *Working Woman*'s Website, fathers are welcome, too.)

Other working parents are able to schedule a compressed work week—three 12-hour days, for example, or four 10-hour days.

There are some drawbacks to telecommuting or working on a compressed schedule, though. Some people find that they end up working a lot more hours on their own. Others simply cannot get work done at home; their kids' demands are too distracting.

Still others find that they must put in significant office time to keep up with meetings and "face time." Some just miss the cameraderie of an office.

On the other hand, working from home—at least part of the time—allows you to save money on commuting, lunch, and wardrobe costs.

If you are interested in learning more about telecommuting, contact your human resources representative, or check out the Working Mother website (www.womanweb.com).

> **Meaning?**
> *Job-sharing* means dividing the duties—and salary—of a single employee between two or more employees.

Finally, working together also works on a shared basis. For example, some businesses allow *job sharing*; that is, dividing up the duties (and salary) of one job between two people. See if your employer would consider it.

Family Leave Laws

These days you're not on your own when it comes to creating a beneficial work schedule. The federal Family Medical Leave Act is just one of many pieces of legislation recently enacted to accommodate the needs of today's working parents.

Family Leave regulations from both Federal and state governments mandate the kind of support that working parents—single or not—need. Early legislation guaranteed leave for family medical needs. Today's rules cover a variety of other needs, including illness of a family members, the needs of aging parents, adoption, pregnancy, childbirth, fatherhood, and even school meetings. Get familiar with the rules in your particular workplace, so that you can take advantage of them. Your state Department of Labor is the best source for information. Check it out in the Yellow Pages or on the Internet.

> **Parent Pitfalls**
> Not all Americans are covered by Family Medical Leave Act legislation. Public-sector employees qualify, but those in small companies may not (depending on local laws). On the other had, smaller companies may be more willing to cut personal deals with employees, to allow for "parental" time off. Whatever the standards in your workplace, it may be worth discussing with your employer.

Optimizing Your Earning Power

Do all of these options sound ideal, but not like anything you could incorporate into a dream job of your own? Take heart, because you may be closer to finding the work you really want than you think. If you have a goal that seems too bogged down by parental responsibilities to be possible, you can get training to move on to something better, or even launch your own business at home. In the following sections, we'll explore these options.

> **Expert-Ease**
> Surveys indicate that less than half of all American workers feel that career success can be combined with a good family life. The benefits wanted by most workers: childcare and time off to care for other family members.

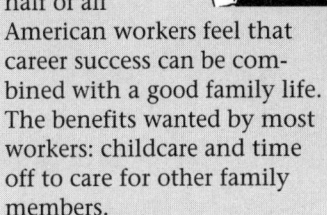

Back to School

Adding yet another major activity to your life may seem ridiculous to an already overstressed single parent. But finding a way to fit learning into your busy life can bring benefits beyond the specific practical value of getting you a better job: It can help you feel good about yourself, and it sends a terrific message to your kids.

Whether they're taking a specific training course (in word processing, say) or a full fledged degree, millions of Americans are taking advantage of adult education to further their careers and enrich their minds.

Part 4 ➤ *Money Matters*

> **Wise Words**
> "I don't know how I'm doing it," comments a single Mom with 4 kids and a full-time job who is headed back to school. Here's how: She has a demanding job but with a flexible schedule; she takes courses via television; and she's found cooperative neighbors and good daycare to watch her kids.

> **Wise Words**
> A working head-of-household Mom, with a son in second grade and a daughter in sixth, started out in a technical program but is now going for her degree: "I don't care if it takes me 10 years. I should have done this long ago."

➤ Almost half of American adults are enrolled in some kind of education program—and surveys indicate that within the next few years that figure will double.

➤ Eight out of ten American workers in every field say education would help them in their work—and most of them are planning to sign up for a course.

➤ Half of all women who are returning to school have at least one child under the age of 18 at home.

So if you sign up for extra education, you won't be alone! And, just as with single parenting, lifelong learning has become such a force in our culture that many companies are learning to accommodate it, both in scheduling and financing.

If you are open to the idea of going back to school, you have to think: What could you learn that would make you more valuable in the job market—and how would you go about it? Here are some suggestions from adult-education specialists:

➤ Before you sign up with any kind of college, training school, or even an employee-ed program at work (even if it's totally free), be sure it's going to enhance your opportunities, not just add a burden.

➤ Know where you're going: Evaluate and clarify your career and life goals.

➤ Be realistic: A step-by-step approach is likely to be more satisfying than a sudden plunge into deep academia. Try one course before signing on for a long-term program. That's a good way to get a clear view of how much time, money, and motivation you have—and how it really affects your family life.

➤ Shop carefully: Compare thoroughly the programs offered by the schools in your area. Is the school convenient, with classes scheduled to fit your already busy day? Are courses designed for more "traditional" college students who are available during the day, or are facilities open at night? What guidance and support are available that you can work into your schedule? Can you take classes from home—via TV or computer?

➤ Count your pennies: Can you afford it? Check with employee tuition programs, school scholarships and financial aid, and grants from churches, unions, and other membership groups. Under some circumstances, tuition is tax deductible. If you qualify, you may also be able to enter public programs that offer job training.

➤ Build support: Make family, friends, co-workers, and kids partners in your effort.

➤ Get organized: Create space and time for your studies.

➤ Ask for help: Don't expect to know it all. Take advantage of counseling or remedial help—and if the courses aren't meeting your needs, say so!

➤ Don't worry about anxiety: Virtually every adult who returns experiences anxiety or a wavering sense of self-confidence. Now you know how your kids feel every fall!

Eighty percent of American adults are going back to school—why not you?

Working at Home

Many single parents find ways to work from their homes. I'm not talking those envelope stuffing scams here; I mean ways to make enough money to keep the cash flow from drying up.

When you work at home, your income needs are lower because you don't have commuting costs, clothes expenses, childcare costs, or even lunch money to think about. Plus, you likely can deduct part of your costs from your taxes.

What might you do? Here's a list of at-home jobs you may not have thought of: news-clipping service, medical transcriptions, repair services, bookkeeping, telephone sales, even franchising (starting an office of a national service business from your own home).

Or, perhaps you can provide "family" services for a fee. Think about what's needed by other families where you live. As more caretakers are going to work outside the home, for example, quality daycare services are at a premium. Maybe you could earn money being a caretaker. Find out what's required.

In fact, any kind of household capabilities can be turned into successful businesses: start a home-cooking business, for example, or run errands for others. All the things you have to do for yourself, you can do for others—for a profit.

Cleaning services can be profitable, too—and cleaning someone else's place is less often taxing than cleaning your own.

Be creative: sure you'd like to work in the field you trained for. Maybe you can develop at-home projects that are connected to your long term goals. Perhaps you can do public relations, graphic arts, or repairs for local businesses or organizations that can become part of a portfolio for "real" work later. Flex your mind!

Entrepreneurship is one of the fastest growing aspects of business today, so if you're thinking about starting your own business, you'll find lots of information and support. The local office of the Small Business Administration, as well as information in your local library or your Chamber of Commerce, can put you in touch with associations and other support groups and services.

The Family That Works Together...

While some of the strongest families are traditionally farm families—in part, perhaps, because they work together toward a common goal—it's also true that family businesses can create friction.

> **Parent Pitfalls**
> Feeling that we're alone in the world is one of the most common single-parent mistakes. Remember, we have community and family available to work with, and public programs to provide job training and guidance.

You may not live on a farm, but perhaps you can still find ways to join forces with family or friends in enterprises that can benefit all of you.

Few of us are heirs to family fortunes—but most of us have family or friends in some kind of business that we could join. If you've got a cousin who owns a restaurant, for example, or a niece who runs a small marketing firm, and you're interested in the business, why not explore working together? Your relatives are more likely than strangers to allow for flexibility in schedules. The key is to be as responsible and helpful to your family members as you would be to any other employer.

Not only is this a practical solution to having too much to do, but it strengthens a sense of community, which in turn brings wider benefits—not the least of which is helping to remind you and your kids that you are NOT alone.

The Least You Need to Know

➤ You can meet your career goals as a single parent, but your timetable may be delayed a bit by parenting demands.

➤ Seek out and negotiate ways to make your employer bend your schedule to accommodate childraising.

➤ If finding an adequate job seems impossible, you may need to be flexible in your goals, creative in your planning—and willing to learn new skills.

➤ Consider going back to school if it will help you advance in your career—or begin a new career.

➤ Consider working at home, which is a great way to stay in touch with your kids and save on commuting, daycare, and other costs.

Part 5
The Buddy System: Friends

Many of the most difficult problems and effects of single parenting arise from the isolation that, at least in the past, has marked the single parent's role.

Today, there are so many single parents that isolation shouldn't be an issue. Unfortunately, it still often is: From a combination of scheduling demands and emotional conflicts, single parents may have a hard time connecting with the supportive networks that surround them. This part shows you how to get by with a little help from your friends.

Chapter 16

Connections: That's What Friends Are For

In This Chapter

- ➤ Finding friends who count
- ➤ Why having a life helps you and your kids
- ➤ How to make new friends—and hang on to old friends
- ➤ Helping your children make friends

In the evening of a too-long day, perhaps filled with frustrations and a bit of fear, alone in the quiet kitchen, it's easy for a single parent to feel "all alone in the world."

Luckily, you aren't alone. You've got a supportive web of friends who understand what you're going through—and can help you get through it.

Many busy single parents, struggling to stay on top of their jobs and keep an eye on their kids, neglect their social lives and forget the importance of friendships. But friendships are important—and for more than just having fun. In this chapter, we'll look at ways you can strengthen your ties to existing friends—and create new ones.

What Friends Are For

What are friends for? Strength, joy, fun, love, and the sharing of life, both its challenges and triumphs. They are well worth the effort, especially for anyone feeling isolated.

Part 5 ➤ *The Buddy System: Friends*

> **Expert-Ease**
> Sometimes children need reassurance about their parents' friendships; some children are threatened by relationships between their parents and others. Many times, children of single parents fear they may lose their custodial parent. One way to alleviate this fear is to share casual information about your friends with your kids, and get them to talk about their social lives, to compare.

> **Parent Pitfalls**
> Some parents are so focused on being parents that they ignore the wider networks they need. Finding friends does not mean cheating your children—it provides enrichment for both.

> **Parent Pitfalls**
> Members of support and therapy groups can be wonderfully supportive and understanding friends. Just be cautious about connecting too fast with someone who may be struggling him- or herself.

Your friendships and social life can also help your children feel safer by creating a ring of connected folks around them. Also, as they see that you have a strengthening network, they will sense that they can relax and let you go. Thus each generation can "get a life" of its own.

Because of the great value friends can bring to your own life and your children's, it's well worth making the effort to find and keep your friends.

Who Are Your Friends?

How wide is your social network? You may have more support than you think. Start listing all the friends you have, and don't overlook people in any of the following categories:

- ➤ People you've been close to for years
- ➤ Neighbors
- ➤ Parents of your children's friends
- ➤ Co-workers
- ➤ Fellow members of single-parenting groups
- ➤ Folks you meet through your hobbies or special interests groups
- ➤ Internet buddies from single-parent or other special interest online communities
- ➤ People in your support and therapy groups
- ➤ Family members
- ➤ Religious fellowships

Make a list of the names and numbers of everyone you can count as a friend—folks who can be there for you in various ways. Use this list to start thinking about your sources for friends.

Look again at the list of categories, and compare it with your list of friends. If any category is a bit thin—if you have few friends, from, say, among your neighbors, ask yourself why and work on cultivating friends from those groups.

Making New Friends

If, like many single parents, you're coming out of a traumatic social situation (a divorce, the death of your spouse), making new friends may be especially important as you develop a new identity and lifestyle. Making friends sounds easy, but it can be tough, even for adults. Here are some suggestions from those who've been there:

➤ Accept that you're nervous instead of telling yourself you shouldn't be.

➤ If you're queasy about accepting an invite or trying out a new social group, force yourself to try it just once. (Imagine you're persuading your child to try a new food she "just has to taste.") Give yourself permission to leave or to not come back if you hate it.

➤ Don't judge your insides by others' outsides. All those folks who look suave or cool on the outside are probably just as timid inside as you are.

➤ At a party or new social scene, introduce yourself or make small talk to at least three people in the group.

➤ Don't approach a social event with unrealistic expectations (i.e., expecting to meet the love of your life). The idea is simply to expand your network of friends for your own sake and your children's.

Here are some easy ways to increase your circle of friends:

➤ Look in your local paper, phone book, or favorite Internet sites for groups that pursue your special interests and hobbies. Think about joining such a group. It's a great way to meet others who share your interests.

➤ Take a class on a topic that interests you, whether it is poetry writing or gourmet cooking. Or take a career-skills class, where you can improve your job opportunities.

➤ Look in your phone book for listings for the local Parents without Partners or other single-parent groups. Start attending meetings.

➤ Volunteer to bring the refreshments to the next scout-group or PTA meeting. Sitting at the cookie table is a great way to meet people.

> **Wise Words**
> "My Mom needs to get a life. She always wants to do stuff with me, spend time with me and my friends. I wish she'd go out and meet people. It's not just boring, but I won't be here forever." —The teenage child of a single parent

> **Expert-Ease**
> Children have been found to benefit from seeing their parent have a positive social life: it makes them feel good about their parent and freer to go off on their own.

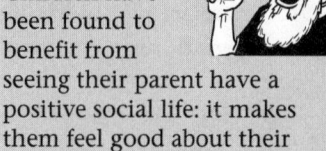

- ➤ Find out when the members of a single-parent online network will get together for their next "in-person" meeting. Try to go.

- ➤ If you are religious, try an activity at your local church or temple.

- ➤ Check out your local health club. Many offer tryout visits. See how you like it (you can also see if it offers activities for your kids).

There may be plenty of other opportunities for socializing in your area. Be sure to check them out.

Getting Your Kids Involved

A common single-parent complaint is not having enough time for fun activities between work, housework, and taking care of the kids. But if you've got other single parents and their kids to hang out with, you can both have fun and spend quality time with your kids.

There are plenty of things you can do with other single parents and your kids. Some suggestions:

> **Wise Words**
> "It started as a babysitting co-op: We took turns caring for each other's kids. Then we got a grocery co-op going. And pretty soon our 'meetings' turned into social events, too—and now we share a lot of life." —A Midwestern single parent

- ➤ Have potluck suppers at each other's houses.

- ➤ Go on picnics and other outings where you share costs and transportation.

- ➤ Hold a group garage sale—and use some of the proceeds to celebrate with dinner or drinks afterwards.

- ➤ Make it a point to gather with the other single parents at all your kid-focused get-togethers like school events or sports matches. Get together before or after for a snack or meal and you've made an outing without adding much time.

(If you have no single-parent groups close by, see the next chapter for suggestions on how to form one.)

Holding On to Old Friends

All of this emphasis on new friends doesn't mean you should let go of your older friends. Being on your own doesn't mean that coupled friends are out of the picture (and if they don't include you, they friendship may not be worth much). These days, research indicates, married couples are very comfortable including single friends.

Chapter 16 ➤ *Connections: That's What Friends Are For*

Some people do have difficulties maintaining friendships in the wake of a separation or divorce. Many couples find that after they split up, their friends split up, too. A newly single parent may have to deal with the fact that he/she may have lost some good friends in the upheaval of the divorce.

If they were your friends to begin with, they will still be. If they weren't, why waste energy trying to hold on to them? Perhaps they were always closer to your spouse than to you. That's fine. Let them be your ex's friends. You might even tell them, "I know this must be awkward for you. I really hope we can stay friends—but if for some reason that's not possible, I'll understand." Then be willing to let the friendship go. Your action might be so well appreciated that you do stay friends.

Also, your married or coupled friends may have some initial adjustment problems relating to you as a newly single parent. Many of the things you all did as couples may now seem off limits—but are they? Did the four of you go hiking, to the movies, to art galleries, bowling? You still can. Nowhere is it written that life has to be lived in even numbers.

> **Wise Words**
> "I learned to give people three tries. If I called three times and they didn't call back, or made three lunch dates and they broke them all, I stopped trying. I can't spend energy on them. I need it to make *new* friends." —Divorced, working mother of two children

This is a time when you will indeed find out who your friends truly are—scary as that may sound. Take a good look at who has stood by you during this traumatic time. Who has logged in hours of phone time, listening to you? Who has offered to watch the kids and give you a break? And who hasn't called since your status changed? Now more than ever, you need REAL friends. And you have less time than ever to waste on people who can't be there for you.

Your Kids' Connections

Your children need a social life at least as much as you—and it's good for them for many of the same reasons.

Your children's friendships are about a lot more than "fun." This is partly true because much of your children's growth and development will occur as they learn to relate to their peers. Single-parent kids in particular can learn important lessons about social life that they may not learn in their single-parent families. Plus they get the same kind of strength from their friendships as you can (or could) get from yours.

While it's important to allow your children the freedom to socialize and explore the world with friends, you still have to keep tabs on their activities. Tough as the scheduling can get, it's important to know who your kids' friends are—both in the playground and in cyberspace. (See Chapter 5 for more on peers and discipline.)

Arrange for regular check-in times and systems; for instance: make it a point to call or check in every day at 4 p.m., no matter where you are (answering machines, cell phones, or beepers are invaluable for keeping tabs like this). Your child should honor curfews and know to call you if she can't make it home on time. Be clear and firm that if she doesn't honor your rules, she won't be allowed to go off on her own. (Remember, you have to honor the same stay-in touch promises, too!)

> **Expert-Ease**
> Single-parent kids should not feel like second-class citizens, so school- and community-related groups need to provide services for them with no comment about their family status.

If you are looking for safe, fun places where your kids can spend time with their friends, there are many possibilities. Many schools and communities offer after-school and weekend activities. Be sure that any after-school activities your kids are involved in combine homework/learning opportunities with supervised socializing.

Like you, your kids may need a bit of a push to get out on their own in new social situations. Aside from after-school activities, your older children may be able to get involved with youth programs at local churches and community centers. If you have younger children, you may have to take them out to friends' homes and recreation centers since they can't get around on their own—but it's worth it.

When Kids Are Home Alone

Kids who are left on their own for part of every day (without a parent in attendance) can feel scared and lonely. First, remind your so-called solo kids that their friends probably envy the privacy they are allowed. Then, suggest some activities your kids can enjoy on their own:

> **Parent Pitfalls**
> You may feel guilty about having to leave your kids alone—and thus overreact and over-reward them. Instead, help them find activities that they can enjoy when they are on their own.

- Keep some long-term projects going, like hobbies or big jigsaw puzzles.
- Become a letter writer or an e-mailer with a pen pal (within limits you set: Make sure you know whom your kids are corresponding with!).
- Visit the library regularly; subscribe to their favorite magazine or join a book club.
- Have some games on hand that just one person can play. Build a collection.
- Have a special place at home to work out.
- Keep yourself company with music, books-on-tape, or parent-approved videos.

Chapter 16 ➤ Connections: That's What Friends Are For

➤ Sign on for after-school work around the house or in the neighborhood.

➤ Plan a schedule to organize your time.

You can be a parent-at-a-distance by working out with your kids a general plan for the time they spend alone. Questions you might talk about include:

➤ How much TV and what shows may kids watch? How much time can they spend on the computer and which sites can they visit?

➤ How much time must they spend on homework before breaking for something else?

➤ What chores must get done?

➤ Can they go out? Where? For how long? How should they keep in touch with you to let you know where they are?

You should also set firm guidelines for safety, so your child knows how to handle any emergency or unusual situation that might come up while you aren't home. See Chapter 9 for more on safety.

> **Parent Pitfalls**
> If either you or your kids (or both) are unable to get out and do things, professional help may be in order. Lack of energy or interest in life can be symptoms of depression. Depression is common; it prevents many people from fully enjoying life. Luckily, it's treatable.

Family Fun: Shared Activities

If after reading this chapter, you and your kids are still having a hard time thinking of things you *like* to do (and that's not so unusual—plenty of people have a hard time thinking of "fun")—or if you want a starting point for finding ways you and your kids can have fun together, here's a list of leisure activities to try.

Fun-Focus Checklist

Check off any activity in this list that you enjoy or that you would like to try. Have your kids do the same. Then review the list together. Items that have two checkmarks are things you can pursue as family activities. Those with one checkmark are ones that each of you can make a center of your individual social lives.

The Arts

❏ Dance   ❏ Painting

❏ Drawing   ❏ Photography

❏ Music, singing   ❏ Sculpture

❏ Music, instrumental   ❏ Writing, poetry

---

continues

169

Part 5 ▶ *The Buddy System: Friends*

continued

Athletics
- ❑ Archery
- ❑ Badminton
- ❑ Baseball
- ❑ Basketball
- ❑ Boccie
- ❑ Bowling
- ❑ Boxing
- ❑ Football
- ❑ Golf
- ❑ Handball
- ❑ Hockey
- ❑ Horseshoes
- ❑ Ping-pong
- ❑ Pool
- ❑ Racquetball
- ❑ Soccer
- ❑ Softball
- ❑ Tennis
- ❑ Track & Field
- ❑ Volleyball
- ❑ Wrestling

Crafts and Hobbies
- ❑ Baking
- ❑ Carpentry/Woodworking
- ❑ Ceramics
- ❑ Cooking
- ❑ Gardening
- ❑ Hobby crafts (models, decoupage, and so on)
- ❑ Knitting, crochet
- ❑ Needlepoint, sewing
- ❑ Quilting

Community Events
- ❑ Concerts
- ❑ Dance
- ❑ Film
- ❑ Museums
- ❑ Readings
- ❑ Theater

Fitness/Individual Sports
- ❑ Bicycling
- ❑ Exercise classes
- ❑ Gymnastics
- ❑ Ice skating
- ❑ Jogging
- ❑ Martial Arts
- ❑ Rollerblading/Rollerskating
- ❑ Swimming
- ❑ Walking
- ❑ Weight lifting
- ❑ Yoga

Chapter 16 ➤ *Connections: That's What Friends Are For*

Games
- ❏ Bingo
- ❏ Board games
- ❏ Cards
- ❏ Checkers
- ❏ Chess
- ❏ Dominoes
- ❏ Video games

Socializing
- ❏ Book clubs
- ❏ Card clubs
- ❏ Chat groups
- ❏ Dances
- ❏ Service clubs, scouts
- ❏ Sports clubs

Outdoors
- ❏ Archery
- ❏ Boating
- ❏ Camping
- ❏ Canoeing
- ❏ Cycling
- ❏ Fishing
- ❏ Hiking
- ❏ Sailing
- ❏ Shooting
- ❏ Skiing

Using those activities as a start, list the following:

Three activities you've stopped doing which you'd like to get back to:
_____
_____

Three activities you'd like to learn:
_____
_____

Three activities you'd like to engage in with your kids:
_____
_____

Three activities that could bring you and other single parents together:
_____
_____

171

Now make a commitment to try at least one activity a week from each category over the next month.

Being a single parent hardly means giving up your own life! In fact, it may open up opportunities for enjoyment and companionship that you never thought of trying.

The Least You Need to Know

- ➤ Friendships take effort to develop and maintain, but their benefits make them worthwhile.
- ➤ Encourage yourself to get out and meet new people, even if you feel awkward or shy.
- ➤ No matter how little time or how little money you have, there are plenty of activities that you can enjoy.
- ➤ Encourage your children to develop friendships of their own. Carefully monitor those friendships to make sure they are good for your children.

Chapter 17

Creating a Single-Parent Community

In This Chapter

➤ How to network to create a safety net for your family

➤ Exploring single-parent support groups

➤ Getting involved in your kids' school

➤ Creating a community with neighbors and friends

Here's some good news for single-parent families: There are vast numbers of folks just like you out there. Today most single-parent kids are growing up emotionally healthy—when they feel the strength drawn from the wider community, their fears and other negative feelings are lessened.

The large number of single parents out there doesn't just mean expanded services and enhanced attitudes. It also means more friends, contacts, connections, and community for you and your kids. By hooking up with others like yourself, you'll feel a part of a greater whole, rather than isolated from the world at large. You'll have strength to draw on, help to turn to, and partnerships for fun.

For many single parents, family ties are loosened or cut, and traditional sources of support and advice are not available. But many other sources of wisdom are accessible. The more that single parents rely on each other and share their experiences, the stronger each single-parent family is.

Part 5 ➤ The Buddy System: Friends

And the more common single parenting becomes, the more knowledge, help, and guidance are available: from professionals, school systems, and employers—many of which make special accommodations for single parenting.

All that's required is for you to reach out. This chapter will show you how.

Networking

Expert-Ease
You can find 12,000 groups offering advice, support, and information regarding single parenting on the Internet.

The most independent and competent single parents know that they need all the help they can get. Linking up with a network of parents in a similar situation will make you that much stronger; shared experience is the most valuable resource of single parents as a group. That network can be within your local community, or around the world via cyberspace.

Over the following pages, you'll meet some key sources of support.

Support Groups

Single-parent support groups provide a great way for you to get information and insight, as well as meet other single parents. Here's just a small sampling of some of the national single parenting support groups you can find:

- The Single Parent Resource Center
- Single Dad Steve Miller's Home Page
- Sole Mothers International
- Gingerbread, Single Parent Support Agency in England and Wales
- Single Parents Association
- Single Parent Project
- Steps Toward Recovery
- Parents Without Partners
- National Organization of Single Mothers, Inc.
- Single Mothers By Choice
- Fathers' Resource Center
- F.R.E.E.
- Single Dads Hall of Fame
- At Home Dads
- Daddy's Home
- The Single Fathers Lighthouse
- Custodial Fathers
- Parents Place
- The Fathers' Forum
- Dads Against Discrimination
- Single and Custodial Fathers Network

Parents Without Partners (PWP) is one national group that provides both socializing and support. There are also single parent service providers at a more local level, through community centers, and certain religious groups. Local mental health departments provide parenting advice and other professional help at low cost while helping create connections with other single parents. See Appendix A for suggestions.

Experts note that it's no surprise that single parents need this kind of support—professional and otherwise—since a single parent has no other adult to provide balance or practical help.

There are as many kinds of single-parent support groups as there are single parents. Let's look at a few different sources of support and socializing that may be right for you.

> **Wise Words**
> "Parents Without Partners involved my whole family in activities and provided support we could all use." —A divorced mother of 5

Religious Groups

Local churches, synagogues, or other houses of worship may run support and social groups for single parents. If the idea of joining a group of single parents with a shared spiritual background interests you, you may wish to explore the offerings of different religious organizations in your area until you find a comfortable group for you and your family (even if it means leaving your current place of worship). If need be, talk to the clergy at your current church about forming such a group.

> **Parent Pitfalls**
> Some religious organizations may have dogmatic ideas about divorce or out of wedlock parenthood, so make sure you find a group that welcomes you.

Clubs—Yours and Your Kids

Social organizations of all sorts may be good for meeting other single parents. Plenty of clubs built around common interests—birding or sailing or theater-going, for instance—can lead to both fun and friendship.

On the other side of the coin, scouts and other youth organizations can serve double duty. Not only are they good for your kids (once you've screened them, of course, by asking around in the community and among your friends), but they can be places where you can participate. Youth groups almost always need parental involvement, and you can bring a reassuring single-parent presence to kids who might be feeling left out of two-parent activities.

> **Parent Pitfalls**
> Social groups may draw people who are specifically there to seek out mates; if you're not interested in that scene, discomfort may make you choose another group.

Starting Your Own Group

If you aren't satisfied with the groups available in your area, you can create your own informal group of single parents. This is a wonderful way to meet people and form a powerful network.

Some single parents enjoy this kind of activity; others feel so isolated they're afraid to try. If you're game, here are some suggestions from The Single Parent Alliance:

- Decide what focus your group will take: Some single-parent groups offer a place where whole families can meet, while others focus more on just adult meetings. Decide whether your group will be for fun, support, or both.
- In advance, plan the specifics of your group: the size, the schedule (how often will your group meet?), the place where meetings will be held, plans for childcare (if children aren't welcome), and the format of the meetings.
- Recruit members, beginning with single parents you know.
- Create a flyer about your group and post it throughout the community.
- Announce your group to the media. You may be able to get your meetings listed in local papers or on the radio.
- As the group grows and new members are added, you may want to add materials and activities.

You can get more details on running a single-parent group successfully by contacting The Single Parent Alliance (see Appendix A for contact information).

True Pals

Many folks living solo (with or without kids) find it useful to have one or two phone buddies—people they talk to on a daily or regular basis. This is a great substitute for the kind of support other parents may get from their spouses—it helps keep you connected and safe.

For single parents this kind of "buddy system" can be even more valuable. If you find another single parent who can be a pal, he or she doesn't have to be your best or most intimate friend, but someone to share a days' worth of information with, as well as a back-up when you need another adult in a hurry.

As you go through your days, keep your eyes and ears open for friends who seem to be on your wavelength; then go out of your way to stay in touch, and see if you can build a common bond with them.

School Days

Your children's school is an outstanding resource for help and social life for both your kids *and* you—so it's that much more important to be sure the school is "singles friendly." For example:

➤ Does the school still have "class mothers" or "class fathers" days? Or "Father-son ball games?" In most cases, this kind of gender bias is illegal; in practical matters, it serves to spread a sense of exclusion among kids as well as parents. Help school officials see that not all parents fit the patterns of the past. Suggest a "class parent" day, or a "parent-child ball game" instead.

➤ Though you probably can't help out during school hours, do your best to participate in some school activities—weekend fairs, evening meetings, school plays—that you can fit into your schedule. The more connections you make at your child's school, the better for all of you.

Fitting school functions into your already busy schedule may seem difficult or impossible. But remember, the more you make your presence known at school, the more willing the school will be to adapt to your special needs and concerns as a single parent.

> **Meaning?**
> Any situation that assumes a certain role can only be filled by one gender or another is an example of *gender bias*.

The People in Your Neighborhood

If, as the saying says, "it takes a village" to raise a child, then you as a single parent can find ways to help your surrounding "villagers" with childcare—as a way to be a good neighbor and receive neighborly support in return. For example:

➤ Be the one to organize a neighborhood clean-up or block party. It's something that you can do in your off hours, especially if you delegate effort—and a great way to make yourself known and needed. (Your kids can get the neighborhood kids involved, too.)

➤ Think of some things that your schedule permits you to do for your neighbors. For example, you can take charge of your neighbors' kids on some weekends and evenings, if they keep your children during the afternoons. Or, you can run errands or do other chores for them on a regular

> **Parent Pitfalls**
> By being "too busy" to participate in life around you, you miss opportunities to let your needs be known. Get involved with school, your family, and your community, and you will find a whole network of people willing to help you and your children in return.

Part 5 ➤ *The Buddy System: Friends*

basis. The more you do for your neighbors, the better you get to know them and the easier it'll be to figure out which ones you want to help you and your kids!

Community-Resource Checklist

No matter where you live, your community is filled with resources for you and your kids. Make a list of all you have access to.

To start, look in your yellow pages under "Social Services," "Community Organizations," and "Youth." Then, check the resources listed in Appendix A. Find local offices for the resources that look most valuable. In the following checklist, jot down the names and numbers of groups you'd like to get involved with or find out more about:

Need to Know Checklist

List the names and phone numbers of all individuals and organizations in your community that may be a source of support to you and your children.

Neighbors

_____

_____

Teachers

_____

_____

PTA members

_____

_____

Religious leaders

_____

_____

Support group members

_____

_____

Doctors

_____

_____

Employers

_____

_____

Social-service agencies

_____

_____

Family members

_____

_____

Others

_____

_____

Chapter 17 ➤ *Creating a Single-Parent Community*

When you make this list, you've accomplished two important goals. One, you've created a handy list of all the key contacts in your community. Two, you've reminded yourself that you do have a community: that there are lots of people close by who provide you and your children with the connection and support you need.

The Least You Need to Know

➤ "Community" is all around you—you just need to discover, or create, your own corner of it.

➤ You may find support in specialized, well-established single-parent support groups.

➤ You may also find ways to fit in with general social groups in your community.

➤ Get involved with the needs of your neighbors and your community, and you will find a willing network of support for yourself and your kids.

Chapter 18

Intimate Arrangements: Sex and Dating

In This Chapter

➤ How much should you tell your children about your dating?

➤ Dealing with your children's fears about your relationships

➤ Setting boundaries with your kids

➤ Introducing your dates into your family life

Romance is tough enough for any one person to deal with. Try to handle dating when you've got the feelings and opinions of your children to consider—and lay all of that on top of what often has been a difficult past with love and dating. Yikes!

More than a few books have been written on this topic alone (see Appendix A for some of them). So here, we'll focus on how dating and single parenting mix.

Are You Ready to Date Again?

Let's stop for a moment and think about how complex and confusing dating can be, even for an independent, single person. Now, reflect on what you've recently been through in the area of relationships. Perhaps someone you loved has died. Perhaps a marriage you had counted on has collapsed. Or, perhaps you've experienced the emotional repercussions of having a child without a partner, a situation you may not have planned on.

In that context, it's understandable that the dating scene may not be *your* scene. If you've decided to go it alone from now on, then you don't need this chapter. If you think you might get involved again, even someday, then this chapter will give you something to think about—but it doesn't mean that as a single parent you have some kind of "duty" to get out there.

If you feel that you "ought" to be dating, slow down. Think about the emotional inner drama you may be experiencing already. Do you really want to add another player to your life right now? You'd be wise to give yourself time—to mourn, to settle down, to get to know yourself again—before you venture onto the relationship stage.

Why? Because now, your children—your very role as parent—make this dating business even trickier than it was when you did it the first time.

It's natural for an adult living "alone" with kids to feel lonely. But maybe you're better off socializing with groups of others (as suggested in Chapters 16 and 17) than in seeking a one-on-one relationship right now.

That's up to you. But whether you're dating now or just considering it for the long-term future, you do have some new things to think about. This chapter will give you a start.

What Will Your Kids Think?

When you are ready to start dating, it's wise to start slowly—go out for a friendly cup of coffee, for example. You may not be willing to get involved in anything serious at the start. However, even though your dating life may be casual to you, it can be a very big deal to your kids.

> **Wise Words**
> Perhaps not surprisingly, the pre-teens and teens of single parents surveyed showed the widest diversity of feelings, attitudes, and opinions about the sex-and-dating aspect of their parent's lives—everything from "I don't care" to "I hate it."

It's easy to forget that what you see as a casual date may look like a major move to your kids. They will have to deal with a host of emotions:

➤ They either badly want (or don't want) a new parent.

➤ They may feel so insecure that any step you take away from them feels like the end of the world.

➤ Young children may struggle with fears of desertion, confusion, and feelings of loyalty toward the absent parent (even when that person has died).

> Older kids have different problems, because adolescence brings its own social and sexual needs and interests that sometimes conflict with those of a single parent.

Fragile feelings and a need for stability are so common among single-parent kids that a relationship between a parent and another adult can create considerable distress. So it's important to reassure your kids, within limits, that your dating is not just about choosing between them and another.

It may be up to you, too, to bring up the subject: "How do you feel about my going out?" is a neutral, direct approach.

If you get a shrug or a non-answer, it's OK to say, "Some kids worry when their parent goes out because they think they're going to get left out somehow. That's not going to happen, you know?"

Or, you may hit a pile of negativity or anger. "How could you do that to Dad/Mom?!" Your answer then might be, "I know you love Dad and care about him… But this isn't about him, it's about me. I'm not going to ask you to choose. Besides, just because I'm going out doesn't mean I'm going to get married or anything."

Or, if you are planning to go out on a date, your kid might ask, "Well, how come I can't come?" Your reply: "I love you to pieces, but sometimes I just like to be with grownups—don't you like to be with kids your age? Besides, you can come with us sometime—that is, if I think this person is worth seeing again. We'll never know unless I try, though."

> **Expert-Ease**
> If you are dating, it's really important that you be as specific as you can about where you're going and when you'll be back—offer to phone during the time you're away, too. Then, stick to the schedule you've set. That way your children learn by your actions that you're still their parent.

Dating: Don't Ask, Don't Tell?

Single parents have at least as many viewpoints on this topic as their kids do. Some simply don't allow dating as a subject of conversation, and say that sex is an adult activity meant only for private, long-term, grown-up relationships. Others take care to keep their social and sexual lives separate from their home lives; they date only when their kids are elsewhere, or spend nights and weekends out only when their kids are away, too. Still others just don't socialize at all for the sake of their kids. While staying at home or compartmentalizing your life may avoid confrontation with your kids, it may also cause you to feel secretly resentful.

Most counselors and other experts recommend being as open as appropriate with your kids about dating (just as you'd talk differently about sex with a small child than with a teen). To a young child, you might say, "I'm having a nice time, spending time with a friend my age, just like you do." To an older one, you can say, "Hey, it's not serious or anything, we're just going out, you know?"

No matter what your child's age when you start dating, it can be a hard adjustment for everyone, and it's better for the kids to have a clear idea about what's happening than to guess or worry—or have a new person sprung on them by surprise.

The Dating Double Standard

What goes on between a married couple behind a closed bedroom door is adult business. The same applies to you as a dating single parent. Your kids don't need to know your private business.

> **Parent Pitfalls**
> Arguing with your teenage children over your own sexual privacy or practices as though they were equals is a mistake, wise parents say, because by erasing boundaries, you erode any authority you have over your teens—on a matter which is none of their business. There can be opportunities for discussion, though, if handled wisely.

> **Meaning?**
> When it comes to single parents and their kids, a *double standard* is one set of sex-and-dating rules that applies to the parent, and another, stricter set, that applies to adolescent children.

One crossover can be tricky—and that's with teens. Whatever rules you expect them to follow in their intimate lives, you need to follow, also. Many two-parent kids may find it easier to accept rules on sexual and dating behavior since the rules clearly apply only to themselves—not their parents. But imagine how it must feel to be a single-parent teen working out your own feelings about relationships and sex—and watching your parent do the same.

Here, a few comments from single-parent kids:

➤ "When I date, my Mom wants me to tell her where, when, who, how, and all that—but why doesn't she do the same?"

➤ "Mom can date, why can't I?"

➤ "If Dad can stay out all night, why can't I?"

➤ "If Mom can bring a man home for the night, how come I can't have a boyfriend over for the afternoon?"

So what do you say if your child challenges you with any of these lines? "Because I'm the parent, that's why!" pretty much sums it up, but to be more constructive, you can talk about the differences between adult dating and young dating. You can also ask your child how he or she would like to see the situation handled. Feeling that they have some say in their environment is often what children want the most.

Chapter 18 ➤ *Intimate Arrangements: Sex and Dating*

Sex and the Single Parent

If dating again requires a healthy dose of time to get into, then having a sexual relationship calls for even more caution. Are you ready? Do you need it? Again, give yourself time. Giving in to pressure—real or imagined—can have results just as painful as when you were a teen yourself. Plus—being a parent means that sex is anything but simple. There's no rush!

Being a "parent first" means, in the views of many single parents as well as psychologists, sleeping with a new partner away from your kids.

Once you're in a stable relationship that looks as though it's long-term, see how comfortable you feel about sharing more of your personal life with your kids: not to let them in the bedroom, any more than you would if you were married, but to be more open about your relationship with your "significant other."

Of course it's OK for you to have intimate relationships somewhere. It's up to you and your ethical beliefs about having sex outside of marriage.

Whatever your dating situation, experts universally agree on several points:

➤ Protect your kids from any fallout. If you and your love-interest are spatting, keep the kids out of the way. If you can't keep your hands off of each other, your kids don't need to be a part of that either.

➤ Practice safe sex. Many formerly married parents may not be used to this rule—but as a single parent back in the dating scene, you have an extra responsibility to protect yourself for the sake of your children.

➤ If you are the noncustodial parent, don't bring your current love interest when the kids are visiting you. It's another story if it's a serious commitment (see Chapter 22) but even then you need to be delicate—and always put your interest in the kids first.

You are entitled to your own love life, to be sure. In fact, if handled carefully, it can enhance your family life, as well. Just be prepared for more complications than dating caused you before you had kids in your life.

Should You Bring Your Kids on a Date?

Some parents feel they always must include their kids in every activity—when the fact is (1) you deserve your own life and (2) dragging your kids along can be uncomfortable for everyone.

If you were married, you wouldn't always include your kids in your activities, would you? NO. So there's no reason to constantly include them in your single-parent social life, either.

185

Sometimes kids of any age can be pesty, even seductive; they may go out of their way to look nice, be around, cater to, and impress their parent's dates. If your kids always seem to be demanding time, attention, and entertainment from your date, it can sometimes mean that they are trying to keep him or her away from you.

What do you do? Make sure they get enough attention from you—and then go about your social life on your own time.

At the other extreme, sometimes kids are justified in feeling left out. Feeling abandoned or ignored is a very natural reaction to a parent's newly developed social life. Most kids are used to being the main focus of their parents' attention, and sharing that attention with someone outside the family can easily cause bad feelings. While the adjustment is especially hard on younger kids, who are still dependent on their parents and who worry about desertion, it's difficult for children of any age.

Kids may act out over feeling left out—or they may pretend they don't care. But if you're dating a lot, or involved in a busy schedule of clubs, courses, organizations, and other activities, try to be sure to leave enough time for your kids—even making your own dates with them for special parent one-on-ones.

Your Kids and Your Dates: Can They All Get Along?

Dating is tough for parents. It's also tough for people who date parents. They may either keep the kids at arm's length because of their discomfort, or they may overreact and try to come on like a parent. Make it clear—to your date, your kids, and yourself—that dating does not necessarily mean marriage. One boy viewed each of his mother's dates—even casual friends—as prospective stepfathers since he really hoped for a "new Dad." As a result, he was often disappointed when his dream father never showed up again. On the other hand, a teenage girl suspected that every woman her father introduced to her was going to be her stepmother, a thought so unpleasant that it made her rude.

Both these reactions are common. But while it's natural for kids to feel loyalty to an absent parent (whether divorced or dead), to wish for the reunion of divorced parents, or to dream of a new two-parent family, kids need to understand that your dates aren't threats.

Research shows that kids with other adults in their lives are better off than those with only a single adult to turn to. So done right, your own involvement with a new partner can also help your kids' development.

This is more likely to be successful if you pick as social partners people who your kids are comfortable with. Few single parents want to spend much time with people who aren't interested in their children.

Chapter 18 ➤ Intimate Arrangements: Sex and Dating

Stick with those partners who are willing to include your kids in appropriate activities—at least sometimes. This is also a good chance to get your kids' feedback on your dates.

First Date Jitters

Okay, so you're bringing a date home for the first time. Nervous much? Best to prepare everyone—your children and your date—in advance. Let the date know your kids are great but are nervous about you going out—so they may act a little, well, off. Meanwhile, tell your date as much about your family as you can, so he or she knows the kids names and a little of what to expect.

Let your kids know they're going to have a guest: don't surprise them with a stranger. Let them know you like this person and value the friendship, and tell the kids as much as they're interested in about your date. And remind them that as with any guest, they need to be polite.

When the first meeting occurs, keep it brief—don't schedule a formal family dinner right away! Be prepared for some uncomfortable moments, but let your kids ask what they need to, even if it's "Are you going to be our new Daddy/Mommy?" Be mature and keep it light. Think of it as animals sniffing each other out. Each person there has a stake in the encounter, and each needs to be very tentative at first about how they feel about each other. That's okay!

> **Wise Words**
> "I don't like it when the date tries to act like a parent." This is a frequent complaint of single-parent kids, and rightly so. It takes a long time before another adult can comfortably interact with authority over your children.

Dating Other Parents

"I learned fast that the best companion/date/lover was one who was a parent, too," most single parents say. And with good reason: Other parents understand priorities. They also tend to be more comfortable people—because parenthood indicates an ability to put someone else ahead of one's selfish needs.

Plus, if you date another parent, you've both got a shared base of experiences to work from. If your date ever deals with your kids in a way you don't accept, for instance, you could always say, "How would you like it if I dealt with *your* children that way?"

> **Wise Words**
> "I found it was much more comfortable dating men who were parents themselves because they understood what it meant to put the children ahead of our own needs or desires." —A divorced mother of a teen and pre-teen.

Intimacy Issues

When you get involved with intimate relationships, those boundary issues really become critical. Your dates may be tempted to cross the line toward your adolescent children, who may be traumatized or prepared to respond in kind—or both.

> **Parent Pitfalls**
> If your children's behavior around a new partner is intense, look closely at how your dates deal with your kids when you aren't around!

Kids may want to be part of a relationship that is really not meant for kids. Parents may want to draw kids into the kind of personal conversation that only adults should be having. The results of this kind of inappropriate interaction can be uncomfortable and even dangerous.

To keep boundaries intact, you may need to set some house rules to guide behavior around your dating:

- Please Knock: Each family member needs to stay on his or her side of the privacy door and ask permission before entering.

- Who's in Charge: Remain a parent, even if you are dating like a kid. Strong parental boundaries keep kids feeling safe with a sound structure.

- Minding Your Own Business: Adult business is adult business; children should not be drawn into inappropriate confidences.

- Make a Wishlist: Have your children make a list of how they wished you and other family members would behave while they are dating. You'd be surprised how much you can learn from that.

The Final Word

Despite the pitfalls and potential problems, almost any kind of social or romantic life can be a positive experience for all as long as you remember to be a parent first. That means…

- Be sure your children know how to reach you when you're out.

- Tell them what time you'll be home and don't be late.

- Watch for erratic behavior in your children and try to deal with its cause—probably fear—rather than react angrily.

- Include kids on appropriate dates sometimes, but if they always want to come, ask, "Do you want me to come with you every day to play with *your* friends?"

- Don't put your kids on the spot by asking "Do you like so and so?" Wait for them to offer their opinion, and watch their behavior for clues.

Chapter 18 ➤ *Intimate Arrangements: Sex and Dating*

➤ Be prepared for—initiate if necessary—honest conversation about this issue. Such talk can make you and your kids more open, honest, and trusting of one another.

The Least You Need to Know

➤ You are entitled to an adult social life.

➤ The basic rule of conduct when dating is to be a parent first. Retain boundaries with your children.

➤ Do not discuss intimate details of your dating life with your children.

➤ If you are raising teenage children, realize that you must abide by the same rules you set for them.

➤ Even when dating, give your children plenty of love, reassurance, and attention.

Part 6
You Are Family

As a single parent, you may feel alone, but that fact is, no matter what your situation, you aren't—or you don't have to be. We all have family—or we can create family. And you need to connect with or create family; if not for yourself, then at least for your children's sake.

Think of the warmth and security the concept of "family" conjures up for you. Then try to imagine what a safe and settled family life can mean to your child. Children thrive under the influence of a supportive, vibrant family life.

This part will help you "discover" and optimize the family you have—and create the family that you need.

Chapter 19

Sharing Your Children—With Their Other Parent

In This Chapter

➤ How to share your children—peacefully and positively—with their other parent

➤ How to manage the child-sharing process

➤ Parenting from a distance

➤ What to do if visitation agreements don't work

Warning: This chapter is not just for divorced parents! How come? Read these examples before moving on…

Marcia became a single mother by choice with the help of a man who stayed, at a distance, in her son's life. Ben adopted a child who, with his encouragement, will be able to seek out his birth parents should he choose to when he's older. When Lisa and Barbara chose to become parents through artificial insemination, they planned to allow their daughter to make contact with her birth father when she was older.

All of the people in these scenarios have "other parents" to deal with; it's not just children of divorce for whom the "other parent" is an issue.

The more "normal" situation, of course, is the sharing of kids between divorced or separated parents. In many divorces, sharing custody creates even more conflict than sharing money does; and it's often the issue that causes the most conflict after the divorce. When that happens, everybody suffers, especially the kids. It's a no-win situation.

Being a parent first for your child pays off—no matter what the circumstances of your adult relationship with your former partner. Putting the child second to the hostility of the relationship is always a bad idea. It's that simple.

In this chapter, you'll learn how to "be a parent first" and find ways to make sharing your kids with their other parent a win-win situation, one that can be good for everyone.

Successful Child Sharing: A Win-Win Situation

> **Expert-Ease**
> Studies repeatedly show that kids thrive in single-parent situations—because they are relieved of the family tensions that occurred before the divorce—that is, as long as those tensions stop with the divorce. When conflicts continue, research demonstrates, the children suffer.

Single-parent families come in a variety of shapes and sizes. Either the mother or the father may have full custody of all children. The parents may share custody and have the kids move from house to house. Or the parents may share custody and have the kids live with one parent and see the other on a liberal visitation schedule. For parents who have more than one child, all children may live with the same parent; or the children may be split up between parents in separate arrangements. There are many different possible arrangements, and whole books are written to discuss each kind.

No matter what your personal circumstance, if you can work out a smooth and amicable childcare arrangement with your children's other parent, everybody wins.

Your kids win because they have the security of knowing that two parents care for them, and the ability to use two adults as role models.

> **Wise Words**
> "I'm still mad at my ex, but I have to see him when I take the kids. So I just try—really *try*—to think of him not as my "ex," but as my children's father. For them, I keep myself calm." —Mother of two, recently separated

You and your ex win because you both benefit from having flexibility and support in your lives.

Face it—no matter how much you love your kids, aren't there times when you would give almost anything for some help in dealing with them? And wouldn't it be nice if you could rely on the regular contribution of funds and time from somebody else?

Who better than the kids' other parent?

Chapter 19 ➤ Sharing Your Children—With Their Other Parent

Immediately after a break-up, child sharing may feel like it's out of the question, but given some time and thought, it creates a sense of wholeness for everyone. It's certainly well worth a try, assuming the other parent is willing, able, and *not* abusive.

Cooperative Parenting

Cooperative parenting, in which parents who live separate lives cooperate when it comes to being parents, is a concept promoted by increasing numbers of counselors. Cooperative parents continue to take equal part in their children's lives: they both turn up at parent-teacher conferences, for example, or participate in school events. Both parents pool their resources to pay for special activities like karate classes or trumpet lessons. They work together to meet the child's needs first. In other words, they are parents together first, even when they live apart.

Cooperative parenting can be worked out in the parenting plan encouraged by many family courts (see Chapter 7 for more on custody agreements), or it can be something developed by each set of parents as they go along.

The same legislation that makes it possible to pursue "deadbeat parents" (see Chapter 13) also includes grants to help support and facilitate non-custodial parents' visitation with, and access to, their children.

Now, if the government recognizes the importance of allowing children to see both parents, shouldn't you be able to do the same?

When you arrange a visitation schedule (see Chapter 7), give the non-custodial parent as much visiting time as possible, and prepare to be flexible to allow for changes as your situation or the children's situation changes.

> **Parent Pitfalls**
> Family crises are traumatic. Trauma of any kind causes damage that requires time to heal. Parents who assume they will always be angry or hurt (or that they will never have anything to do with their ex again) would do well to calm down and wait for their pain to heal rather than dig a hole too deep for their kids to crawl out of. Change happens.

> **Expert-Ease**
> If you arrange a cooperative parenting agreement with your ex, be sure to put it in writing so everyone is aware of their responsibilities.

> **Wise Words**
> "I was really afraid I'd never see my Dad again. And I felt like it was my fault. When he kept coming, I felt better."
> —Child whose parents divorced when she was very young

Part 6 ➤ *You Are Family*

Sharing Fairly

It's widely agreed—at least through lip service—that children should never be tools or pawns in their parents' conflict. This may seem so obvious that it doesn't need to be repeated, but it does. Not only is putting children in the middle unfair and cruel, but repeated studies show that kids whose parents live apart but don't tear each other apart are just as healthy and secure as kids from intact, happy homes. And isn't that what being a parent first is all about?

If you use your children as weapons against their other parent, two bad results may occur: your children may be damaged—probably permanently—and you will ultimately lose their respect and trust.

If you view visitation as an opportunity for revenge or punishment against your ex-spouse, you hurt your children. Those who are parents first know that their first duty is making life better for their children.

Here are a few more rules that should govern your behavior toward both your children and their other parent:

> **Meaning?**
> The formal arrangement allowing for connection between non-custodial separated parents and their children is referred to as *visitation*. It's a rigid, formal word, but parental visits should be a friendly, flexible activity.

> **Wise Words**
> "Never damn or curse the other parent. Never force your kids to take sides—they love you both! Never make them—or let them—feel responsible for your dismay or struggle."
> —A single Dad who shares custody of his son

> **Wise Words**
> When her Dad started asking 12-year-old Shawna difficult questions about her mother, she responded: "Why don't you just ask Mom that, OK?" He never tried to put her in the middle again.

➤ Visitations should not be opportunities to unnecessarily spoil or bribe children. The parent-child interaction is what's most important.

➤ Visitations do not have to be filled with action-packed adventures and activities. In fact, normal activities and quiet time is more reassuring and valuable to children.

➤ Don't discuss financial arrangements or other business with your ex-spouse when you pick up or drop off the children.

➤ Don't use children as messengers or delivery people.

➤ Children should never be pumped for any information about the other parent's lifestyle.

➤ Don't speak badly of your child's other parent. If you start badmouthing, you will eventually alienate your kid.

➤ Children and the visiting parent should be allowed to develop their own relationship, even if the custodial parent doesn't understand or agree with the relationship.

Chapter 19 ➤ Sharing Your Children—With Their Other Parent

➤ Each parent should refrain from criticizing what the other parent does with the kids—so long as the kids are safe, cared for, and having a good time.

➤ Make sure you work out a clear, consistent pick-up/drop-off ritual—and stick with it. Both of you should be prompt when it comes to picking up and dropping off the kids. Your children—even older ones—need to be able to predict your comings and goings. For them, every coming together ends in another separation, and can lead to *separation anxiety* (inappropriate or excessive anxiety over separation from a parent). So the smoother and more predictable it is, the better for all.

➤ Be alert to the children's behavior, specifically problems that indicate serious difficulties with the other parent. If you suspect trouble, investigate it independently of the kids.

> **Meaning?**
> *Separation anxiety* refers to an inappropriate or excessive anxiety concerning separation from home or from those to which an individual is attached (for example, parents).

In an ideal world, child sharing is mostly done with great goodwill. In the real world, it *can* be, but it takes a lot of work. (It's worth it, though!)

Consistency Counts

Whatever arrangements you make, it's important that you and your ex send consistent messages to your kids. Separated parents need to agree on major parenting issues, just like married couples do. When my son complained, "You sound just like Dad," that was good news: it meant we were guiding the kid along the same wavelength and keeping confusion to a minimum. Here are some consistency issues you and your ex should agree on:

> **Parent Pitfalls**
> Some parents use visitation time as a way to harass their exes. The custodial parent who doesn't have the children ready at pick-up time and the visiting parent who doesn't bring the kids back on time are two examples. Games like these have a very negative impact on the kids—so much so that in some cases, parents who cannot resolve visitation schedules may choose to go back to court to resolve their conflicts.

➤ House rules. Keep house rules (curfews, TV limits, etc.) as consistent as possible between homes.

➤ Snack rules. Foods and eating habits that are off-limits in one house should be off-limits in both.

➤ Bedtimes. Bedtime should be the same in both households.

➤ Homework rules. Both of you should decide how much value you place on having homework done properly and on time, and you should set rules that reflect that value.

197

➤ **Allowance.** Both parents should offer similar financial gifts and payments to the kids.

➤ **Activities.** Activities that are off-limits in one home should be off-limits in both.

Counselors suggest holding regular meetings—once a month is good—with the other parent to discuss how the kids are doing and to get sticky matters into the open in an adult, business-like fashion. Some recommend making the meeting as organized as possible, with agendas and timetables—which is not a bad idea, especially if your relationship is bumpy.

"Business-like" meetings between you and your ex about issues regarding the children may seem cold—but if it allows you and the other parent to get together to discuss the children, then it's worth it.

Staying in the Loop

Because they don't see the children on a daily basis, many non-custodial parents report feeling shut out of their children's lives. These parents need encouragement to get more involved. Here are some ways each parent can help the other stay in the picture.

Custodial parents:

➤ Discuss problems your kids may be dealing with in school, in their social lives, or at home with the other parent. Go to parent-teacher conferences together if at all possible.

➤ Keep the other parent up to date on your kids' report cards and other school work. Get the kids involved; have them put the material together for mailing, or encourage them to discuss school issues on the phone with their other parent.

> **Wise Words**
> "My ex and I had an extra set of all family pictures made so we could keep albums at both our homes. Whatever else went on in our lives, we were parents and these children were family."—Divorced Mom

Non-custodial parents: Remember that even though you do not live with your kids, you are still their Mom or Dad. Your kids need your guidance and they need to know you're there for them. You may need to make an extra effort to do that. Here are some ideas:

➤ Get on the school's mailing list for all materials and announcements of school activities. Show up at parent-teacher conferences and events!

➤ Work with your kids to set up a visitation schedule; get them a calendar to mark for visits. Keep to the schedule! Being a parent first and keeping a child's faith requires reliability.

> ➤ Encourage your child to bring homework or school projects along on visits. This way you can help out and keep up with your child's interest. This also makes the visit seem more like a part of "real, regular, daily life" to your kids than it really is.

> ➤ Keep some of your child's wardrobe and supplies at your house so it feels like another home to them. (Set your home up along the lines suggested in Chapter 9 to make your kids comfortable.)

> ➤ If you have more than one child, do what you would do if you were all living together: Arrange some individual time with each child.

> ➤ Stay positive. This isn't easy for you or the kids—but the more you can make your children's visits feel like a "normal" part of their lives, the better.

> ➤ If you must cancel a visit with your kids, it should be for a very good reason—and let them know immediately. Arrange right away for a make-up meeting.

Here's a rule for both parents: The more consistency and stability you can give your children, and the less emotional drama you present to them, the better they will grow.

Parenting from a Distance

If you live far away, you can still stay in your children's lives. Here are some suggestions:

> ➤ Send little notes to your children on a regular basis.

> ➤ Send your children video or audio taped renditions of bedtime stories or other activities to give your long-distance connection a personal touch.

> ➤ Don't swamp your kids with big gifts, but make a practice of sending them little trinkets or articles of clothing—it's a reminder that you're thinking of them, wherever you are.

> ➤ Send photographs regularly, too. Get your children to respond by enclosing large self-addressed stamped envelopes, so they can send you schoolwork and pictures.

> ➤ Make it easy for your children to call you, anytime, in private. Consider installing a phone in your children's room, or getting an 800 number. Provide phone cards for your kids to use.

> ➤ If you and the kids have computers (and can afford it), think about getting Internet or e-mail service installed on your systems. Be willing to

Wise Words
"Having felt 'trapped' myself with a difficult single parent, I made sure my son had a train ticket so that he could always come to me if he needed," a single Mom explains. "He never had to use it, but knowing that it was there gave us both a good feeling."

pay for some of that service and you have a terrific, low cost, and very personal way of keeping in touch.

When you live far away from your children, visits present a special opportunity to bond and renew your connection. Here are some suggestions on making the most of visits:

➤ Prepare financially for visits. Set aside a regular amount to pay for travel, and keep your eye out for low-cost fares if necessary. Don't let the kids down by saying they can't come because you can't afford it.

➤ Be prepared for the extra costs visits will incur. It's not that you're going to entertain the kids lavishly, but you will need to pay for added groceries and a movie (or three). Non-custodial parents who must pay support frequently gripe (with justification) about having to pay for all this—but it's not your kids' fault. This is a prime example of needing to put adult resentments aside for the sake of staying close to your kids.

➤ If you visit often enough, vary the formats with your children. Take them camping or traveling or someplace fun. If there are relatives or friends nearby, see about making that your regular visiting spot.

Finding a place where you can relax and enjoy yourselves together is good. Just make sure the custodial parent knows where that place is. In some cases, acceptable visitation places and activities are specified in visitation agreements. In any case, it's only right for you to share information about your visitation plans with the custodial parent in advance.

> **Meaning?**
> *Psychosomatic* (*mind-over-body*) ailments—complaints of illness or sickness that have no physical validity—are sometimes thought of as phony, when actually, they are ways that children and teens express conflict and pains they cannot verbalize. These pains need to be treated with care. In treating them, the first step is to be sure all physical causes are ruled out. Then, an emotional source can be pinned down and adjusted.

When Visitation Doesn't Work

Sometimes, the visitation arrangements parents make with the best of intentions are difficult for their kids. Your kids may not verbally tell you that they aren't happy, either out of loyalty for the other parent or because they really don't know how they feel. But their bodies and behaviors will send signals.

When establishing a visitation pattern, watch out for stress-related symptoms, including:

➤ Sleep problems

➤ School problems

➤ Acting-out problems

➤ Behavioral manipulation (for example, "Mom lets me do it all the time," or "Dad lets me do it at his house.")

➤ *Psychosomatic* complaints (stomach aches, headaches, rashes, and other physical symptoms caused by emotional or psychological tension).

If there is tension, or your children are resisting visitation, find out what's going on. Perhaps the other parent isn't appropriately involved with the kids, or there's a conflict going on that needs to be looked into.

Should Children Choose?

It's generally agreed that children shouldn't be asked to choose which parent to live with, because the conflict that decision could create is potentially too painful. But some couples do build into their visitation agreements a timetable by which children can choose to change living arrangements.

And of course, if couples can't decide who should get custody, a court will step in and make the decision—often by asking the children what they want.

Sometimes, generalized unhappiness expresses itself in a desire to live with the other parent. This may be something the child genuinely wants. On the other hand, it may be a ploy, designed to get attention or concern from the current custodial parent.

If a child suggests that he wants to live with the other parent, the custodial parent may be shocked, hurt, upset, and angry. These are understandable reactions, but they are reactions that need to be hashed out with other adults, friends, counselors, and family.

If your child expresses an interest in living with the other parent, work through your own hurt feelings with other adults. Then, help your child think it through. Here are some of the ramifications he may not have thought about:

➤ Does the other parent *want* him to live there? Is she or he capable to care for him?

➤ Is he ready to give up his school and neighborhood friends?

➤ What kind of community would he be moving to? Would he really be happy there?

➤ Does the other parent have a spouse or serious partner? Does the child get along with this person?

➤ Ask him to make some honest lists. First, have him write down all the things he likes and dislikes about staying put. Then have him write down all the things he would like and dislike about the new home. Then ask him to compare the lists and decide truthfully if he wants to move.

Part 6 ➤ *You Are Family*

> **Singular Successes**
>
> My ex-husband and I arranged a separation agreement in which we gave our son the right to choose his living arrangements when he turned 15. That helped him feel in control. At 15, he was settled in his new school and life, so he said he'd like to stay put. We decided his decision was fair all around.

The Least You Need to Know

- Share your children amicably with your ex for the sake of your children; don't withhold or complicate visitation out of your own self-interest or anger.
- Venting negative feelings about your ex around or through your children will only backfire on you.
- Cooperative parenting makes optimum use of each parent's assets to maximize the benefits for the child.
- Both the custodial and visiting parent should set consistent rules and limits on the children.
- Take as many practical steps as necessary to make the transition between custodial and visiting parent as smooth and friendly for the child as possible.

Chapter 20

Sharing Your Children—With All of Their Family

In This Chapter

➤ Why extended family is a critical factor in the lives of your kids *and* you

➤ How to encourage a good relationship between your kids and their other family

➤ How to improve your relationship to your other family

➤ How to encourage the other family to help you and your children

If children feel and act better from having two parents on the scene, just think how good it is for them to be surrounded by an entire network of family. Unfortunately, in cases of divorce and unmarried parenthood, often that wider network of family (including cousins, aunts, uncles, and grandparents) gets left out of the picture. These days, many grandparents and other relatives have started fighting for—and winning—THEIR rights to involvement with these children.

Seeing that it's good for everyone involved, the wise single parent will actively seek to create and strengthen family bonds for their children. This chapter will show you how.

Part 6 ➤ *You Are Family*

Extending the Net

In earlier days (and still in many cultures), the wider family is a physical part of a child's life; various generations and collateral relations live under the same roof. In contemporary American culture, that doesn't happen, but it's no less necessary—especially for children who live with a sole parent. Aunts, uncles, cousins, and grandparents all bring something special to a child in their unique style of loving attention.

> **Wise Words**
> "My Dad's aunt provided the snuggling my Mom didn't have time for—and it made a huge difference in my life."
> —An adult child of a single parent

Security is a big worry for single-parent kids, and stability is a prime requirement for their healthy development. For those reasons, the more folks in the family net, the better the kids feel.

Your children deserve the largest family possible—and just because you and their other parent are no longer connected is no reason why they should be cheated.

> **Singular Successes**
>
> Here are some examples of single parents who've kept family ties intact. Monica is a single mother by choice, but she keeps in touch with her son's father, who has regular visitation privileges. Peter is a widower who has remarried, but has kept his late wife's family in his children's lives. Joan's daughter always visits her Dad at his mother's or sister's homes.
>
> When Mark's wife died, her family became the kids' caretakers while Mark got his life organized. Good for Mark and good for the kid's sense of safety.
>
> Sally's divorce didn't cut her off from her ex-husband's family—so her son could spend the summer on Uncle Bob's farm, giving everybody a break and a positive feeling.
>
> All of their kids have strong family identities, and all the parents benefited from having that family back-up—as do all single parents who let the "other family" in.

How can your children's "other family" help you and your kids? Let's count the ways:

➤ The more family the kids have, the more solid will be their own sense of self and future family life. Even though they may not see how a couple works together at home, they can see it elsewhere in their family.

Chapter 20 ▶ Sharing Your Children—With All of Their Family

- ▶ Instead of having only one model to identify with or imitate, children who are in touch with a wide range of family members have a choice.

- ▶ As we learn more about the genetic influences on such non-physical traits as personality and talent, we understand that kids are indeed the product of their entire birth families. The more your kids know about their heritage, the more they can accept and express themselves. For example, your child may say, "I love how Uncle Harry plays the saxophone. Maybe I could try music," or "I love Great Aunt Martha. She loves to cook, and her kitchen is so cozy!"

- ▶ Extensive family bonds are good for parents, too. The more people in your children's life, the more strength for you.

So there may be good reasons to help kids stay connected with their entire family.

> **Wise Words**
> "When we separated, we were able to tell our son that nothing else had changed in his life. Hearing that he could still visit his aunts and uncles, he let out a huge sigh of relief." —A divorcing couple

> **Wise Words**
> "Getting to know my 'other' family helped me see why I am the way I am— and makes me feel that I'm not an oddity in the world." —Single-parent teen, on meeting his father's family

What's Holding You Back?

Even after you realize all the advantages to keeping a wide family network available for your kids, you may still be reluctant to open up these connections. You may have good reasons: the hostility and negativity on the other side may be on-going and may make your kids more uncomfortable than cozy. But, if your children's other parent has a family, you'll need to find a way to make it OK for your kids and not bad for yourself.

> **Meaning?**
> *Identity* is an individual's sense of who he or she is as a consistent personality in an in-depth sense. Identity is derived from a sense of continuity and connection.

Experts remind us to be sure you as a parent know the extended family and feel comfortable with them. Just because they are family does not mean you trust them with your children. And children should feel free to tell you if they are uncomfortable with any relative that may indicate abuse.

It may well be that other relatives are negative, and do make the kids uncomfortable (for example, by putting you down or asking your kid to take sides). You can avoid this by getting your former spouse involved to try to keep things neutral, for the kids' sake. Or it

> **Wise Words**
> "Even after the divorce, my grandpa taught me to swim and helped me with my research papers..."—Child of a single parent

may be just your own feelings—of negativity, perhaps, or of pride in not wanting to get "outside" help.

Perhaps it's just fear that your kids will need or love you less if they have other family members to turn to. Actually, it's more likely to be the opposite: The more giving you can be, the more you will get back. Besides, remember that being a parent first means putting your feelings aside so your kids have the freedom to make their own lives.

Making the Most of What You've Got

Aside from the psychological stability that extended family brings, there are other reasons to keep your children surrounded by relatives who love them. The more people helping with the raising of your children, the more of everything—from material things to love—there is to go around. And that can't be bad.

For example, more and more grandparents—even in "intact" families—are willing to help with the younger generation's education, or take the kids on trips that parents simply don't have the time or the money to arrange. If you maintain friendly relationships with them you'll likely find that there's lots they can do for the kids, from buying computers or Christmas gifts to traveling with the kids on camping or vacation trips. Later on, they may even help with college tuition.

On the less materialistic side, simply the time that non-live-in relatives have can be valuable for you and your kids. Your kids will benefit from spending fun time with their family, and you will enjoy the temporary break from parenting.

If this all sounds somewhat materialistic or selfish, remember, it's not about "giving" to *you;* your children represent the family's best shot toward the future—so relatives have their own reasons for being supportive.

When Families Fight for Rights

In fact, many relatives are so concerned about staying in touch with the children in cases of death or divorce that they are willing to fight for the privilege of contact with the next generation.

In recent cases, grandparents have been found by the courts to have rights to access to their grandchildren despite divorce or paternity suits. In some cases grandparents have been allowed to seek visitation in their own names. When trying these cases, the courts generally take a number of factors into considerations, including:

- Evidence of affection
- Amount of time spent together
- The relatives' care-taking abilities
- Family traditions
- Collateral family connections with aunts, uncles, and cousins.

But there's no need to make a fight out of the extended family's right to see your children. In fact, it might well be something to discuss as you work out a separation agreement with your ex.

Or you might want to make it a bit formal, by simply writing a note to the relatives confirming arrangements for the kids to visit on some regular basis.

> **Wise Words**
> "Having holiday scheduling written into our separation agreement avoided an ongoing hassle, and got us started on creating a natural network for our kids."
> —Divorced parents of teens

> **Wise Words**
> "I was so angry at my ex that I couldn't bear the thought of my daughter being a part of his family. The result was that she had to make a choice—and there was a period when she needed to be with them and felt she had to cut me off. It was awful."
> —Divorced single Mom

Keeping It All in the Family

Here are some tips for how to best make—and improve—your children's connections with their other family:

- Develop specific schedules or traditions for your kids to share with their other family: summers at the grandparents'; one holiday a year with the aunts and uncles; vacation trips with the cousins; every Thursday night at your ex-mother-in-law's. Whatever works best for your extended family and your children.

- But just as you shouldn't speak badly of their other parent in front of your kids, you should also be positive about their other family. Say only good things to your kids about them—and they should do the same. If you have good relations, thank them and let them know you appreciate it.

- Watch your kids—if they're reluctant to spend time with their other family, there may be conflict going on that you aren't aware of. You may want to initiate a discussion with them to find out what's going on.

- Keep photographs of the "other" family members in your home—and keep them in your conversation so the kids know it's OK to talk about them.

207

> ➤ If you live far away from other family members, keep the connections open with regular correspondence and exchange of photographs. Encourage your kids to phone or e-mail them. And be sure your kids say "thank you" for whatever they receive from relatives.

The Least You Need to Know

- ➤ Extended family connections benefit you, your children, and their other family.
- ➤ Children who connect to their entire family relate better to themselves and to you.
- ➤ The techniques for keeping your kids connected to their other family are really very simple: Work out a system in advance, schedule time, and be positive about the other family in front of the kids.
- ➤ Even if you do not want to connect, the other family has rights they can fight for—so why not avoid the fight?

Chapter 21

Family First

In This Chapter

- "Home" is where you make it
- "Family" is what you define it
- How to create a family that matters—and how to enjoy it

Often, it's found, single parents view their status as merely transitional. They'll be a "whole" family again someday. And for many, that's true: In the United States, more than ³/₄ of all divorces end in remarriage. On the other hand, looking toward that as "happily ever after" could also be a mistake since some 40 percent of all remarriages end in divorce.

Whatever your dreams for the future, remember that you're living now. This is not a dress rehearsal. This is especially true when it comes to dealing with your children, who won't be with you for long. Remember, this is *their* life.

As mentioned before, research shows that when single-parent kids display negative characteristics or encounter serious emotional roadblocks, it's not because they have "only" one parent. It's due to a variety of other factors that add up to constant instability. When they can stay put, count on reliable caretaking, and experience a reasonably peaceful environment, they compare very favorably to children of intact families.

Part 6 ➤ *You Are Family*

> **Wise Words**
> "I always felt there was somebody missing at that dinner table," one child of a single parent recalls, "I felt we weren't a 'home,' I guess, but when my Mom got organized to paint the house and put up wallpaper—and I helped—it made me feel really good."

> **Wise Words**
> "Understand that not all families have two parents—concentrate less on what's wrong with your life and more on what's right with it."—Teenage child of a single parent

> **Expert-Ease**
> Therapists and counselors agree: "We need to understand and remind our children that *all* families are whole."

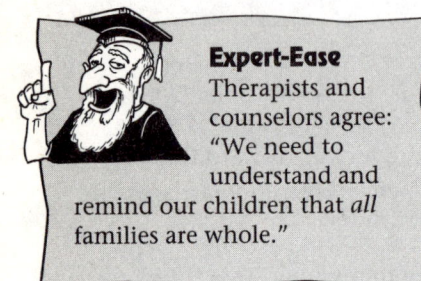

The implication here: Instead of thinking of what's missing from your family, figure out how best to MAKE it family. That's what this chapter is all about.

Making a Permanent Home

By focusing on what you don't have, you may blind yourself to what you do (or could) have. Here are some ways to make the best of what you've got:

➤ Think about not being so transient. If you're staying with friends or relatives, make getting a place of your own your first goal. (Lots of people manage to accomplish this goal. According to the Census Bureau, nine million of the nation's 11+ million single parents own or rent for themselves).

➤ Getting a place that's yours may not be out of the question, even if money seems tight. Many localities have subsidized housing, and given the income rates of most single-parent families, you may be able to qualify—and get a decent home that you and your kids can stay in.

➤ If you don't qualify for subsidized housing, but you do want to own a home, look into *Fanny Mae*, the federal home mortgage lender that offers subsidized mortgages for first-time owners.

➤ If you are renting, make your place yours. Get your kids in on it. What can you do to improve the place? Get the kids to help you decorate, paint, scrape, hang curtains. Then, no matter where you live, your place has become yours.

➤ Go back to Chapter 9 for tips on creating comfort in any circumstances. Follow your own tastes and instincts.

Building a Future

Throughout this book, I've tried to show you how to not only survive, but thrive. To be a successful single parent, you must be able to get your finances stable, to put resentments and other negative feelings behind you (or at least set them aside), and look past today toward the future that you can build for yourself and your children.

Your kids, like all kids, need to plan and prepare for the next stages in their lives. They need a parent to help with that—not one who's too wrapped up in other matters.

Help your kids start finding the direction they want their lives to take. Do they want to go to college? Do they want to pursue a special talent? Get them thinking ahead with confidence, and the troubles of today or yesterday may seem to ease. Together, you can help them visualize and work toward their dreams.

And you need to plan and prepare for your own future after your kids are out on their own. The time to start building that future is now: and the process provides momentum to bring positive energy to your life.

> **Wise Words**
> "He doesn't have to do *everything*! He comes home from his job, cooks, cleans, does laundry, everything. I try to help and he won't let me. Why not? I mean, we are a family."—An 11-year-old daughter of a single Dad

> **Parent Pitfalls**
> Many single parents are so focused on getting through "today" that they can focus even less easily than others on preparing for a future. Don't neglect your future in your struggle to get through today.

What Matters Most

Ask most parents what matters most to them, and they say "my kids." Yet sometimes we get so bogged down and boggled up in other issues—spousal battles, financial status, social insecurity, whatever—that we forget about our kids. And instead of focusing on an emotionally rich life for our kids, we leave those kids with a sense of bitterness.

We get so crotchety as we fight today's battles that we become people our kids can't wait to get away from.

Secure, united, loving, supportive: A family of any shape can meet these criteria, but it takes a focus uncluttered by past hurts and future fears.

Happy Kids

Successful single parents avoid burdening their kids with their problems. And while they understand that nobody can be "happy" all the time, they're attentive to the kids' moods.

> **Expert-Ease**
> "Successful" children learn that their family, whatever its shape, can work out a unique system of love and support. A positive self-image is the most critical factor for family success. Despite ups and downs, what matters is the feeling that the family can create its *own* success and validation for its own members.

> **Wise Words**
> Looking back, a divorced mother of four comments: "You'll have plenty of time for your own life after the kids leave—plenty! Focus now on creating a special life for them now."

If your children—or you, for that matter—can't seem to *ever* get happy, then some outside help is called for. Having a professional psychological check-up after a life-trauma is not a bad idea anyway.

But if you continue to be a "parent first" and focus on helping your kids maintain a fairly even (and cheerful) keel, something amazing happens—you start to feel better yourself.

Joyful Journey

Are you having fun yet? If not, stop. Step back, Take a deep breath. What's bothering you most—worrying you, making you crankiest—this week? How important is it? Is it important enough to keep you from enjoying (and being enjoyable to) your family—the family you have right now?

Probably not. Try smiling, doing something silly.

Go back to Chapter 16 and check out the list of fun activities. Try one today. Try another one this weekend.

Single-parent families can have as much fun, pleasure, and joy as any others—if you let yourself.

Making Memories

Some parents, made single by death or divorce, find it painful to look through picture albums from the past or to live through holidays and other events that bring up memories of happier days. That pain passes eventually…

But in the meantime, it's important to make new memories: Start new photo albums and scrapbooks. Develop new traditions. At holiday times think of special ways to celebrate that are yours alone. Make new birthday and vacation rituals that will create memories for your children to look back on.

The "Ideal" Family: Yours!

Family is what you make it. The meaning of "family" depends on how you define it. It might be a good idea to talk to your children about this: If they feel that something or someone is missing from their home, they may have a hard time coping, without knowing why. Discover ways you can tighten family bonds by working and playing together.

Chapter 21 ➤ *Family First*

A useful approach to help you all feel more like a family is to look at what you do have, rather than what you don't. Teach your children that you aren't different, you're special.

Answer the following questions to focus on what makes your family a happy family:

➤ What makes your family special?

➤ Three things you're proudest of:

➤ Three things you enjoy the most:

➤ Three adjectives that best describe your family:

Get the whole family involved so that all of you can discuss what makes yours a special family.

The Least You Need to Know

➤ Single-parent families can be as successful and nurturing as intact families.

➤ Don't let everyday struggles keep you from planning the future for yourself and your kids.

➤ Create an environment that's "yours" to live in.

➤ Work up activities and traditions that involve everyone as a family.

Chapter 22

Re: Marriage

In This Chapter

- ➤ Are you ready for remarriage?
- ➤ How can you tell if your new partner is good for your kids?
- ➤ Predictable problems of blended families

Probably little is more longed for—or more feared—by both single parents and their children than the marriage or remarriage of the parent.

You may long for a marriage because of your need for love and for someone to share your workload. Your children may long for it because they need a sense that they will be whole and safe, and also because they think that you would be happier.

On the other hand, you may fear marriage, perhaps because of previous bad experiences or because you are unwilling to give up the power and pride that you derive from being the "sole proprietor" of your own family. Your children may fear it because they don't want to lose your love and attention, and they fear the intrusion of a stranger.

Your exhilaration over the possibility of marriage may be great, but as a "parent," you don't want to risk inflicting emotional danger on your kids or yourself.

Part 6 ➤ *You Are Family*

> **Wise Words**
> "I really wanted my Mom to get married again. But then, I really didn't, too."—An eight-year-old child of a single parent

> **Parent Pitfalls**
> Realize that you may not be ready for a new attachment. As a single parent, you may have felt so lonely and miserable that any possibility of companionship looked good. But if you haven't gone through all the stages of becoming detached from a previous partner, or of mourning a previous marriage, it can be very difficult to enter a new relationship. It often happens that people who date happily even for a long time seem to turn into two entirely different individuals once the arrangement is made permanent by marriage.

Well, here's the good news—there are plenty of factors that you can evaluate before taking this tremendous step into the next phase of your life. In this chapter, I'll show you what they are.

Should You Get Married?

Some single parents are determined to go it alone; some are constantly seeking spouses. The attitudes of most of the rest fall somewhere in between. But one thing that's easy to agree on: It's not a good idea to get married just for the sake of being married, or to depend on another person as a support (financial or otherwise). That rarely works, and if you try it's often your kids who will suffer.

So how do you decide whether marriage is right for you? Here are rules of thumb, courtesy of single parents who've been there:

➤ Marry for love. "Marry because it matters, not just for the sake of attaching to someone."

➤ Make sure your partner is prepared to be a parent, too. "What's most important to me is how my partner relates to my kids."

➤ Think about your interests. Do you and your partner have enough in common to enjoy life together?

➤ Make sure your partner is stable. "Can he take care of himself, or am I just getting another kid?" wondered one single parent about a potential partner.

➤ Take time. Give yourself time to feel good about yourself. Give the relationship enough time to really get to know each other, warts and all.

What about your kids? While their needs must be taken into consideration, beware of making assumptions about "what's good for them." Research indicates that children with two parents are "better adjusted" than those with one parent, irrespective of their biological relationship to their parents. But before you rush to the altar, consider that that finding doesn't take into account the quality of the two-parent relationship: Remember that according to statistics most remarriages end in divorce.

On the other hand, children who are accustomed to having you all to themselves are not going to jump with joy at the prospect of sharing—so if you ask them, they may not be enthusiastic. They shouldn't be asked ahead of time to approve anyway—it's your decision. As soon as you have decided for sure, you need to let them know of your plans. Then take careful measures of their reactions.

Just give everyone a lot of time to adjust to the possibility. Let your kids see that they won't be losing you to another person; instead, they will gain someone—and that, as a happily married parent, you will be better able to enjoy your life and share the resulting positive feelings with them.

Living Together

Living together is another option—at least for the interim. Some parents—especially those with teens—are uncomfortable with the idea of living with a partner because of the double standard implied. If you caution your teenager against pre-marital sex, you may be open to challenge if you share a bed with someone you aren't married to. If you can come to terms with this issue, however, co-habitation does give a sense of how life as a new family could work.

Many recent studies indicate that though the number of single-parent families is growing, and the number of kids apparently living with one parent is huge, in reality, many live with non-married couples. Other studies show that living with two unrelated adults in the household can benefit the child—again, if the adults share a positive relationship.

The one clear rule that applies to living together (as to all other types of situations) is that you remain the parent. Sometimes your partner may need to take charge, but no matter what the relationship between you, the relationship between you and your child needs to stay the same.

Having someone to share your home can be convenient and useful for many practical reasons: You share costs, childcare, and other chores.

> **Parent Pitfalls**
> Be sure that you are in a committed relationship with your partner before you invite him or her to live with you. Having a string of live-in relationships will leave your children with no feeling of security or consistency.

> **Parent Pitfalls**
> As a single parent, you've worked hard to create an appropriate atmosphere in your home, and a good structure for your kids. Then, if you aren't careful, you may open your home to share with someone who cannot follow the same rules. Make sure you and your partner have similar ideas about childraising and everyday living before you make a commitment. Sharing a home takes more care than you might think.

But some things need to be carefully spelled out. Who's in charge, for instance. If it's your house, you get to make more of the rules. You and your new housemate have to agree on discipline: If your housemate lets her kids do what yours may not, you have a difficult conflict.

> **Parent Pitfalls**
> Parents can and should expect support and back-up from their new spouses, but they make a mistake if they turn over too many of the parenting responsibilities too quickly to another.

As you add a new adult to your household, remember, your kids were there first. So don't be surprised if they start acting out—breaking house rules and arguing constantly, for example, or getting ultra-clingy or making you feel guilty for sometimes leaving them behind or closing the door on them.

It's best to get all this out in the open, ahead of time if possible, and make your own set of rules that applies to your own unique situation. The same kind of limit-setting applies when you are the ones moving in, too. Both parents need to be supportive of all concerned.

You're Still a Parent First

Whatever the form of these reattachments, remember that you are a parent first. That means that no matter how much you love a new spouse or live-in, your first responsibility is to your children. And you are the one who is the parent, not the newcomer.

> **Wise Words**
> The teenage children of single parents were asked how they felt about their parents remarrying or living with a lover. About one-third said they would be in favor of their parent's remarriage; about one-third said they'd be against it; and another one-third said "it depends."

Your role as parent is critical in protecting your kids—from physical threats or from financial threats that can arise when another adult is added to the household. A new spouse may turn out to be abusive, or a leech looking only for support. A parent needs to keep a clear enough view of the household to understand when a newcomer is not what he or she pretended to be. Children and families have been thrown into turmoil by the wrong person being added to the family.

If after one or two warnings, your new partner is still a negative presence in your household, the only solution may be to ask him or her to leave.

> **Wise Words**
> "When my Dad didn't have as much time for me, I found a coach at the after-school club that I could talk to. It worked out OK." —A 13-year-old boy whose father remarried

You are also responsible for being sure that your family is comfortable, emotionally as well as physically. This means making sure the kids feel as safe and loved and involved as when there was no new person, but also seeing that your new partner is helped to feel welcome in the family.

It may take a while, but spending the right amount of time and attention on each is an important goal to strive for.

Blending Families: Can't You All Just Get Along?

Reattachment often radically increases the size and shape of families, depending on how many kids come with the new spouse. This can bring complications that need to be handled with tact—by parents as well as by kids.

Remarriage runs into complications because it requires adjustments different from those of the familiar family unit. "Because we see a family with two married adults and kids, we assume it will follow the same rules and patterns as intact families," explains a remarriage counselor. "But it won't—it's a whole new ball game."

Kids for example, may feel very sad and depressed, though they think they "should" be happy. Perhaps without realizing it, many children of divorce dream of a reunited ideal family that is better than their own actually ever was. Remarriage pops this fantasy. If a child's parent has died, the presence of a new parent may stir up memories of the dead parent, and act as a reminder that he or she is indeed gone forever.

Sometimes children of a new step-parent are frightened that their natural parent will desert them and turn all their attention to the newcomer. This is an understandable feeling and one that you should be aware of and not belittle.

> **Meaning?**
> Once called *step-families*, the family units that arise when parents bring their own children into a remarriage are now called *blended families*. (If the original parents have also remarried others, you have a *blended extended family*.) The term blended families avoids the "wicked" connotations of step-family.

Parents need to encourage family equality and cooperation, no matter whom "came first" or is related "by blood."

Playing Favorites

If one parent is playing favorites, it's something the two parents need to discuss in private and try to work out: Adults who care about each other and about their kids need to find a balance between themselves and the rest of the family. If this kind of conflict arises, counseling would be a wise step.

Dealing with Jealousy

It's also understandable that your children may feel jealous, either of the step-parent or of the step-parent's children (whether they live with you or not).

Beware of complaints that are really expressions of jealousy in disguise. How can you tell the difference and how do you know when serious trouble might be ahead? If your new partner is much closer to your kids' age than to yours, or if he or she has never had any experience dealing with kids, you may run into problems that will probably just take time to resolve. Meanwhile, be sure your kids are getting the attention they need.

> **Expert-Ease**
> Don't expect friendships among the kids to develop too quickly. Bonding takes time, and the kids need to be able to sort out their feelings about their new family. Encourage contact, but be careful not to push.

Sibling Rivalry

You can help your blended family get along by helping them find some small point of contact, something they have in common, and using this as a basis of friendship.

Don't expect the kids to immediately love one another; make it gradual and introduce your prospective spouse's kids gently! If you are the custodial parent and you have married someone with children whose primary residence is with their other parent, you are now the step-parent to those children, and you and your children will be welcoming those children to your home. If you are the non-custodial parent, you will be helping your children adjust to your new home, a new step-parent, and new step-brothers and step-sisters.

> **Expert-Ease**
> Remarriage even under the best of circumstances represents a big change, and any change in life can be upsetting. Also, it may come at a time when you're still coping with the loss of your previous family. Some research suggests that it can take as long as five years to get over a family break-up, and many single parents remarry within three years.

Relationships among your children require respect and care. Sexuality may arise among your kids—that's an issue to be aware of and to deal with carefully but not punitively: Punishing the children for natural (and not really *wrong*) instincts is counterproductive because society likely sees this as taboo. However, it probably needs to be curtailed. Outside counseling is especially useful here.

New Parent, Old Parent

And even under the best of circumstances, it's difficult to know how to feel about new family members and how to fit them in with your past. Your kids may wonder if the new adult, for example, is supposed to take the place of their other parent. Kids may ask, "Are those other kids supposed to be my siblings or your boyfriend's?"

Let your own children be able to seek reassurance and confess their fears ("I'm afraid you won't have time left for me"). In response, go out of your way to arrange a regular or special get-together-lunch once a week, the fishing trip you've always promised one another, a trip to the theater or a shopping excursion, or whatever suits your interests.

The emotional needs of the children must be placed ahead of those of the new spouse who is an adult and can adapt. Time will smooth things out if the kids feel comforted now.

Testing, Testing

Trying to undermine a marriage just by being unruly is a normal overreaction to stress. Kids can undermine a relationship indirectly, too—sometimes without realizing it because of a natural emotional state, but sometimes, let's face it, they do it on purpose. For instance, kids are often apt to put step-parents or live-in lovers to even tougher tests than they set for their parents. One teen sneered about her mother's various boyfriends, "Either he wanted to run my life, or he went and asked Mom everything." If your new partner has never had any experience in dealing with kids, he or she is especially likely to fail the in-house challenge.

Kids may also heavily test you to see if you still love them. "The first year Mom's boyfriend lived with us, we really made life hell for her," two sisters reported.

If your kids start acting up or acting out, try to be open and calm about it. Say, "You know, some kids get nervous when their parents remarry. I just want you to know that I love you, and I hope you'll be able to deal with this." Then just give it time.

> **Wise Words**
> "Keep an open mind," one teen recommends, and this may be the best advice of all. Try to avoid building up good or bad expectations in advance. A lot of children of single parents seem convinced, long before their parent is even considering a reattachment to anyone, that it's going to be "terrific" or "terrible." Instead, take it step-by-step.

> **Singular Successes**
> "Put yourself in their shoes" is advice that works for both parents and kids of blended families. One single-parent teen says when she could think about how she had felt in situations similar to her parents', whether it was falling in love or starting out on some new adventure, she could imagine how excited and confused her parents must feel.
>
> Likewise, a new step-parent, pregnant and trying to deal with her husband's obstreperous eight-year-old, suddenly saw what a shock all this newness must be to the little boy, and could be sympathetic instead of angry at him.

If you've given the new relationship time and your children are still not happy, or the family is still not working, consider getting counseling. Too few people do this, but it can be vital at such a troublesome time. Family therapists or marriage counselors can be useful, as can the books and organizations listed in Appendix A. Remember that adding a family member can be as difficult as losing one.

When Your Ex Remarries

The advice in this chapter applies if it's your spouse that's getting married. You still need to give your children (and yourself!) time to adjust to the idea. You still have to set limits on their behavior and respect their feelings. Your kids may have to grapple with jealousy in this case, since they will see that a new spouse (and possibly new children) are physically closer to their parent than they are. Your ex should try to give the kids as much special, one-on-one attention as is possible.

None of your family problems can be resolved easily or overnight. Remember, real life is not prime–time TV or the afternoon soaps. For single parenting and remarriage, as for any other major life change, real people need time, awareness, and communication to adjust to new ways of living.

The Least You Need to Know

- ➤ The decision to remarry is an adult decision, one you should make.
- ➤ Don't remarry just for the sake of having physical and financial support. Make sure your new partner will be good for your kids and yourself.
- ➤ When you have a blended family, you will have to make sure that you and your new partner treat all children fairly.
- ➤ If your blended family is not working—even after lots of time—consider therapy.

Appendix A

Resources

In-depth information on many of the subjects covered in this book is available from more specialized sources. Use this section as a beginning for further fact-finding.

Print, online, and in-person resources for information and support are arranged according to topic.

This is far from being a complete list. There are almost as many books related to parenting and life management as there are parents or families. But as you browse this list, the bookstore, or the Internet, look for resources that meet your needs.

You Are NOT Alone: Single-Parent Info and Support

Millions of single parents like you are parenting on their own, sharing common concerns and joys—and as the numbers grow, so does the support available in the form of groups, networks, and books. Here are a few resources to try.

Hotlines

The following organizations can offer immediate assistance or guidance when you or your kids are really feeling in trouble.

Boys Town (parenting help): 800-448-3000

Child Help: 800-422-4452

Missing Children: 800-426-5678

National Clearinghouse on Family Support and Children's Mental Health: 800-628-1696

National Council on Child Abuse and Family Violence: 800-222-2000

National Council on Family Relations: 888-791-9331

National Resource Center on Domestic Violence: 800-537-2238

National Youth Crisis Center: 800-448-4663

Planned Parenthood: 800-230-7526

Psychiatric Networks: 800-222-3151

Relationship Help: 800-432-6454

Teenline: 800-832-9623

Websites

The World Wide Web has many sites of value to single parents. These offer information, advice, and links to other resources, including networks of other single-parent families. The following are especially useful because they provide such a variety of links to related topics.

www.parentsoup.com

Highlight: its directory of relevant organizations.

www.parentsplace.com

For parenting of all kinds. Try the "Single Parents Reading Room" and "Single Parent Resource" e-zine and online chat groups.

www.hughson.com

"The Divorce Page" links to every aspect of this issue, including a Fathers' Page with extensive network of father-related sites.

www2.aaak.com

This "All About Kids" site features a single-parent forum.

www1.tmisnet.com

Highlight: Parents resource center includes useful links to other sites.

Single-Parent Groups

Contact these organizations for information, support, and advice; note that many have local chapters, so there may be one in your town.

National Organization of Single Mothers, Inc.
P.O. Box 68
Midland, NC 28107
(704) 888 2337

Parents Without Partners
401 N. Michigan Ave.
Chicago, IL 60611
(800) 637-7974

Single Mothers By Choice
P.O. Box 1642
Gracie Square Station
New York, NY 10028
(212) 988-0993
E-mail: mattes@pipeline.com

Books

Growing Up With a Single Parent: What Hurts, What Helps. Sara McLanahan, Gary Sandefur. Harvard University Press, 1996.
Professional advice based on national survey and decade-long research.

Mom's House, Dad's House: A Complete Guide for Parents Who Are Separated, Divorced, or Remarried. Isolina Ricci. Fireside/Simon & Schuster, 1997.
An updated classic on the legal, financial, and emotional realities of shared custody.

Positive Discipline for Single Parents: A Practical Guide to Raising Children Who Are Responsible, Respectful, and Resourceful. Jane Nelsen, et al. Prima, 1993.
Advice on creating a partnership between parent and child and toward developing responsibility in children.

Raising Sons Without Fathers: A Woman's Guide to Parenting Strong, Successful Boys. Leif G. Terdal, Patricia Kennedy. Birch Lane Press,1996.
Boys without fathers tend toward low achievement; this book offers guidance.

Single Fatherhood: The Complete Guide. Chuck Gregg. Sulzberger and Graham, 1995.
All about single parenting—for men.

Single Mothers by Choice: A Guidebook for Single Women Who Are Considering or Have Chosen Motherhood. Jane Mattes. Times Books, 1997.

The first handbook for a growing number of parents, by the president of the Single Mothers by Choice organization.

Whose Rights? What's Right? Support and Custody

The letter of the law is often filled with typos, but by paying attention, you can make optimal use of it anyway. Here are some additional resources offering advice and guidelines, with an emphasis on those resources that help you avoid damaging legal battles.

Websites

www.acf.dhhs.gov/ACFPrograms/CSE

This site, offered by the Office of Child Support Enforcement, provides links to states that have their own home pages providing information on child-support and custody issues.

www.divorcesupport.com

This "Divorce Page" links to a wide network of other resources concerned with support and custody, from various angles.

Groups

Academy of Family Mediators
4 Militia Dr.
Lexington, MA 02173
(617) 674-2663

Association for Children For Enforcement of Support (ACES)
2260 Upton Ave.
Toledo, OH 43606
(800) 537-7072

Grandparents Rights Organization
555 S Woodward Ave.
Birmingham, MI 48009
(248) 646-7191

Joint Custody Association
10606 Wilkins Ave.
Los Angeles, CA 90024
(310) 475-5352

National Center for Missing and Exploited Children
2101 Wilson Blvd
Arlington, VA 22201
(800) THE-LOST
Website: www.missingkids.org

Organization for the Enforcement of Child Support
1712 Deer Park Rd.
Finksburg, MD 21048
(410) 876-1826

Society of Professionals in Dispute Resolution
815 15th St. NW, Suite 530
Washington, DC 20005
(202) 783-7277

Books

The Best Interests of the Child: The Least Detrimental Alternative. Joseph Goldstein (Editor), et al. Free Press, 1996.
How to agree on custody with a minimum amount of intrusion by the legal system.

Child Custody: Building Agreements That Work. Mimi E. Lyster. Nolo Press, 1996.
Workbook that encourages parents to make a joint effort to avoid custody battles.

Child Support Survival Guide: How to Get Results Through Child Support Enforcement Agencies. Bonnie M. White, Douglas Pipes. Career Press, 1997.
An up-to-date guide. (See the Office of Child Support Enforcement Website, above).

Divorced Parent's Guide to Managing Custody & Visitation. Peter Favaro. Poseidon Press, 1996.
Valuable advice for every parent concerned about custody.

A Father's Rights: Hard-Hitting & Fair Advice for Every Father Involved in a Custody Dispute. Jeffery Leving, et al. HarperCollins, 1997.
Comprehensive guide for fathers seeking fair custody, by an expert in family law.

Grandparents' Rights: With Forms (Take the Law into Your Own Hands). Traci Truly. Galt Press, 1995.
Background and worksheets for grandparents to gain visitation or custody, organized by state.

Joint Custody and Co-Parenting: Sharing Your Child. Miriam Galper Cohen. Running Press, 1991.
A sensible approach to parenting apart.

Reinventing the Family: The Emerging Story of Lesbian and Gay Parents. Laura Benkov. Crown Publishing, 1994.

With millions of children in gay or lesbian families, this guide covers a wide range of topics, including issues of managing custody.

Being a Parent First: Guides to Raising Healthy, Confident Kids

Parentsoup, parentsplace, and the other sites listed earlier are good resources for all parenting issues. Check out the following sites, too.

www.aspensys.com/eric

This is ERIC (Education Resources Information Center), an excellent site sponsored by the U.S. Department of Education that covers every aspect of childraising. Check it out for links that include:

www.family.com

The Disney family site offers a variety of resources.

Groups

These professional organizations provide information as well as valuable, low-cost publications.

American Academy of Pediatrics
Department of Publications
141 Northwest Point Blvd.
Elk Grove Village, IL 60009-0927
E-mail: kidsdocs@aap.org
Website: www.aap.org

Big Brothers/Big Sisters of America
230 N 13th St.
Philadelphia, PA 19107
(215) 567-7000
E-mail: bbbsa@aol.com
Website: www.bbbsa.org

Child Welfare League of America
440 First St. NW
Washington DC 20001
(202) 638-2952
E-mail: hne898@handsnet.ort
Website: www.handsnet.org/cwla

Father Flanagan's Boys Home
14100 Crawford St.
Boys Town, NE 68010
(800) 321-4171
E-mail: helpkids@boystown.org
Website: www.boystown.org [Good parenting advice]

Foster Grandparents Program
1201 New York Ave. NW
Washington DC 20525
(800) 365-0153

Grandparents as Parents
P.O. Box 964
Lakewood, CA 90714
(562) 924-3996

National Association for Family Child Care
206 6th Ave.
Des Moines, IA 50309
(800) 359-3817

National Association for the Education of Young Children
1509 16th St. NW
Washington DC 20036-1426
(800) 424-2460

National Association of Child Care Resource and Referral Agencies
1319 F St. NW
Washington DC 20004
(800) 570-4543

National Council on Family Relations
3989 Central Ave. NE
Minneapolis, MN 55421
(888) 791-9331
E-mail: ncfr3989@ncfr.com
Website: www.ncfr.com

National PTA
330 N. Wabash Ave.
Suite #2100
Chicago, IL 60611
(312) 951-6782

Parents Anonymous
675 W Foothill Blvd.
Claremont, CA 91711
(909) 621-6184

Parents Helping Parents
3041 Olcott St.
Santa Clara, CA 95054
(408) 727-5775
Website: www.php.com

Books

101 Ways Parents Can Help Students Achieve. K. Amundson. American Association of School Administrators, 1991.
Advice on support without interference.

Between Parent and Child. Haim G. Ginott. Avon Books, 1982.
A classic of child "management"; still of great value.

Child Behavior: The Classic Childcare Manual from the Gesell Institute of Human Development. Frances L. Ilg, Louise B. Ames, Sidney Baker. Harper Perennial Library, 1997.
A careful guide through childhood, still among the best.

The Complete Idiot's Guide to Grandparenting. Walter and Marilyn Hartt with Will Cross. Alpha Books, 1997.
How today's grandparents can maintain bonds in spite of divorce, separation, and remarriages.

Dr. Spock on Parenting. Benjamin Spock. Pocket Books, 1995.
Trusted expert on issues related to *today's* parents.

Don't Take It Out On Your Kids. Katherine Kersey. Berkley Books, 1994.
Guide to positive discipline.

Grandparenting in a Changing World. Eda LeShan. Newmarket Press, 1997.
Revered parenting expert turns her attention to a new form of parenting.

The Little Things Make a Big Difference: How to Help Your Children Succeed in School. National Association of Elementary School Principals, 1991.
A helpful guide to encouraging academic achievement.

P.E.T. Dr. Theodore Gordon. New American Library, 1990.
Parent Effectiveness Training from a professional.

Princeton Center for Infancy and Early Childhood Series on Child Development. Theresa and Frank Caplan. Bantam, 1983.

A thorough, factual description of development and behavior at each stage of young development: separate volumes cover the first year, second year, and ages 2 to 6.

Professional Help and How to Find It

If your family's problems are too much to bear, counseling or therapy may be the answer.

Websites

Web pages provide information, links, and in some cases, counseling. A word to the wise: These sites are fine places for blowing off steam, but be wary of anonymous cybertherapy.

To get an idea of the kinds of things people "have on their minds," and to find links to specific health matters, visit:

www.counselingnet.com

www.psych-web.com

www.wantree.com.au

Groups

The following professional associations provide information and referrals.

American Association for Marriage and Family Therapy
1133 15th St. NW
Washington DC 20005
(800) 374-2638
Website: www.aamft.org

American Counseling Association
5999 Stephenson Ave.
Alexandria, VA 22304
(800) 347-6647
Website: www.counseling.org

Facing Your Financial Facts

Dealing squarely with money matters can be scary. These resources can make the effort less painful.

Websites

www.cccsdc.org

The Consumer Credit Counseling Service is a non-profit, community service organization that provides free professional guidance. This Website helps you figure where you are and where you're going financially.

Books

1,001 Bright Ideas to Stretch Your Dollars: Pinch Your Pennies, Hoard Your Quarters, Collar Your Dollars. Cynthia G. Yates. Vine Publishing, 1995.
A handy how-to.

Bonnie's Household Budget Book: The Essential Workbook for Getting Control of Your Money. Bonnie Runyan McCullough. St Martins Press, 1996.
A classic, practical guide, updated and revised.

The Budget Kit: The Common Cents Money Management Workbook. Judy Lawrence. Dearborn Press, 1997.
Easy-to-use system for organizing a budget.

The Complete Idiot's Guide to Managing Your Money. Robert Heady, Christy Heady. Alpha Books, 1995.
Everything you want to know about keeping track of your finances and how to invest wisely.

The Consumer Reports Money Book: How to Get It, Save It, and Spend It Wisely. Janet Bambord, et al. St Martins Press, 1997.
Detailed, solid guidance.

Living on a Shoestring. Ann Fox Chodakowski, Susan Fox Wood. DTP Publishers, 1998.
"The Tightwad Twins" on how to live comfortably without spending a lot.

Making the Most of Your Money. Jane Bryant Quinn. Simon & Schuster, 1997.
Best-selling down-to-earth expertise.

What Works

Of course, single parents can have careers! Here, some heads-up resources and a few of the multitudinous career-advice books. (Dads, don't be discouraged if some of the sources mention "working moms": the advice within applies to all working single parents.)

Groups

Working Mother Magazine
P.O. Box 5240
Harlan, IA 51593-2740
(800) 627-0690
Website: www.womanweb.com

Families & Work Institute
330 7th Ave.
New York, NY 10001
(212) 465-2044
Website: www.familiesandwork.org

Books

The Best Home Businesses for the 90s: The Inside Information You Need to Know to Select a Home-Based Business That's Right for You. Paul Edwards, Sarah Edwards. Tarcher, 1995.
Hands on advice from self-employment experts.

Career Change: Everything You Need to Know to Meet New Challenges and Take Control of Your Career. David P. Helfand. VGM Career Horizons, 1995.
Information and hand-on access, career-guidance materials, plus resource lists and Website.

Work of Her Own: A Woman's Guide to Success Off the Career Track. Susan Wittig Albert. Tarcher, 1994.
How to re-examine and reclaim one's worklife.

The Working Parents Handbook. Katherine Murray. JistWorks, 1996.
"How to succeed at work, raise your kids, maintain a home and still have time for you."

First Things First: Getting Organized

Books

Confessions of a Happily Organized Family. Deniece Schofield. Betterways Publishing, 1997.
A commonsense how-to.

The Essential Home Record Book: Ready-to-Use Forms for All Your Personal, Medical, Household, and Financial Information. Pamela K. Pfeffer. Plume, 1997.
Does the necessary for you.

Organize Your Home!: Simple Routines for Managing Your Household. Ronni Eisenberg, Kate Kelly. Hyperion, 1994.
Step-by-step system for keeping things simple.

How to Clean Practically Anything. Editors of *Consumer Reports*. Consumers Union, 1993.
A practical and thorough guide.

Re: Marriage

Marriage with children can be a special challenge. Here's some guidance toward meeting that challenge.

Websites

Many of the Websites listed previously have information on and links to "blending" families—worth checking out.

www.flyingsolo.com

Groups

StepFamily Association of America
6240 Maryland Dr.
Los Angeles, CA 90048
(213) 935-7529

Books

The Complete Idiot's Guide to Stepparenting. Erika Lutz. Alpha Books, 1998.
A warm, humorous guide to successful stepparenting.

Developing Healthy Stepfamilies. Patricia Kelley. Haworth Press, 1995.
Families tell their own stories.

Positive Discipline for Blended Families. Jane Nelson, Ed. D. Prima, 1997.
How to develop partnerships among children in remarriages.

Appendix B

Meaning? Glossary

Acting out   Behavior (usually negative) that children and teens use to express feelings they can't explain verbally.

Alimony   Payment to a former spouse or partner agreed to at separation; not usually collectible by public agency.

Blended families   Once called "stepfamilies"; this term is used to describe the pseudo-sibling relationships that arise when parents bring their own children into a remarriage. (The original parents may have also remarried others, making a blended extended family.)

Boundaries   The appropriate psycho-emotional separation of individuals, allowing for the development of independent identities.

Childcare in a home setting   Refers to childcare workers, such as babysitters or nannies, who come to the home in order to watch the children. Not usually regulated or licensed by the state.

Child support   Money owed by the non-custodial parent to the custodial parent to pay expenses for childcare; collectible by public agencies if necessary.

Child Support Enforcement Program   An office of the Federal government that enforces child support.

Chronic depression or **major depression**   A serious emotional disorder requiring professional help.

Co-dependent   An unhealthy, overly close relationship in which each party is made to "live for" the other and made to feel incapable of freedom.

Cognitive development   Growth in the ability to learn.

Counselor   Advisor; generic word for therapist or other person giving guidance.

Custodial parent   The parent who holds the child in custody.

Custody   The condition of caring for a child. Custody is not ownership.

Developmental tasks   A behavioral achievement appropriate to a given stage or age: grasping is one of the developmental tasks of early infancy; walking, of early toddlerhood.

Discipline   The word is related to "disciple," or one who follows a teacher. Discipline means teaching, not punishment.

Discretionary income   Money left over after living expenses are paid; discretionary income is used for unnecessary items like entertainment.

Displaced anger   Anger that is expressed toward people or objects other than the actual source of the anger. Kids who get into many fights on the playground, for instance, may be driven by anger toward a parent who they feel has let them down.

Double standard   In terms of single parents and their kids, the double standard refers to one set of sex-and-dating rules that applies to the parent, and another, stricter set that applies to the children.

Family   A group of people related by blood or marriage or living together within the same household.

Family daycare   Daycare provided in the home of another person who may care for several children at once. Family daycare providers may or may not require licensing. This is often the preferred type of out-of-home care for infants and very young children.

Family-friendly employer   One that provides benefits and options, such as on-site childcare or flextime—that make it comfortable to be both a parent and an employee.

Flextime   Employers' means of adapting job schedules to fit family demands.

Garnished   Having a portion of a paycheck set aside to pay off a debt, usually as the result of a court order.

Gender bias   Any situation that assumes a role can only be filled by one gender or another.

Group family care   Daycare provided in a caregiver's home; usually regulated by government authorities.

Identity An individual's sense of who he or she is as a consistent personality.

Income withholding The prior allocation of salary from each paycheck for the purpose of making payments elsewhere.

Intact A word used in social service professions to refer to married, never-divorced families with children. As such, it's a useful shorthand term, but the suggestion that divorced or non-married parents with kids are "broken" is a holdover from a previous era.

Internalizing A feeling or state of mind that refers to taking the love, comfort, protection, and security that a parent or early caretaker provides externally to an infant or toddler, and developing a solid sense of that affection and support to strengthen the child as he or she grows.

Job sharing Dividing the duties—and salary—of a single employee between two or more employees.

Joint custody Both parents share in legal custody, physical custody, or both.

Latchkey children Children left at home alone by working parents. The name derives from the house key they must carry—often around their necks—to let themselves in after school.

Legal custody The right and obligation to make decisions about the child's care.

Mediation Intervention in a dispute by a neutral party trained in negotiation.

Non-custodial parent The parent who does not hold the child in custody. The noncustodial parent usually (although not always) is granted *visitation*, which means the right to visit the child according to a certain schedule.

Obsessive-Compulsive Disorder (OCD) A combination of obsessions (recurrent and persistent thoughts, impulses, or images that cause marked anxiety or distress) and compulsions (repetitive behaviors or mental acts that the person feels driven to perform in response to an obsession) aimed at preventing or reducing distress.

Out-of-home care Childcare that takes place at public or private childcare centers. Can be full- or parttime. Licensing is usually required.

Parent To care for, defend, and take responsibility for a child into adulthood. Comes from the Latin for "giving birth."

Physical custody A parent's right to have a child live with him or her.

Positive identification The incorporation into one's self of the characteristics of another.

Psychiatrist A psychotherapist with a medical degree.

Psychologist   A psychotherapist without an M.D. who may hold a Ph.D. or lesser degree.

Psychosocial boundaries   These define who we are as separate from each other. They are critical for healthy development, especially as children separate from parents.

Psychosomatic ailments   Physical responses to emotional or psychological stress.

Regression   Returning to more babyish patterns in one or more areas of behavior (for example, when a school-age child reverts to thumb-sucking).

Role reversal   When a child takes over some (or all) of the functions normally expected of a parent, even to the point of becoming in some sense a parent or caretaker of the adult.

School-age childcare   Childcare for children ages 5 to approximately 12 that takes place during non-school hours (often referred to as "before and after-school care") is found in a variety of settings. Often state licensed and formally programmed.

Self-esteem   A combination of how we feel about ourselves and how we believe that others perceive us, also as a sense of being both capable and worthy of love.

Separation anxiety   Inappropriate or excessive anxiety concerning separation from home or from those to whom an individual is attached, marked by signs of distress, fear of the loss of or harm to the attachment figure, fear of being alone, reluctance to leave home or go to school, recurrent nightmares, and being physically upset when attachment figure is absent.

Sequential organization   A business management term for doing first things first.

Single parent   Any adult raising one or more children for a period of time without the aid of a partner. Includes single Moms, single Dads, and single grandparents raising grandchildren.

Situational depression or **reactive depression**   A down phase tied to a specific event, like loss from death or divorce.

Social worker   A professional counselor who often works as a therapist.

Telecommuting   Working from home on a computer, modem, phone, and fax in areas such as editorial, telemarketing, and database management jobs, where being on-site is not essential.

Visitation   The formal arrangement allowing for connection between non-custodial separated parents and their children.

Visitation order   The court decree defining the visitation rights of the non-custodial parent.

Visitation schedule   The schedule by which visitation occurs.

Appendix C

Checklist Checkup

Now that you've worked through *The Complete Idiot's Guide to Single Parenting*, you can use it to create your *own* guide to single parenting. Go back to the worksheets and questionnaires in each chapter and review your responses. How far have you (and your family) progressed since you first filled them out? Maybe you've worked through some difficult issues in recent weeks and months. On the other hand, perhaps you now have to face new crises that have developed.

As you know through your experiences as a single parent, self-discovery is an ongoing process that can help you locate untapped inner resources. By repeatedly returning to the checklists and personal inventories included here, you can continually review the strengths you and your family have developed—and the challenges you all face.

How Do You Feel About Single Parenting?

Are you a single parent by:

_____ Choice   _____ Chance   _____ Death   _____ Desertion

Was your separation from your partner—or decision to not attach to him/her—made:

____In an amicable context?   ____In a hostile context?

What kind of difference does that make in your attitude toward your situation—and perhaps toward your children as well?

Biggest positive impact: _____
_____
_____
_____
_____
_____

Biggest negative impact: _____
_____
_____
_____
_____
_____

Checklist Checkup

Single Parent Worry Worksheet

Write down the issues that you are most concerned about in each area of your life:

Your kids _____
_____
_____

Your finances _____
_____
_____

Your family's security _____
_____
_____

Your family's health and safety _____
_____
_____

Your legal problems _____
_____
_____

Your job _____
_____
_____

Your physical and mental health _____
_____
_____

Your relationships _____
_____
_____

Your romantic life _____
_____
_____

Personal Style Self-test

Use a scale of 1 to 8 to profile your own personal style. Begin by rating each descriptive line with "1" for "least like me" to "8" for "most like me."

          least like me   most like me

I...

P	Tend to work quickly, often impatiently	1 2 3 4 5 6 7 8
O	Like to have a plan to work by	1 2 3 4 5 6 7 8
R	Prefer to use old skills rather than learn new ones	1 2 3 4 5 6 7 8
A	Value making other people happy	1 2 3 4 5 6 7 8
L	Enjoy analyzing things (problems and people)	1 2 3 4 5 6 7 8
S	Enjoy working by myself	1 2 3 4 5 6 7 8
E	Adapt to change easily	1 2 3 4 5 6 7 8
N	Dislike routine	1 2 3 4 5 6 7 8

I...

R	Am precise and detail-oriented	1 2 3 4 5 6 7 8
A	Like to feel that people are getting along well	1 2 3 4 5 6 7 8
E	Tend to take on too many projects to finish comfortably	1 2 3 4 5 6 7 8
P	Focus on results more than process	1 2 3 4 5 6 7 8
O	Dislike working on more than one project at once	1 2 3 4 5 6 7 8
N	Rush work even to the point of carelessness	1 2 3 4 5 6 7 8
S	Find it difficult to remember faces and names	1 2 3 4 5 6 7 8
L	Am uncomfortable interacting emotionally with others	1 2 3 4 5 6 7 8

I...

E	Am influenced in decision-making by personal feelings	1 2 3 4 5 6 7 8
L	Appreciate fairness and rational orderliness	1 2 3 4 5 6 7 8
S	Often have trouble communicating with others	1 2 3 4 5 6 7 8
N	Enjoy learning new techniques more than putting them to use	1 2 3 4 5 6 7 8
A	Tend to work in spurts rather than steadily	1 2 3 4 5 6 7 8
R	Proceed step by step to a result	1 2 3 4 5 6 7 8
O	Need minimal info to initiate projects	1 2 3 4 5 6 7 8
P	Enjoy variety	1 2 3 4 5 6 7 8

Checklist Checkup

I...

A	Am sensitive to other people's needs	1 2 3 4 5 6 7 8
R	Don't enjoy being presented with new problems	1 2 3 4 5 6 7 8
O	Come to quick decisions about things and people	1 2 3 4 5 6 7 8
S	Dislike being interrupted	1 2 3 4 5 6 7 8
L	Am able to take the "personal" component out of a job	1 2 3 4 5 6 7 8
E	Feel comfortable with open-ended projects and situations	1 2 3 4 5 6 7 8
P	Enjoy working with other people around	1 2 3 4 5 6 7 8
N	Follow my intuitions	1 2 3 4 5 6 7 8

I...

L	Don't have much need for others' approval	1 2 3 4 5 6 7 8
O	Need to come to conclusions about people & situations	1 2 3 4 5 6 7 8
E	Am curious and excited about new situations	1 2 3 4 5 6 7 8
S	Need a quiet setting for work	1 2 3 4 5 6 7 8
A	Avoid unpleasant communications	1 2 3 4 5 6 7 8
N	Can deal calmly with complicated processes	1 2 3 4 5 6 7 8
P	Enjoy interacting with people	1 2 3 4 5 6 7 8
R	Don't rely on intuition	1 2 3 4 5 6 7 8

Now, total the rank-number "scores" for each letter-code:

P = _____

E = _____

R = _____

S = _____

O = _____

N = _____

A = _____

L = _____

Circle the four letter-items with the highest number scores.

Write down those four corresponding letters here:

_____

continues

continued

> Each letter represents an aspect of your PERSONAL style:
>
> **P** or **people-oriented** types tend to turn attention outward, to others, and the environment.
>
> **E** or **enthusiastic types** are generally spontaneous, curious, and available for new experiences. (They occasionally have difficulty completing more mundane tasks.)
>
> **R** or **right-now types** dwell in the present and rely on directly observed information.
>
> **S** or **self-focused types** look inward and focus on their own emotions and ideas. (They may have some difficulty dealing with others.)
>
> **O** or **organized types** plan step by step approaches to life and appreciate arriving at decisions (and are sometimes put off by unexpected change).
>
> **N** or **new-facing types** have faith in possibilities and the future (and may perhaps pay less attention to the present).
>
> **A** or **appreciative types** operate from personal judgments (and sometimes ignore hard facts).
>
> **L** or **logical types** base their decisions and opinions on rational analysis and tend to focus closely on tasks (sometimes to the exclusion of human factors).
>
> When you tally up your scores, stop and give them some thought. What do they say about how you get along in the world and with other people—about how you feel about your own value?
>
> Career experts know that if your career goals don't match your personality type, success may be elusive (and perhaps not even satisfying, even when you do achieve it). You will have a better chance at happiness when you allow your goals to grow out of your personality.

Checklist Checkup

Dream Analysis Worksheet

To get a clear view of your personal and emotional assets and liabilities, open up your dreams and take a look at some personality possibilities.

DREAMS

Begin with what you liked playing as a kid. What's your earliest memory of a life-dream? Write it down, even if it seems silly.

_____
_____

MORE DREAMS

What did you want to be when you were in elementary school?
_____

In junior high? _____

In high school? _____

What do you do in your free time? Note what kinds of activities you most enjoy watching or reading about:
_____

What kinds of activities send you into daydreaming? _____
_____

And now, today, if you could do anything at all in life, what would it be? (Forget what you think it OUGHT to be—or what would be good for your children. For just this moment, focus on what YOU want.) _____
_____

What do your dreams, then and now, have in common? Describe in a few words:
_____

DOING: Are you doing something actively, with your hands or body?
_____

RELATING: Are you relating with other people? In what context? (Groups, helping, supervising, one on one...) _____

EXCELLING: What marks excellence in your dreams? Creating a product? Completing a project? Winning at something? Hearing applause?
_____

ACTIVITY LEVEL: How active are you in your dream: Are you sedentary? Vigorous? Moderate? _____

THINKING: How much of your dream work relies on your mind more than the rest of you? (As in creating, thinking, planning, etc.)
_____

SETTING: Where does your dream take place? Outdoors? Inside? In a specific location?
_____

Charting Your Goals Worksheet

With your "dreams" in mind, write down one major life-goal for each area:

Relationship-related goal: _____
_____
_____

Work-related goal: _____
_____
_____

Self-related goal: _____
_____
_____

Now, write down three specific steps you could take toward achieving those goals:

Relationship-related goal: _____
_____
_____
_____

Work-related goal: _____
_____
_____
_____

Self-related goal: _____
_____
_____
_____

Now, from the information you've put down, make some to-do lists.

What are the three qualities or characteristics about yourself that you like the most?
_____
_____
_____
_____

List three ways you'll put them to good use:
_____
_____
_____

What are the three that you like the least?
_____
_____
_____

List three ways you'll work to change them:
_____
_____
_____

Where would you like to be in:
5 years: _____
_____
_____

10 years: _____
_____
_____

15 years: _____
_____
_____

And three actions you can take right now toward getting there:
_____
_____
_____

Watching the Kids Worksheet

If your single-parent status is new, list three behaviors of your child/children that are different than previously.

1. _____
_____

2. _____
_____

3. _____
_____

Have others—family, teachers, neighbors—commented on changes in your children's behavior? What are they? _____
_____
_____

If you've been a single parent for a while, has any change in status occurred that might cause reaction in kids? _____
_____
_____

My child wants most from me as a parent:

_____ Unconditional Love   _____ Caring firmness

_____ Consistency   _____ Understanding of his/her needs

_____ Respect   _____ All of the above

_____ My presence

Checklist: What's Fun?

Three activities my kids really enjoy (away from me) are:
_____
_____
_____
_____

Three activities I really enjoy away from my kids are:
_____
_____
_____
_____

Three activities I can plan now to share with my kids are:
_____
_____
_____
_____

If you have a very hard time answering those questions, something's missing. So step back and evaluate:

My kids and I (check one):

_____ work well together

_____ play well together

_____ seem to always be in each other's way

_____ should spend more time together

_____ should spend less time together

This checklist should give you an idea of how you can better spend time with your kids. Single parents must be creative with their time because they don't have a lot of it. In the next few chapters, I'll show you how to organize your time with your children so you all can make the most of it.

Legal Issues Worksheet

Why am I continuing my legal struggles?

_____ Because I need what I'm demanding

_____ Because I want to hurt my former partner

What do my children really want?

_____ To be with me alone

_____ To be with their other parent alone

_____ To have time with both of us

Do I know what they really want? _____Yes _____No

Have I ever used my children as bait to get something from their other parent? _____Yes   _____No

Why do I want custody?

_____ Because I love the kids

_____ Because I hate their other parent

Am I truly willing to let go of the other parent—or struggling to NOT let go?

_____

_____

Am I comfortable letting my children go? _____Yes   _____No

Have I tried every non-confrontational procedural aid—or gone straight to court?

_____

_____

Do I always meet MY terms of the agreements in question?

_____

_____

Do I ever use any of our points of conflict to point the finger at my former spouse or other family members in front of the kids?

_____

_____

Wish List Worksheet

If you could arrange our living space any way you wanted, what would you wish for?
_____
_____
_____

If we could furnish our living space anyway we wanted, what would you wish for?
_____
_____
_____
_____

Now for each wish think of a do-able step to take toward it: (For example, "Someday I'd like to re-decorate the whole place." OK, go to a paint store and pick out some paint colors and wallpaper patterns to play with.)
_____
_____
_____
_____

List 5 household items we NEED:

What we need	What it costs	How do we get it?
1.		
2.		
3.		
4.		
5.		

List 5 household items we WANT:

What we want	What it costs	How do we get it?
1.		
2.		
3.		
4.		
5.		

Chores To Do:

Yearly: _____
_____
_____
_____
_____
_____

Semi annually _____
_____
_____
_____
_____
_____

Monthly: _____
_____
_____
_____
_____
_____

Weekly: _____
_____
_____
_____
_____
_____

Daily: _____
_____
_____
_____
_____
_____

Weekly Assignment List

Chore	Who Does It	When It Gets Done

Where Does Your Money Go?

Living Expenses   **Monthly Payment**

Housing
- Rent or Mortgage   _____
- 2nd Mortgage   _____
- Condo/Co-op Fee   _____

Utilities
- Gas/Heating Oil   _____
- Electric   _____
- Water   _____
- Telephone   _____
- Cable   _____

Food
- Groceries   _____
- Household Supplies   _____
- Dining Out   _____

Transportation
- Auto payment   _____
- Auto maintenance   _____
- Gas/Oil   _____
- Parking   _____
- Commuter fares   _____

*Alimony/Child Support

Childcare
- Sitter   _____
- Tuition, school fees   _____
- Daycare/After-school fees   _____
- Transportation   _____
- Lunches, snacks   _____

Living Expenses   **Monthly Payment**

Personal
- Cosmetics/Hair Care   _____
- Tobacco/Alcohol   _____

Checklist Checkup

Books/Papers/Magazines _____
Clothing
  Your clothing _____
  Your children's clothing _____
  Laundry/Dry Cleaning _____
  Other _____

Recreation
  Entertainment _____
  Membership fees (i.e. gym) _____
  Other _____

Periodic Expenses (divide into monthly amounts)

*Insurance
  Life _____
  Health _____
  Disability _____
  Homeowners/Renters _____
  Auto _____

*Taxes
  Personal Property _____
  Income Taxes _____
  Other local taxes _____
  Emergencies/Repairs _____
  Vacations _____

*Medical Expenses
  General medical visits _____
  Dental/Eye Care _____
  Medications _____
  Other _____

Miscellaneous
  Gifts _____
  Dues _____
  Contributions _____

Other items not listed here: _____

TOTAL Monthly Expenses: _____

*Don't include amounts that already may be deducted from your paycheck.

Where Does Your Money Come From?

Source	Amount
Paycheck (from first job, less deductions)	_____
Paycheck (from second job, less deductions)	_____
Alimony	_____
Child Support	_____
Social Security	_____
Insurance Settlement	_____
Dividend Income	_____
V.A. Benefits	_____
Rental Income	_____
Interest Income	_____
Unemployment Income	_____
Freelance Income	_____
Other	_____
TOTAL	_____

Budget Sheet

Expense Item	Planned Cost	Actual Cost
Household costs	_____	_____
Utilities	_____	_____
Food	_____	_____
Transportation	_____	_____
Childcare/Support	_____	_____
Insurance	_____	_____
Credit cards	_____	_____
Other	_____	_____
	_____	_____
	_____	_____
	_____	_____
Total	_____	_____

Fun-Focus Checklist

Check off any activity in this list that you enjoy or that you would like to try. Have your kids do the same. Then review the list together. Items that have two checkmarks are things you can pursue as family activities. Those with one checkmark are ones that each of you can make a center of your individual social lives.

The Arts
- ❏ Dance
- ❏ Drawing
- ❏ Music, singing
- ❏ Music, instrumental
- ❏ Painting
- ❏ Photography
- ❏ Sculpture
- ❏ Writing, poetry

Athletics
- ❏ Archery
- ❏ Badminton
- ❏ Baseball
- ❏ Basketball
- ❏ Boccie
- ❏ Bowling
- ❏ Boxing
- ❏ Football
- ❏ Golf
- ❏ Handball
- ❏ Hockey
- ❏ Horseshoes
- ❏ Ping-pong
- ❏ Pool
- ❏ Racquetball
- ❏ Soccer
- ❏ Softball
- ❏ Tennis
- ❏ Track & Field
- ❏ Volleyball
- ❏ Wrestling

Crafts and Hobbies
- ❏ Baking
- ❏ Carpentry/Woodworking
- ❏ Ceramics
- ❏ Cooking
- ❏ Gardening

Community Events
- ❏ Concerts
- ❏ Dance
- ❏ Film
- ❏ Museums
- ❏ Readings
- ❏ Theater

Fitness/Individual Sports
- ❏ Bicycling
- ❏ Exercise classes
- ❏ Gymnastics
- ❏ Ice skating
- ❏ Jogging
- ❏ Martial Arts
- ❏ Rollerblading/Rollerskating
- ❏ Swimming
- ❏ Walking
- ❏ Weight lifting
- ❏ Yoga

Games
- ❏ Bingo
- ❏ Board games
- ❏ Cards
- ❏ Checkers
- ❏ Chess
- ❏ Dominoes
- ❏ Video games

Socializing
- ❏ Book clubs
- ❏ Card clubs
- ❏ Chat groups
- ❏ Dances
- ❏ Service clubs, scouts
- ❏ Sports clubs

Outdoors
- ❏ Archery
- ❏ Boating
- ❏ Camping
- ❏ Canoeing
- ❏ Cycling
- ❏ Fishing
- ❏ Hiking
- ❏ Sailing
- ❏ Shooting
- ❏ Skiing

Need to Know Checklist

List the names and phone numbers of all individuals and organizations in your community that may be a source of support to you and your children.

Neighbors

_____

_____

_____

Teachers

_____

_____

_____

PTA members

_____

_____

_____

Religious leaders

_____

_____

_____

Support group members

_____

_____

_____

Family Members

_____

_____

_____

Appendix D

Single Parent Problem Solver

Being a single parent means single-handedly juggling your responsibilities at work, taking care of your kids, running your household, managing the family budget, and still trying to carve out time for your own goals and dreams. It can seem impossible to handle—but not if you tackle one problem at a time. This guide shows you how to find answers to some of the most pressing problems single parents face.

Part One: You Are NOT Alone

If you want to…	See page
Understand and face the fears common to many single parents	16
Understand your personal style—and what it means for your career and your life	24
Analyze your dreams—and plan to make them come true	28

Part Two: Keeping an Eye on the Kids

If you want to…	See page
Understand what to do when your kids act out	36
Learn what it means if your kids show regressive behavior	37
Discipline your teenager effectively	44
Decide whether or not to use physical punishment as a disciplinary tool	49
Choose a therapist if your family problems are too difficult to handle alone	53

Develop self-esteem in your kids 57
Understand what co-dependency is—and avoid a co-dependent relationship
with your kids 60
Understand the custody process 68
Work out a fair joint custody plan with your ex 69
Discover how to calculate child support 72
Mediate custody and support battles—without going to court 76
Learn how to write your will 80
Understand your childcare options 84
Discover creative ways to finance quality childcare 85
Evaluate the safety of your children's child care 86

Part 3: Finding Space and Time

If you want to…   See page

Discover creative ways to furnish your space on a low budget 94
Set up private space for each family member—even in close quarters 95
Make your space safe for your kids 97
Get your entire family to help keep your place clean and organized 103
Simplify your life 105
Choose household chores that your kids can do 109
Delegate chores amongst your family so everything gets done 110
Save time on errands 118
Keep track of your kids' schedules 120
Rearrange custody and visitation rights 121
Beat burnout 122

Part 4: Money Matters

If you want to…   See page

Discover where all your money goes 128
Collect child support and alimony 132
Uncover other sources of support for your family 133
Use credit carefully 134
Put the importance of money in its proper perspective 136
Set a realistic budget—and stick to it 141

Brainstorm ways to make more money 143
Save on expenses (without living like a monk) 144
Set financial goals for the long term 148
Boost your savings accounts 149
Find a job that's right for you 151
Learn what a family-friendly company is—and why you want to
work for one 154
Learn how to negotiate with your employer to make your work
hours more flexible 155
Decide whether or not to go back to school 157
Explore ways of working at home 159

Part 5: The Buddy System: Friends

If you want to…   See page

Build your social network 165
Find other single parent families you and your kids can spend time with 166
Encourage your kids to make friends 167
Brainstorm fun activities you can enjoy with your kids 169
Discover a single parenting support group that's right for you 174
Start your own group for single parents in your area 176
Decide when you are ready to start dating 181
Feel free to date—without upsetting your kids 182
Help your kids and your dates to get along 186

Part 6: You Are Family

If you want to…   See page

Learn how to share your children with your ex—peacefully 195
Make sure you and your ex enforce consistent disciplinary rules
and regulations 197
Arrange visitation fairly 199
Learn how to parent successfully even if you live far from your kids 199
Discover the signs that visitation may not be working out 200
Let your ex's family stay in touch with your kids 204

Decide whether or not to get married—and determine its effect on
your kids 219
Build a successful blended family.. 219
Handle sibling rivalry, favoritism, and other issues that arise in newly
blended families 220

Index

A

abuse (child)
   National Council on Child Abuse and Family Violence hotline, 224
   Parents Anonymous, 50
Academy of Family Mediators, 226
acting out behaviors, 36-37, 235
adult education
   criteria, 158-159
   increasing earning power, 157-159
after-school activities
   children, 85, 167-168
   misbehavior, 48
age and discipline, 42-43
alcohol abuse by teenagers, 48
alimony, 235
   eligibility as custodial parent, 132
All About Kids Web site, 224
American Academy of Pediatrics, 228
American Counseling Association, 231
anger, displaced, 18
arts as children's leisure activities, 169, 258
assets, calculating, 131-132
assigning chores to children, 110-111
At Home Dads, 174
at-home jobs, 159-160
athletics as children's leisure activities, 170, 258

B

babies, abnormal behavior, 43-44
baby-sitting co-ops, 86
bedrooms, space-saving tips, 93
behavior
   abnormal behavior
      babies, 43-44
      pre-teens, 44
      teenagers, 44
   acting out, 36-37
Child Behavior: The Classic Childcare Manual from the Gesell Institute of Human Development, 230
   children, acting out, 36-37
   pre-teens, abnormal behavior, 44
   professional assistance, 52-53
   regression, 37
   teenagers, 44
The Best Interests of the Child: The Least Detrimental Alternative, 227
Between Parent and Child, 230
Big Brothers/Big Sisters of America, 54, 228
blended families, 235
   children's jealousy, 220
   defined, 219
   dynamics, 219
   emotional complications, 219
   goals, 219
   perceived emotional neglect, 220-221
   playing favorites by adults, 219
   sibling rivalries, 220
   testing behaviors by children, 221-222

bonding activities with family, 212-213
Bonnie's Household Budget Book: The Essential Workbook for Getting Control of Your Money, 232
books
- 101 Ways Parents Can Help Students Achieve, 230
- 1,001 Bright Ideas to Stretch Your Dollars: Pinch Your Pennies, Hoard Your Quarters, Collar Your Dollars, 232
- The Best Interests of the Child: The Least Detrimental Alternative, 227
- Between Parent and Child, 230
- Bonnie's Household Budget Book: The Essential Workbook for Getting Control of Your Money, 232
- The Budget Kit: The Common Cents Money Management Workbook, 232
- Career Change: Everything You Need to Know to Meet New Challenges and Take Control of Your Career, 233
- Child Behavior: The Classic Childcare Manual from the Gesell Institute of Human Development, 230
- Child Custody: Building Agreements That Work, 227
- Complete Idiot's Guide to Grandparenting, 232
- Complete Idiot's Guide to Managing Your Money, 232
- Confessions of a Happily Organized Family, 233
- Divorced Parent's Guide to Managing Custody & Visitation, 227
- Don't Take It Out On Your Kids, 230
- Dr. Spock on Parenting, 230
- Grandparenting in a Changing World, 230
- Growing Up With a Single Parent: What Hurts, What Helps, 225
- How to Clean Practically, 234
- Joint Custody and Co-Parenting: Sharing Your Child, 227
- Little Things Make a Big Difference: How To Help Your Children Succeed in School, 230
- Living on a Shoestring, 232
- Making the Most of Your Money, 232
- Mom's House, Dad's House: A Complete Guide for Parents Who Are Separated, Divorced, or Remarried, 225
- Organize Your Home!: Simple Routines for Managing Your Household, 234
- Positive Discipline for Blended Families, 234
- Princeton Center for Infancy and Early Childhood Series on Child Development, 231
- Raising Sons Without Fathers: A Woman's Guide to Parenting Strong, Successful Boys, 225
- Reinventing the Family: The Emerging Story of Lesbian and Gay Parents, 228
- Single Fatherhood: The Complete Guide, 225
- Single Mothers by Choice: A Guidebook for Women Who Are Considering or Have Chosen Motherhood, 226
- Work of Her Own: A Woman's Guide to Success Off the Career Track, 233
- Working Parents Handbook, 233

boundaries (individuals), 235
Boys Town, 58, 223
The Budget Kit: The Common Cents Money Management Workbook, 232
budgeting
- books, 232
- discretionary income, 140
- goals
  - long-term, 148
  - mid-term, 148
  - short-term, 148

Index

guidelines, 142-143
income boosters, 143-144
money saving ideas, 144-146
priorities, 141-142
record keeping, 147-148
savings plan, developing, 149
spending advice, 142-143
wants versus needs, 140-141
building self-esteem, 56-59
burnout (emotional), preventing, 122-123
Business Week magazine, 155

C

calculating
  assets, 131-132
  expenses, 128-131
  net worth, 137
Career Change: Everything You Need to Know to Meet New Challenges and Take Control of Your Career, 233
careers
  home alone children, guidelines, 97-98
  resources, 232-233
  see also jobs
Charting Your Goals Worksheet, 28-30, 246-260
childcare
  National Association for Family Child Care, 229
  National Association of Child Care Resource and Referral Agencies, 229
  time, advice, 119

Child Custody: Building Agreements That Work, 227
child support, 235
  age of majority, 74
  Association for Children For Enforcement of Support (ACES), 226
  collecting, 132-133
  Cost of Living Adjustment (COLA) clauses, 73
  "deadbeat dad" regulations, 133
  effects of adoption, 74
  eligibility as custodial parent, 132
  emancipation, 74
  evolution of law, 72
  factors, 73
  Federal Parent Locator Service, 75
  formulas, 72-73
  governmental enforcement
    federal, 74-75
    local, 74-75
    state, 74-75
  increasing, 133
  Organization for the Enforcement of Child Support, 227
  permanent changes, 73
  public governmental assistance, 134
  statistics, 72
  temporary changes, 73
  versus visitation issues, 73-74
Child Support Enforcement (CSE) Program, 74, 132, 235
Child Welfare League of America, 228
child-rearing resources
  books, 230-231
  Web sites, 228
childcare
  baby-sitting co-ops, 86
  consistency, 84
  cost
    employment resources, 85
    government resources, 85
  environment, 87
  evaluation questions, 86-87
  health problems, 87
  parental guilt, 84
  potential health problems, 87
  research studies, 84
  settings, 84-85
  when to start, 84
  worker qualifications, 87
children
  accompaniment on your dates, 185-186
  acting out, 36-37
  as first priority, 211
  babies, regression, 43-44
  breakups, effect of, 8-9
  chore assignments, 110-111
  comfort levels with your date, 186-187
  conflicts with custodial parents, 201-202
  cooperative parenting
    economic resources, 195
    social resources, 195
  creation of schedules, 120-121

267

custody
  court battles, 77-78
  court denial of parental claim, 71
  duties, 198-199
  elements of agreement, 70
  factors in final decision, 69
  legal issues questionnaire, 78-80
dating
  feelings of double standards, 184
  sharing with, 183-184
denial of problems, 39
depression, 18, 169
development
  cognitive development, 34
  developmental tasks, 34
  internalizing feelings, 34
  problems, 44
  stages of development, 35
divorced parents' relationship, 8-9
effects of dating
  concern for other bioparent, 182
  fear of desertion, 182
  insecurity, 182
effects of remarriage, 216-217
emancipation age, 74
extended families
  benefits, 204
  improving connections between, 207-208

fears, 18, 164
  common, 14
  overcoming, 19-20
future planning, 211
hardships, intact families versus single parent homes, 10
home alone activities, 168-169
housecleaning
  benefits, 108-109
  guidelines, 109-110
jealousy within blended families, 220
legal protection, 67-68
leisure activities
  arts, 169, 258
  athletics, 170, 258
  community events, 170, 258
  crafts, 170, 258
  games, 171, 259
  outdoors, 171, 259
  social groups, 171, 259
  sports, 170, 259
listening to, 39
monitoring effects of dating, 188-189
non-custodial parents
  duties of, 198-199
  visitation arrangements, 200
parenting from a distance, 199-200
perception of emotional neglect in blended families, 220-221
pre-teens and abnormal behavior, 44
protection
  economic, 67
  physical, 67

provisions in wills, 80
psychological counseling, 67, 211-212
regression, 37
  in babies, 43-44
role reversals, 37
sense of identity, 205
sexual identity crises, 38
sibling rivalries in blended families, 220
social activities
  after-school, 167-168
  commitment, 171-172
  locating, 178-179
  parental involvement, 175
  with other single parents, 166
stress proofing, 38
teenagers, abnormal behavior, 44
testing behaviors in blended families, 221-222
U.S. Office of Child Support Enforcement, statistics, 72
visitation arrangements
  extended families, 206-207
  rearranging, 121-122
  sample agreement, 70
  stress-related symptoms, 200-201
Watching the Kids Worksheet, 40, 248-260
well-being, 9
worries, 18
chores
  checklist, 114-115
  children, assigning, 110-112

Index

frequency, 114-115
neighbors, exchanging with, 113
chronic depression, 235
classes, parenting, 39
clutter in homes, organizing, 105-106
co-dependency, 236
   prevention strategies, 60-61
cognitive development, 34, 236
cohabitation
   children, treating as first priority, 218-219
   economic advantages, 217
   effects on children, 217
   house rules, developing, 218
   role as biological parent, 217
   role of partner, 218
collecting child support, 132-133
community events as children's leisure activities, 170, 258
Complete Idiot's Guide to Grandparenting, 230
Complete Idiot's Guide to Managing Your Money, 232
Confessions of a Happily Organized Family, 233
conflict resolution, 76-77
confronting fears, 16-17
consistency in discipline, 42, 52
Consumer Credit Counseling Service (CCCS), 146
   Web site, 232

cooperative parenting, 195
   economic resources, 195
   house rules, 197-198
   social resources, 195
corporal punishment, 49-50
Cost of Living Adjustment (COLA), 73
counseling
   American Association for Marriage and Family Therapy, 231
   American Counseling Association, 231
   fears, overcoming, 19
   for parents and children, 211-212
   Web sites, 231
crafts as children's leisure activities, 170, 258
creating
   home with sense of permanancy, 210
   new memories, 212
   positive self-images within families, 212
   schedules for children, 120-121
credit cards
   credit ratings, 134-135
   debt, reducing, 135-136
   when to use, 134-135
custodial parents, 236
   conflicts over living arrangements, 201-202
   eligibility
      alimony, 132
      child support, 132
   organization of life, 102
   versus non-custodial parents, 198-199

custody
   courts
      appeals, 71
      battles, effects on children, 77-78
   arrangements, proper behavior, 196-200
   decision factors, 69
   defined, 68, 236
   denial, 71
   elements of agreement, 70
   geographic moves, 76
   interference, 78
   joint custody, 227
   legal issues questionnaire, 78-80
   legal representation, 77
   mediation of disputes, 76-77
   negotiations, 68
   provisions in wills, 80
   resources
      books, 227-228
      organizations, 226
   role of courts, 68
   types
      joint, 68-69
      legal, 68-69
      physical, 68-69
   Uniform Child Custody Jurisdiction Act, 68

D

Daddy's Home, 174
Dads Against Discrimination, 174

dating
  children
    accompanied by, 185-186
    meeting the "other" person, 186-187
    monitoring effects, 188-189
  considerations, 181-182
  double standard, 184
  effect on young children, 182
  effects on teenagers, double dating standard, 184
  house rules, establishing, 188
  jitters, 187
  partner's reaction to your children, 186-187
  sexual relationships, expert advice, 185
  sharing with children, 183-184
daycare
  National Association for Family Child Care, 229
  National Association of Child Care Resource and Referral Agencies, 229
debt reduction on credit cards, 135-136
decorating guidelines, 94
decreasing spending (budgets), 144-147
denial, 39
dependency, 60-61
depression, 18, 169
developing
  extended family connections with children, 207-208
  savings plan, 149
development (child)
  Child Behavior: The Classic Childcare Manual from the Gesell Institute of Human Development, 230
  cognitive development, 34
  developmental tasks, 34
  internalizing feelings, 34
  Princeton Center for Infancy and Early Childhood Series on Child Development, 231
  problems, 44
  stages of development, 35
developmental tasks, 34, 236
discipline, 41, 236
  abnormal behavior
    babies, 43-44
    pre-teens, 44
    teenagers, 44
  age-related issues, 42-43
  consistency from ex-spouses, 42, 52
  defined, 42
  extremes, 42
  grounding, 46
  picking battles, 50
  pre-teens, 43, 46
  professional assistance, 52-53
  resources, 230
  rules
    breaking, 47-48
    consistency with ex-spouse, 52
  stepfamilies, 234
  strategies
    guidelines, 51-52
  "I" messages, 50
  picking battles, 50
  positive consequences, 49
  spanking, 49-50
  teenagers, 43, 47
    breaking rules, 47-48
    grounding, 46
  toddlers, 43-46
discretionary income, 140, 236
Disney Web site, 228
displaced anger, 18, 236
divorce
  before/after situations with friends, 166-167
  child support
    books, 227
    organizations, 226-227
  custody issues
    books, 225-228
    fathers, 227
    organizations, 226
  loss of friends, 166-167
  remarriage statistics, 209
  resources
    books, 225
    organizations, 226-227
    Web sites, 224
  visitation, 227
Divorce Page Web site, 226
Divorced Parent's Guide to Managing Custody & Visitation, 227
Don't Take It Out On Your Kids, 230
"down and out" rule (housecleaning), 112-113
Dr. Spock on Parenting, 230
dream jobs, 152-153
drug abuse by teenagers, 48

Index

E

e-mail addresses
  American Academy of Pediatrics, 228
  Big Brothers/Big Sisters of America, 228
  Child Welfare League of America, 228
  Father Flanagan's Boys Home, 229
  Single Mother's By Choice, 225
earning power (wages), increasing, 157-159
emotions
  children
    acting out, 36-37
    anger, 18
    depression, 18
    expressing, failure to, 35-36
    fears, 18
  failure to express, 35-36
  fears
    acknowledging, 16
    common, 14
    confronting, 16-17
    overcoming, 19-20
    unproductive fears, 14-15
employers, childcare costs, 85
ERIC (Education Resources Information Center) Web site, 228
errands, advice, 118
Essential Home Record Book: Ready-To-Use Forms, 233

establishing rules
  cooperative parenting, 197-198
  dating, 188
evaluating
  childcare, 86-87
  needs versus wants, 140-141
ex-spouses
  disciplining children, 42, 52
  remarriage of, 222
exchanging chores with neighbors, 113
expenses
  calculating, 128-131
  categories
    child support, 129, 254
    food, 129, 254
    housing, 129, 254
    insurance, 130, 255
    living, 130, 254
    medical, 130, 255
    recreation, 130, 255
    taxes, 130, 255
    transportation, 129, 254
    utilities, 129, 254
  types
    fixed, 128
    variable, 128
expressing emotions (children)
  acting out, 36-37
  failure to, 35-36
extended families
  benefits
    as models to children, 204-205
    family structure, 204-205
    genetic influences, 204-205
    material, 206
    psychological, 206
  old feelings and hostilities, 205-206
  visitation rights, 206-207

F

families
  accumulation of junk, 104
  areas for organization, 104
  bonding activities, 212-213
  children, treating as first priority, 218-219
  fun activities, 212
  health, 9
  intact families
    defined, 9
    hardships, 10
    versus single-parent families, 10, 93
  new memories, creating, 212
  organization, 103-104
  positive self-images, 212
  poverty statistics, 127-128
  safety, 9
  security, 9
  single-parent families
    cognitive development, 34
    development stages, 35
    family time, 96
    home size, 93

hotlines, 223-224
versus intact families, 93
strategies for organization, 105-106
Families & Work Institute Web site, 233
family daycare, 85, 236
Family Medical Leave Act
eligible employees, 156-157
provisions, 156-157
family-friendly jobs, 154-155, 236
Fannie Mae loans for first-time home owners, 210
Father Flanagan's Boys Home, 229
fathers
custody issues, 227
hardships, 8
Single Fatherhood: The Complete Guide, 225
versus mothers, statistics, 5
Fathers' Forum, 174
Fathers' Resource Center, 174
fears
acknowledging, 16
children, 18
common, 14
confronting, 16-17
overcoming, 19-20
unproductive fears, 14-15
Federal Parent Locator Service, 75
finances
assets, calculating, 131-132

Consumer Credit Counseling Service, 232
credit cards, 134-136
expenses, calculating, 128-131
home-equity loans, 135-136
money
emotional issues, 136-137
wants versus needs, 140-141
net worth, calculating, 137
see also money-saving tips
first date jitters, 187
fixed expenses, 128
flextime scheduling, 155, 236
Foster Grandparents Program, 229
friends
categories, 164
new, 165-166
old, pre/post divorce situations, 166-167
parents as, 62
phone pals, 176
purpose, 163-164

G

games as children's leisure activities, 171, 259
garnished wages, 236
gay/lesbian couples, 228
gender bias, 236

goals
budgeting
long-term, 148
mid-term, 148
short-term, 148
Charting Your Goals Worksheet, 28-30, 246-260
elements
accountable, 102-103
measurable, 102-103
realistic, 102-103
specific, 102-103
timed, 102-103
government
child support enforcement
federal, 74-75
local, 74-75
state, 74-75
childcare costs, 85
children, legal protection, 67-68
Grandparenting in a Changing World, 230
grandparents
Complete Idiot's Guide to Grandparenting, 230
Foster Grandparents Program, 229
Grandparenting in a Changing World, 230
visitation, 206-207, 227
Grandparents as Parents Organization, 229
Grandparents Rights Organization, 226
grounding teenagers, 46
group family childcare, 85, 236

Growing Up With a Single Parent: What Hurts, What Helps, 225
guilt, 6
   overindulgence, 45

H

handling (advice)
   child care, 119
   errands, 118
   housework, 119-120
   money, 136-137
hiring professional cleaning services, 113
hobbies
   children, 59
   determining, 63-64, 249-260
home alone activities for children, 168-169
home-equity loans, 135-136
homes
   decorating, 94
   environmental stability, 93-95
   family times, 96
   kitchens, 94
   loans (Fannie Maes), 210
   necessities, 99, 251
   privacy
      personal spaces, creating, 95
      private time, creating, 95-96
   psychosocial boundaries, 95
   sense of permanancy, 210
   sleeping spaces, 93
   storage spaces, 93
   versus intact families, 93

Wish List Worksheet, 98-99, 251-260
hotlines
   Boys Town, 223
   Child Help, 223
   Missing Children, 223
   National Clearinghouse on Family Support and Children's Mental Health, 224
   National Council on Child Abuse and Family Violence, 224
   National Council on Family Relations, 224
   National Resource Center on Domestic Violence, 224
   National Youth Crisis Center, 224
   Planned Parenthood, 224
   Psychiatric Networks, 224
   Relationship Help, 224
house rules
   cohabitation, 218
   dating, 188
housecleaning
   benefits
      discipline, 108-109
      gender roles, 108-109
      practical skills, 108-109
   children
      boundaries, 109-110
      chore assignments, 110-111
      guidelines, 109-110
   chores
      checklist, 114-115
      frequency, 114-115
   participation of children, 111-112

professional cleaning services, hiring, 113
household tasks
   groceries, 111
   laundry, 111
   meal preparation, 111
How to Clean Practically, 234

I - J - K

"I" messages, discipline strategies, 50
identifying support network, 164
identity, 205
income
   boosting, 143-144
   job type, 153
increasing
   child support, 133
   circle of friends, 165-166
   earning power
      adult education, 157-159
   income, 143-144
intact families, 9, 237
   defined, 9
   hardships, 10
   home sizes, 93
internalizing, 237
Internet, support groups, 174
introducing children to your date, 186-187
inventories (personal)
   Charting Your Goals Worksheet, 28-30, 246-260
   Personal Style Self-Test, 24-25, 242-243

273

job sharing, 156, 237
jobs, 9
   at-home types, 159-160
   earning power, increasing, 157-159
   Family Medical Leave Act provisions, 156-157
   family-friendly elements, 154-155
   flextime scheduling, 155
   goals
      actions, 152
      income, 152-153
      practical realities, 153-154
      schedule, 152
   resources
      books, 233
      organizations, 232
joint custody, 68-69, 237
   Joint Custody Association, 226
   visitation schedules, 69, 121-122
Joint Custody and Co-Parenting: Sharing Your Child, 227
Joint Custody Association, 226
joys of single parenthood, 10-11

kitchens
   money-saving tips, 94
   space-saving tips, 94

L

latchkey children, 237
legal custody, 68-69, 237
legal issues, 9
legal protection of children, 67-68
legal status (single parents)
   cohabitation, 66-67
   custodial, 66-67
   divorced, 66-67
   non-custodial, 66-67
leisure activities (children)
   arts, 169, 258
   athletics, 170, 258
   community events, 170, 258
   crafts, 170, 258
   games, 171, 259
   outdoors, 171, 259
   social groups, 171, 259
   sports, 170, 259
lesbian/gay couples, 228
Little Things Make a Big Difference: How To Help Your Children Succeed in School, 230
living arrangements
   homes
      decorating, 94
      family times, 96
      kitchens, 94
      necessities, 99, 251
      personal spaces, creating, 95
      privacy, 94-96
      psychosocial boundaries, 95
      sleeping space, 93
      stability, importance of, 93-95
      storage spaces, 93
      versus intact families, 93
      Wish List Worksheet, 98-99, 251-260
   statistics, 6
   with custodial parents, 201-202
   with non-custodial parents, 201-202
Living on a Shoestring, 232
living together, *see* cohabitation
locating
   quality childcare, 86-87
   support groups, 178-179
long-distance parenting, 199-200

M

maintaining friendships in wake of divorce, 166-167
major depression, 235
making new friends, 165-166
Making the Most of Your Money, 232
material benefits
   extended families, 206
mediation, 76-77, 237
   Academy of Family Mediators, 226
misbehavior
   after school activities, 48
   causes, determining, 45
   see also discipline
Missing Children Hotline, 223
Mom's House, Dad's House: A Complete Guide for Parents Who Are Separated, Divorced, or Remarried, 225

Index

money
  emotional issues, 136-137
  poor spending habits, 137
  wants versus needs, 140-141
money saving ideas
  books, 232
  clothing, 145
  entertainment, 146
  food, 145
  medical care, 145
  reducing loan debts, 146
  sleeping areas, 93
  storage spaces, 93
  transportation, 145
  utilities, 144
mothers
  hardships, 8
  Raising Sons Without Fathers: A Woman's Guide to Parenting Strong, Successful Boys, 225
  Single Mothers by Choice: A Guidebook for Single Women, 226
  versus fathers, statistics, 5
  working resources, 233
multitasking, 118

N

National Association for Family Child Care, 229
National Association for the Education of Young Children, 229
National Association of Child Care Resource and Referral Agencies, 229
National Center for Missing and Exploited Children, 227
National Clearinghouse on Family Support and Children's Mental Health, 224
National Council on Child Abuse and Family Violence, 224
National Council on Family Relations, 224
National Organization of Single Mothers, Inc., 174, 225
National Resource Center on Domestic Violence, 224
National Youth Crisis Center, 224
needs versus wants, 140-141
negative feelings and self-esteem, 56
neighbors
  exchanging chores, 113
  support groups, 177-178
net worth, assets versus liabilities, 137
new friends, making, 165-166
new spouses as threat to your children, 218-219
non-custodial parents, 237
  long-distance relationships, 199
  organization of life, 102
  versus custodial parents, 198-199
  visits from children, 200

O

Obsessive-Compulsive Disorder (OCD), 237
Office of Child Support Enforcement Web site, 133, 226
old friends in pre/post divorce situations, 166-167
organizations
  Academy of Family Mediators, 226
  American Academy of Pediatrics, 228
  American Association for Marriage and Family Therapy, 231
  American Counseling Association, 231
  Big Brothers/Big Sisters of America, 54, 228
  Child Welfare League of America, 228
  Consumer Credit Counseling Service, 232
  Families & Work Institute, 233
  Father Flanagan's Boys Home, 229
  Foster Grandparents Program, 229
  Grandparents as Parents, 229
  Grandparents Rights Organization, 226
  Joint Custody Association, 226
  National Association for Family Child Care, 229
  National Association for the Education of Young Children, 229

275

National Association of Child Care Resource and Referral Agencies, 229
National Center for Missing and Exploited Children, 227
National Organization of Single Mothers, Inc., 225
Organization for the Enforcement of Child Support, 227
Parents Anonymous, 50, 230
Parents Helping Parents, 230
Parents Without Partners, 37, 225
Single Mothers By Choice, 225
Society of Professionals in Dispute Resolution, 227
StepFamily Association of America, 234
Organize Your Home!: Simple Routines for Managing Your Household, 234
organizing
   families
      accumulation of junk, 104
      goals, 103-104
      strategies, 105-106
      structure, 103-104
   for custodial parents, 102
   for non-custodial parents, 102
   goals, 102-103
   household tasks
      groceries, 111
      laundry, 111
      meal preparation, 111

sequential organization, 102
out-of-home childcare, 85, 237
outdoors as children's leisure activities, 171, 259
overcoming fears, 19-20
overindulgence and guilt, 45

P-Q

parental kidnapping, 78
parents
   books, 230-231
   classes, 39
   custodial versus non-custodial, 198-199
   geographic moves, 76
   provisions for children in wills, 80
   resources, 228
Parents Anonymous, 50, 230
Parents Helping Parents, 230
Parents Place, 174
Parents Without Partners, 37, 174, 225
Parentsoup Web site, 224
Parentsplace Web site, 224
permanent homes, creating, 210
personal inventories, 23
   Charting Your Goals Worksheet, 28-30, 246-260
   Personal Style Self-Test, 24-25, 242-243

personal spaces, creating, 95
Personal Style Self-Test, 24-25, 242-243
personal time
   creating, 95-96
   hobbies, 63-64, 249-260
   success as single parents, 60
   unrealistic concerns, 61
physical custody, 68-69, 237
Planned Parenthood, 224
planning
   activities for home alone children, 169
   for future
      children's education, 211
      finances, 211
Positive Discipline for Blended Families, 234
positive identification, 237
positive self-images within families, 212
poverty statistics for single-parent families, 127-128
praise, building self-esteem, 57-59
praising children, "4-to-1" rule, 58
pre-teens
   abnormal behavior, 44
   discipline, 46
pregnancies
   unexpected, Planned Parenthood, 224
   unintentional, 8
Princeton Center for Infancy and Early Childhood Series on Child Development, 231

Index

priorities
　children versus finances, 211
　parental responsibilities, 62-63
　putting children first, 38-39
　setting, 62-64
privacy
　homes, 94
　personal spaces, creating, 95
　private time, creating, 95-96
problems for single parents
　abnormal behavior
　　babies, 43-44
　　pre-teens, 44
　　teenagers, 44
　alcohol, 48
　children
　　abnormal behavior, 43-44
　　acting out, 36-37
　　denial of problems, 39
　　regression, 37
　　role reversals, 37
　　sexual identity crises, 38
　　warning signs, 44
　denial, 39
　drugs, 48
　pre-teens, abnormal behavior, 44
　sex, 48
　teenagers
　　abnormal behavior, 44
　　alcohol, 48
　　drugs, 48
　　sex, 48
　　warning signs, 44

professional assistance
　American Association for Marriage and Family Therapy, 231
　American Counseling Association, 231
　discipline, 52-53
　financial issues, Consumer Credit Counseling Service, 232
　therapists, questions to ask, 53-54
professional cleaning services, hiring, 113
profiles
　personal, 23
　　Charting Your Goals Worksheet, 28-30, 246-260
　　Personal Style Self-Test, 24-25, 242-243
　typical, 6
Psychiatric Networks, 224
psychological benefits of extended families, 206
psychological counseling for parents and children, 211-212
psychosocial boundaries, 95, 238
psychosomatic illnesses, 200, 238

R

reactive depression, 238
real fears, 15
rearranging visitation schedule (joint custody), 121-122

record keeping and budgeting, 147-148
reducing credit card debt, 135-136
regression, 238
　babies, 43-44
　young children, 37
Reinventing the Family: The Emerging Story of Lesbian and Gay Parents, 228
Relationship Help Hotline, 224
religious support groups, 175
remarriage
　blended families
　　dynamics, 219
　　problems, 219-220
　　sibling rivalries, 220
　　testing behaviors by children, 221-222
　children, treating as first priority, 218-219
　effects on children, 216-217
　failure statistics, 216-217
　guidelines for single parents, 216-217
　of ex-spouse, 222
　parental responsibility to children, 218-219
　recovery period from previous relationships, 220
　statistics, 209
role reversals, 238
　children
　　co-dependency, preventing, 60-61
　　parents as pals, 62
　　problems, 37

277

defined, 37
parents as pals, 62
rules
   consistency
      in households, 197-198
      with ex-spouse, 52
   cooperative parenting, 197-198

S

safety for home alone children, 97-98
savings plan (budgets)
   developing, 149
   goals, 149
   wants versus needs, 149
schedules
   burnout, 122-123
   important elements, 120-121
school
   101 Ways Parents Can Help Students Achieve, 230
   childcare, 238
   Little Things Make a Big Difference: How To Help Your Children Succeed in School, 230
   parent-child activities, 177
self-esteem, 238
   children, building
      guilt, unnecessary, 56-57
      hobbies, 59
      importance, 55-56
      praising, 57-58

guilt, unnecessary, 58-59
importance, 55-56
parents, 58-59
self-sacrifice, 22
self-worth, building, 57-59
separation anxiety, 197, 238
sequential organization, 102, 238
setting
   budget priorities, 141-142
   goals for organization, 102-103
setting priorities, 62-64
sexuality
   dating advice, 185
   identity crises, 38
   teenagers, 48
sharing children with other parent
   overview, 194-195
   proper behavior, 196-200
   purpose of dating, 183-184
sibling rivalries, 220
Single and Custodial Fathers Network, 174
Single Dad Steve Miller's Home Page, 174
Single Dads Hall of Fame, 174
Single Fathers Lighthouse, 174
Single Mothers By Choice, 174
   e-mail address, 225
   organization, 225
Single Mothers by Choice: A Guidebook for Single Women Who Are Considering or Have Chosen Motherhood, 226

Single Parent Alliance, 176
Single Parent Project, 174
Single Parent Resource Center, 174
single parents
   accompaniment on dates, 185-186
   cooperative parenting, 195
   custody arrangements, proper behavior, 196-200
   dating other single parents, 187
   defined, 4
   depression, 169
   extended families, benefits, 204
   increase, societal changes, 5-6
   legal status
      cohabitation, 66-67
      custodial, 66-67
      divorced, 66-67
      non-custodial, 66-67
      unmarried, 66-67
   mothers versus fathers, statistics, 5
   new spouses as threat to your children, 218-219
   psychological counseling, 211-212
   remarriage guidelines, 216-217
   sexual relationships
      effect on children, 185
      protection, 185
   social activities with other single parents, 166
   support groups
      locating, 178-179
      starting, 176
   typical profiles, 6

Index

Single Parents Association, 174
single-parent families
  children
    acting out, 36-37
    cognitive development, 34
    denial of problems, 39
    development stages, 35
    expressing emotions, 35-36
    internalizing feelings, 34
    listening to, 39
    regression, 37
    role reversals, 37
    sexual identity crises, 38
    stress proofing, 38
  family time, 96
  home size, 93
  poverty statistics, 127-128
  resources
    hotlines, 223-224
    Web sites, 224
  success, 38-39
situational depression, 18, 238
sleeping spaces in homes, 93
social activities
  child and parental involvement, 175
  for children
    after-school, 167-168
    commitment, 171-172
    weekend, 167-168
    friends, making, 165-166
    neighborhoods, 177-178
    schools, 177
  with other single parents, 166
Social Security Administration, 134
societal changes, 5-6
Society of Professionals in Dispute Resolution, 227
Sole Mothers International, 174
solo kids
  home alone activities, 168-169
  rules, 169
space-saving tips
  kitchens, 94
  privacy, 94
  sleeping spaces, 93
  storage spaces, 93
spanking, discipline strategies, 49-50
spending, decreasing (budgets), 144-147
sports as children's leisure activities, 170, 259
stages of development, 35
  Child Behavior: The Classic Childcare Manual from the Gesell Institute of Human Development, 230
  Princeton Center for Infancy and Early Childhood Series on Child Development, 231
statistics, 4
  living arrangements, 6
  mothers versus fathers, 5
stepfamilies
  discipline, 234
  resources
    organizations, 234
    Web sites, 234
StepFamily Association of America, 234
Steps Toward Recovery, 174
storage spaces in homes, 93
strategies for discipline
  guidelines, 51-52
  "I" messages, 50
  positive consequences, 49
  spanking, 49-50
stress
  stress-proofing, 38
  symptoms in children, 200-201
support groups
  At Home Dads, 174
  Custodial Fathers, 174
  Daddy's Home, 174
  Dads Against Discrimination, 174
  Fathers' Forum, 174
  Fathers' Resource Center, 174
  friends
    categories, 164
    purpose, 163-164
    social activities, 165-166
  Internet, 174
  locating, 178-179
  National Organization of Single Mothers, Inc., 174
  Parents Place, 174
  Parents Without Partners, 174
  religious organizations, 175
  Single and Custodial Fathers Network, 174
  Single Dad Steve Miller's Home Page, 174
  Single Dads Hall of Fame, 174

Single Fathers Lighthouse, 174
Single Mothers By Choice, 174
Single Parent Project, 174
Single Parent Resource Center, 174
Single Parents Association, 174
Sole Mothers International, 174
Steps Toward Recovery, 174

T

teenagers
  abnormal behavior, 44
  discipline, grounding, 46-47
  double dating standard, 184
  National Youth Crisis Center, 224
  rules, 47-48
Teenline, 224
telecommuting, 238
  disadvantages, 156
  job types, 156
  personality types, 156
  work week schedule, 156
therapy
  American Association for Marriage and Family Therapy, 231
  American Counseling Association, 231
  fears, overcoming, 19
  questions to ask, 53-54
  Web sites, 231
time
  advice
    care for children, 119
    errands, 118
    housework, 119-120
  burnout, preventing, 122-123
  family time, 96
  multitasking, 118
  personal time
    success as single parents, 60
    unrealistic concerns, 61
  schedules, creating, 120-121
  visitation schedules, rearranging, 121-122
toddlers, discipline, 45-46

U - V

U.S. Office of Child Support Enforcement, 72
Uniform Child Custody Jurisdiction Act, 68
unintentional pregnancy, 8
unproductive fears, 14-15

variable expenses, 128
Veteran's Administration, public governmental assistance, 134
visitation agreements, 238
  grandparents, 227
  rearranging, 121-122
  schedules
    court ordered, 70
    joint custody, 69
    sample agreement, 70
stress-related symptoms, 200-201
visualization, 153

W-Z

wants versus needs, 140-141
Watching the Kids Worksheet, 40, 248-260
Web sites
  All About Kids, 224
  American Academy of Pediatrics, 228
  American Counseling Association, 231
  Big Brothers/Big Sisters of America, 228
  Child Welfare League of America, 228
  Consumer Credit Counseling Service, 232
  counseling, 231
  Disney, 228
  Divorce Page, 226
  ERIC (Education Resources Information Center), 228
  Families & Work Institute, 233
  Father Flanagan's Boys Home, 229
  National Center for Missing and Exploited Children, 227
  Office of Child Support Enforcement, 133, 226
  Parents Helping Parents, 230
  Parentsoup, 224
  Parentsplace, 224

    single parent issues, 224
    stepfamilies, 234
    The Divorce Page, 224
    Working Mother Magazine, 156, 233
well-being of children, 9
widows/widowers, 8
wills, provisions for children, 80
Wish List Worksheet, homes, 98-99, 251-260
Work of Her Own: A Woman's Guide to Success Off the Career Track, 233
working
    children home alone, guidelines, 97-98
    resources, 232-233
Working Mother Magazine, 154
    Web site, 233
Working Parents Handbook, 233
worksheets
    Charting Your Goals Worksheet, 28-30, 246-260
    Checklist: What's Fun?, 63-64, 249-260
    Watching the Kids Worksheet, 40, 248-260
    Wish List Worksheet, 98, 251

Don't miss these other parenting titles in the Complete Idiot's Guide® series!

The Complete Idiot's Guide® to Bringing Up Baby
by Kevin Osborn and Dr. Signe Larson
$16.95
ISBN: 0-02-861957-9

The Complete Idiot's Guide® to Parenting a Preschooler and Toddler, Too
by Keith Boyd, M.D. and Kevin Osborn
$16.95
ISBN: 0-02-861733-9

The Complete Idiot's Guide® to Parenting a Teenager
by Kate Kelly
$16.95
ISBN: 0-02-861277-9

The Complete Idiot's Guide® to Stepparenting
by Ericka Lutz
$16.95
ISBN: 0-02-862407-6

The Complete Idiot's Guide® to Grandparenting
by Walter and Marilyn Hartt with Wilbur Cross
$16.95
ISBN: 0-02-861976-5

The Complete Idiot's Guide® to Adoption
by Chris Adamec
$18.95
ISBN: 0-02-862108-

The Complete Idiot's Guide® to Surviving Divorce
by Pamela Weintraub and Terry Hillman with Elayne J. Kesselman, Esquire
$16.95
ISBN: 0-02-861101-2